FORMS OF MODERN FICTION

FORMS of MODERN FICTION

Essays collected in honor of Joseph Warren Beach

Edited by **WILLIAM VAN O'CONNOR**

A MIDLAND BOOK

Indiana University Press • Bloomington

*The chapter by Mark Schorer on "Technique as Discovery" is
reprinted from the* Hudson Review, *Volume I, Number 1, Spring
1948, copyright 1948 by the* Hudson Review, Inc. *The chapter
by Robert Penn Warren on "William Faulkner" (copyright 1946
by Robert Penn Warren) appears in a revised form in* Selected
Essays *by Robert Penn Warren, Random House, 1958. The chapter by Morton Dauwen Zabel on "Graham Greene," as included
in this volume, was originally written for* The Nation, *Vol.
CLVII, pages 18-20 (July 3, 1943). Mr. Zabel has since then
revised and expanded the essay to include a discussion of Graham
Greene's work down to 1957, and has included it in his book,*
Craft and Character, Viking Press, 1958, pages 276-296.

Note

FORMS OF MODERN FICTION *was first published in the spring of 1948. It had been put together rather hurriedly during the preceding fall and winter so that the University of Minnesota Press might have it ready to present a copy to Professor Joseph Warren Beach upon his retirement. In retrospect it is clear that it was a fortunate enterprise. At that time the criticism of fiction, of the sort that had been devoted to poetry, was relatively rare; since then it has become a commonplace, and there are whole magazines given over to publishing this sort of criticism. Almost all of our contributors have continued to write significant criticism, much of it about the novel. Several of the essays have been quoted from over and over again in books and articles published in the intervening decade; they have become, to use an abused phrase, seminal studies in the criticism of modern fiction. Along with a number of other pieces in the book they are likely to be studied for a good while to come.*

In this Midland Book edition the essay by Robert Wooster Stallman on "Life, Art, and 'The Secret Sharer' " has been omitted at the author's request.

January 1959   W. V. O'C.

WILLIAM VAN O'CONNOR

MARK SCHORER

ALLEN TATE

JOSEPH WARREN BEACH

DAVID DAICHES

FRANCIS FERGUSSON

WILLIAM TROY

RAY B. WEST, JR

RICHARD CHASE

T. S. ELIOT

ROBERT PENN WARREN

LIONEL TRILLING

E. K. BROWN

CARLOS LYNES, JR

FREDERICK J. HOFFMAN

C. W. M. JOHNSON

ROBERT BECHTOLD HEILMAN

WARREN BECK

CHARLES CHILD WALCUTT

ERIC BENTLEY

MORTON DAUWEN ZABEL

C. H. RICKWORD

Table of Contents

✑§ WILLIAM VAN O'CONNOR

The Novel in Our Time

GEORGE SAINTSBURY, writing as late as 1926, could see little point in all the contemporary concern with technique. In art, he said, "technique will be of little use to you and of no little danger." The employment of technique will mean self-conscious writing and stillborn characters. A novelist cannot be taught technique. Either he can catch his story and create appropriate characters or he cannot—either he is a novelist or he is not. We can only infer that to Saintsbury a novel, whether written in the eighteenth, nineteenth, or twentieth century, was simply a story with interesting characters and exciting action. Saintsbury did not believe, apparently, that the kinds of knowledge or the views of reality held by the novelists and their century obligated the novelists to find forms best suited to express them.

It is surprising that his acquaintance with the work of James and Conrad, if with that of no others, did not make evident to Saintsbury the value of certain techniques, such as James' rendering rather than reporting and Conrad's putting the narrator inside the story to refract and interpret it. Ford Madox Ford called the work of James and Conrad an "alien cloud" that in passing over the landscape of the English novel left behind a feeling that the simple story was gone forever. Thereafter the novelist had a greater self-consciousness. And he was likely, to use

1

Joseph Warren Beach's expression, to produce a "well-made novel." Since 1885, Beach adds, there has been an ever-increasing preoccupation with form, an effort to make the novel "as different as possible from the philosophical essay, the historical chronicle, with which in the beginning it was so closely associated."

In its turn, however, the "well-made novel" was seen to have its limitations: a rigorously delimited subject matter, a formalized neatness, a conscious gentility, and a lack of emotional and intellectual exuberance. The reactions were many. Among them was the break with gentility, as in the realism of Lewis and Dreiser; the attempt to capture the feelings that border and merge with the unconscious and the currents of sensation passing between characters, as in Lawrence; the effort to bring into some kind of focus the heterogeneous complexity of ideas, feelings, and impressions in individual minds, as in Joyce and Virginia Woolf; and the concern to bring into juxtaposition multiple points of view, as in Gide and Huxley. Each of these novelists has attempted to find a form whereby he might appropriately objectify or dramatize his understanding of our time.

All of us are, whether we especially like it or not, of our own age. We belong to it and to no other because it has formed us. Having lived in it, we could not be fully at ease in any other. In responding to the knowledge and expressions of our time our sensibilities, to some extent, are created for us. The art of all periods will have similarities, but the art of each period will have, in addition, a character peculiar to it. More than human fickleness is behind genres assuming varied forms or falling into desuetude. Certainly something more than fashion is involved, more than an aping of an *avant-garde* that is bent only on change for the sake of change. The spirit and kinds of knowledge informing these genres change and thus necessitate new forms. The contemporary reader can enjoy a *novella* or a heroic drama, but he cannot enjoy either if written by a twentieth-century short story writer or dramatist. To be true to his art a man must be true to his age. He must use the resources it presents to him.

The paradox that artists create their age or make their world, in the sense that before they have caught its aspects in an art form it has been unstated and therefore not clearly perceived, is related of course to the problem of form. It is hardly an exaggeration to say that we do not know what kind of world we live in until we have experienced it through the coherent and meaningful configurations of our most original and perceptive artists. W. H. Auden somewhere comments that the difference between a mediocre and a great poet is that the one reminds us how we feel about many matters, while the other makes us realize for the first time how we feel about them. "From now on, thanks to this poem, I shall feel differently." To this we might add that the poet sometimes makes us aware for the first time of the very existence of matters characteristic of an age. But the artist who makes us understand and feel differently is not distinguished necessarily from the rest of us in his capacity for abstract thought about these matters—he is distinguished in his capacity for devising and probing a form in such a manner that his perceptions are not only objectified but enlarged and qualified through his having to discover the relationships of meanings within the limits of his form. The form, a symbolic structure, is not a transcript of life; it is a representation which equips us to understand more fully aspects of existence outside of art. Form is the objectifying of idea, and its excellence, it would seem, depends upon its appropriateness to the idea.

It has become a commonplace of contemporary criticism that poets like Eliot, Marianne Moore, and E. E. Cummings have discovered and employed exquisitely appropriate forms. More critics have applied themselves to the study of poetic forms than to the forms of the novel, possibly because the novel, for whatever reasons, is more difficult for the critical mind to assimilate. Yet an equivalent intense criticism is necessary for the novel because it, like other genres, has lost much of its nineteenth-century character through attempts to serve twentieth-century needs.

In "Graham Greene," Morton D. Zabel explains the appropriateness of horrors arising out of the ideological conflicts in the twentieth century being caught in the mystery-thriller form.

3

What was, in the tragedy of blood or the Gothic romance, sheer melodrama is now the actuality reported in the daily newspaper. For the stock and artificial motivations necessary to the mystery-thriller, there remains merely to substitute motivations appropriate to the actual world. The point, of course, is that Greene has found a way of expressing the character of our time in an appropriate art form.

Virginia Woolf, among the modern innovators, objected to the forms employed by Bennett, Wells, and Galsworthy. Immersed in the new awareness of the strange associational workings of the mind, in the twentieth-century preoccupation with flux and the shifting centers of personal identity, Mrs. Woolf wanted to emphasize a personal, subjective sense of reality. The structures of Bennett, Wells, and Galsworthy, like those of most of their Victorian predecessors, undoubtedly served to present a Victorian sense of reality, a world in which things are what they seem, and in which neither moral values nor a sense of identity was to be questioned. They would not serve Mrs. Woolf, who was not at all sure that either values or a sense of identity could be kept stable.

She required a form in which the individual's sense of flux, of sensory impressions, sometimes clear, sometimes blurred, could be caught. Her characters do not move in an ordered, stable world and derive therefrom a personal sense of order; they seem, rather, to live in themselves and to cause the external world to flow, in nicely patterned or in disconnected impressions, through their minds and sensibilities. By using the waves, for example, as a recurrent and multi-meaningful symbol, she could evoke the sense and recognition of change, and the pull of inexorable forces drawing us into an impersonal nothingness. And by using the stream of consciousness technique she could evoke the disconnected, blurred, and shimmery experiences that compose our consciousness. To repeat our point: the world as perceived by Mrs. Woolf had lost its stability and order. The Victorian forms, devised to express an earlier sense of reality, did not serve her purposes.

Nor did they serve James Joyce, who possessed, perhaps to a

greater degree than any of his contemporaries, a tremendous capacity for suggesting the centrifugal forces leaping away from man's mind and the shadowlike memories left behind them. We are held fascinated by the little world of confused sensation whirring or quiescent in the head of each character. It does not follow that Joyce felt no need for bringing order or meaning out of such chaos. He knew, as Eliot suggests, that the modern world must create its own order and its own conscience. In employing a parallel between the world of the *Odyssey* and the world of Stephen Dedalus and Leopold Bloom, he found, Eliot remarks, "a way of controlling, or ordering, of giving a shape and a significance to the immense panorama of futility and anarchy which is contemporary history." Joyce, Harry Levin adds, "evoked the past to illuminate the present." This constant comparison between two worlds is among the chief techniques employed by Joyce.

The sense certain novelists, among them André Gide and Aldous Huxley, have had of living in a world of conflicting or at least complementary ideas has given rise to the novel of ideas. "I am like a composer," Gide wrote, "who seeks to juxtapose and overlap, in the manner of César Franck, an andante motif with an allegro." Like many of his contemporaries, Gide was aware that in a world of ideas he could not safely commit himself to a single idea. In the beliefs of Huxley and in his statements about this matter we find strong echoes from Gide. Philip Quarles in *Point Counter Point* is made to say that to achieve the "musicalization of fiction" he, the novelist, needs "a sufficiency of characters and parallel, contrapuntal plots. . . ." Huxley found the novel of ideas *modern* because "the new way of looking is multiplicity." We may object, as the older Huxley apparently has, that this way of seeing encourages us to view all things as meaningless flux— but we must also admit that since the vision of world and man as flux is so considerable a part of the contemporary mind the novelist cannot ignore it. The weakness in the novel of ideas, as the critics of Huxley have repeatedly said, is that it fails to evoke those parts of experience that affect the sensibilities.

Both Conrad and James have been credited, each in his own

way, with the mastery of tone, with creating a unity of feeling and mood by sustaining the emotional vibrations, at appropriate degrees of intensity, through each of their novels. This preoccupation is necessary to the novelist who would give us either the *feel* of a given situation or the tone of his society. Theme and subject are caught not abstractly or as surface events but with their emotional resonance and overtones. Upon analysis one finds, quite frequently, that the vibrations and the resonance are caused by a central symbolism or by an interrelated body of metaphors.

Conrad's "The Secret Sharer," to take a fairly simple example, exists at the level of dramatic, adventurous action, and at the level of a more significant meaning, concerned with the kinds of awareness various minds have of the disaster that encircles our security and successes. The young captain who helps Leggatt escape is not merely a sensitive young man from Conway—he is a large segment of aware humanity. Other characters symbolize an abject or an obtuse reverence for the law. The ship in its narrow escape from being wrecked and the sea itself, dark with mystery or sunlit like brave hopes and a new destiny, are as always more than adequate symbols.

After a close, intensive reading of *Remembrance of Things Past,* C. W. M. Johnson has shown that the tone is evoked not only through the attitudes of the narrator but through a "matrix of images related to each other in subtle ways." In the fiction of James, there frequently are—as in *The Figure in the Carpet, The Golden Bowl,* and *The Beast in the Jungle*—centrally pervasive symbols. And he, of course, is also concerned with what in Hawthorne he called "the deeper psychology," not with cerebration alone but with the tones and overtones set up by a sensibility reacting to a situation or character. In examining the language of an inward-looking Jamesian character, one discovers that the tone appears to have been evoked through the seemingly incidental employment of deft metaphor and subtle gradations of meaning. These qualities in James, we may assume, have made it easier for later novelists, like Edith Wharton, or, more recently, Lionel Trilling, to suggest not merely the emotional quality in the speech of a given character or situation, but the tonality of their respective societies.

The novelists, then, who have been intensively concerned with problems of technique have been attempting to discover means whereby heterogeneous situations are best dramatized for us. In his analysis of *Madame Bovary*, for instance, Allen Tate centers his attention upon a single incident—the whirring of a lathe—which enables us to experience what is occurring in the mind of Emma. Flaubert is employing a technique that Eliot was to call the "objective correlative." It is through this and similar techniques, Tate says, that "the novel has at last caught up with poetry."

Technique is also seen as the "manipulation" of subject matter, to arouse within it a vitality in accordance with its singular kind, in the matter of style. Robert Penn Warren has demonstrated the appropriateness of the tight-lipped, monosyllabic style of the early Hemingway who believed in *nada*. And Mark Schorer notes that it is instructive to observe how this style breaks down, becomes inappropriate, when Hemingway's subject matter changes to social affirmation. The earlier style of Hemingway was appropriate to a body of attitudes that developed after World War I. "One should correct Buffon," Schorer says, "and say that style is the subject." Or, perhaps, we should say that style at its best is the product of a worth-while mind and sensibility expressing itself in terms appropriate to a given subject, and that style, when appropriate, is a part of the meaning. Style is also the expression of a motivating spirit and therefore of an era or a culture.

William Butler Yeats observed that a certain passivity in literature began when "Stendhal described a masterpiece as a 'mirror dawdling down a lane.'" The "mischief," to use Yeats' term, probably had its sources in a philosophy and in events generations before Stendhal. Whatever its causes, naturalism in modern fiction has been a large and influential movement. Through it the twentieth-century mind has been free to indulge in the debunking of many traditional forms and beliefs and to exchange, as someone has said, "fictions, faiths and constructed systems" for the "hard, cold facts." More positively, it has enabled modern literature to effect a break with gentility and to achieve a power of description equal to that of the expert photographer. Progressively, however, critics have leveled protests similar to that made by Yeats against the naturalists. Those concerned with myth, for example, see in it a way of organizing and giving a transcendent meaning to otherwise delimited actions and characters described by the naturalistic novelists. The realm of "hard, cold facts," in other words, should not be the exclusive concern, the only realm, of the novelist.

❧ MARK SCHORER

Technique as Discovery

MODERN criticism, through its exacting scrutiny of literary texts, has demonstrated with finality that in art beauty and truth are indivisible and one. The Keatsian overtones of these terms are mitigated and an old dilemma solved if for beauty we substitute form, and for truth, content. We may, without risk of loss, narrow them even more, and speak of technique and subject matter. Modern criticism has shown us that to speak of content as such is not to speak of art at all, but of experience; and that it is only when we speak of the *achieved* content, the form, the work of art as a work of art, that we speak as critics. The difference between content, or experience, and achieved content, or art, is technique.

When we speak of technique, then, we speak of nearly everything. For technique is the means by which the writer's experience, which is his subject matter, compels him to attend to it; technique is the only means he has of discovering, exploring, developing his subject, of conveying its meaning, and, finally, of evaluating it. And surely it follows that certain techniques are sharper tools than others, and will discover more; that the writer capable of the most exacting technical scrutiny of his subject matter will produce works with the most satisfying content, works

NOTE. Reprinted from the *Hudson Review,* 1948, by permission of the editors and the author.

with thickness and resonance, works which reverberate, works with maximum meaning.

We are no longer able to regard as seriously intended criticism of poetry which does not assume these generalizations; but the case for fiction has not yet been established. The novel is still read as though its content has some value in itself, as though the subject matter of fiction has greater or lesser value in itself, and as though technique were not a primary but a supplementary element, capable perhaps of not unattractive embellishments upon the surface of the subject, but hardly of its essence. Or technique is thought of in blunter terms than those which one associates with poetry, as such relatively obvious matters as the arrangement of events to create plot; or, within plot, of suspense and climax; or as the means of revealing character motivation, relationship, and development; or as the use of point of view, but point of view as some nearly arbitrary device for the heightening of dramatic interest through the narrowing or broadening of perspective upon the material, rather than as a means toward the positive definition of theme. As for the resources of language, these, somehow, we almost never think of as a part of the technique of fiction — language as used to create a certain texture and tone which in themselves state and define themes and meanings; or language, the counters of our ordinary speech, as forced, through conscious manipulation, into all those larger meanings which our ordinary speech almost never intends. Technique in fiction, all this is a way of saying, we somehow continue to regard as merely a means to organizing material which is "given" rather than as the means of exploring and defining the values in an area of experience which, for the first time *then*, are being given.

Is fiction still regarded in this odd, divided way because it is really less tractable before the critical suppositions which now seem inevitable to poetry? Let us look at some examples: two well-known novels of the past, both by writers who may be described as "primitive," although their relative innocence of technique is of a different sort — Defoe's *Moll Flanders* and Emily Brontë's *Wuthering Heights*; and three well-known novels of this century — *Tono Bungay,* by a writer who claimed to eschew technique; *Sons and Lovers,* by a novelist who, because his ideal of subject matter ("the poetry of the immediate present") led him at last into the fallacy of spontaneous and unchangeable composition, in effect eschewed technique; and *A Portrait of the Artist as a Young Man,* by a novelist whose practice made claims for the supremacy of technique beyond those made by anyone in the past or by anyone else in this century.

Technique in fiction is, of course, all those obvious forms of it which are usually taken to be the whole of it, and many others; but for present purposes, let it be thought of in two respects particularly: the uses to which language, as language, is put to express the quality of the experience in question; and the uses of point of view not only as a mode of dramatic delimitation, but more particularly, of thematic definition. Technique is really what T. S. Eliot means by "convention": any selection, structure, or distortion, any form or rhythm imposed upon the world of action; by means of which, it should be added, our apprehension of the world of action is enriched or renewed. In this sense, everything is technique which is not the lump of experience itself, and one cannot properly say that a writer has no technique, or that he eschews technique, for, being a writer, he cannot do so. We can speak of good and bad technique, of adequate and inadequate, of technique which serves the novel's purpose, or disserves.

II

In the prefatory remarks to *Moll Flanders,* Defoe tells us that he is not writing fiction at all, but editing the journals of a woman of notorious character, and rather to instruct us in the necessities and the joys of virtue than to please us. We do not, of course, take these professions seriously, since nothing in the conduct of the narrative indicates that virtue is either more necessary or more enjoyable than vice. On the contrary, we discover that Moll turns virtuous only after a life of vice has enabled her to do so with security; yet it is precisely for this reason that Defoe's profession of didactic purpose has interest. For the actual morality which the novel enforces is the morality of any commercial culture, the belief that virtue pays—in worldly goods. It is a morality somewhat less than skin deep, having no relation to motives arising from a sense of good and evil, least of all, of evil-*in*-good, but exclusively from the presence or absence of food, drink, linen, damask, silver, and timepieces. It is the morality of measurement, and without in the least intending it, *Moll Flanders* is our classic revelation of the mercantile mind: the morality of measurement, which Defoe has completely neglected to measure. He fails not only to evaluate this material in his announced way, but to evaluate it at all. His announced purpose is, we admit, a pious humbug, and he meant us to read the book as a series of scandalous events; and thanks to his inexhaustible pleasure in excess and exaggeration, this element in the book continues to amuse us. Long before the book has been finished, however, this element has also become an absurdity; but not half the absurdity as that which Defoe did not intend at all—the notion that Moll could live a rich and full life of crime, and yet, repenting, emerge spotless in the end. The point is, of course, that she has no moral being, nor has the book any moral life. Everything is external. Everything can be weighed, measured, handled, paid for in gold, or expiated by a prison term. To this, the whole texture of the novel testifies—the bolts of goods, the inventories, the itemized accounts, the landlady's bills, the lists, the ledgers—all this, which taken together comprises what we call Defoe's method of circumstantial realism.

He did not come upon that method by any deliberation; it represents precisely his own world of value, the importance of external circumstance to Defoe. The point of view of Moll is indistinguishable from the point of view of her creator. We discover the meaning of the novel (at unnecessary length, without economy, without emphasis, with almost none of the distortions or the advantages of art) in spite of Defoe, not because of him. Thus the book is not the true chronicle of a disreputable female, but the true allegory of an impoverished soul, the author's; not an anatomy of the criminal class, but of the middle class. And we read it as an unintended comic revelation of self and of a social mode. Because he had no adequate resources of technique to separate himself from his material, thereby to discover and to define the meanings of his material, his contribution is not to fiction but to the history of fiction, and to social history.

The situation in *Wuthering Heights* is at once somewhat the same and yet very different. Here, too, the whole novel turns upon itself, but this time to its estimable advantage; here, too, is a revelation of what is perhaps the author's secret world of value, but this time, through what may be an accident of technique, the revelation is meaningfully accomplished. Emily Brontë may merely have stumbled upon the perspectives which define the form and the theme of her book. Whether she knew from the outset, or even at the end, what she was doing, we may doubt; but what she did and did superbly we can see.

We can assume, without at all becoming involved in the author's life but merely from the tone of somnambulistic excess which is generated by the writing itself, that this world of monstrous passion, of dark and gigantic emotional and nervous energy, is for the author, or was in the first place, a world of ideal value; and that the book sets out to persuade us of the moral magnificence of such unmoral passion. We are, I think, expected, in the first place, to take at their own valuation these demonic beings, Heathcliff and Cathy: as special creatures, set apart from the cloddish world about them by their heightened capacity for feeling, set apart, even, from the ordinary objects of human passion as, in their transcendent, sexless relationship, they identify themselves with an uncompromising landscape and cosmic force. Yet this is absurd, as much of the detail that surrounds it ("Other dogs lurked in other recesses") is absurd. The novelist Emily Brontë had to discover these absurdities to the girl Emily; her technique had to evaluate them for what they were, so that we are persuaded that it is not Emily who is mistaken in her estimate of her characters, but they who are mistaken in their estimate of themselves. The theme of the moral magnificence of unmoral passion is an impossible theme to sustain, and what interests us is that it was device—and this time, mere, mechanical device—which taught Emily Brontë—the needs of her temperament to the contrary, all personal longing and reverie to the contrary, perhaps—that this was indeed not at all what her material must mean as art. Technique objectifies.

To lay before us the full character of this passion, to show us how it first comes into being and then comes to dominate the world about it and the life that follows upon it, Emily Brontë gives her material a broad scope in time, lets it, in fact, cut across three generations. And to manage material which is so extensive, she must find a means of narration, points of view, which can encompass that material, and, in her somewhat crude concept of motive, justify its telling. So she chooses a foppish traveler who stumbles into this world of passionate violence, a traveler representing the thin and conventional emotional life of the far world of fashion, who wishes to hear the tale; and for her teller she chooses, almost inevitably, the old family retainer who knows everything, a character as conventional as the other, but this one representing not the conventions of fashion, but the conventions of the humblest moralism.

What has happened is, first, that she has chosen as her narrative perspective those very elements, conventional emotion and conventional morality, which her hero and heroine are meant to transcend with such spectacular magnificence; and second, that she has permitted this perspective to operate throughout a long period of time. And these two elements compel the novelist to see what her unmoral passions come to. Moral magnificence? Not at all; rather, a devastating spectacle of human waste; ashes. For the time of the novel is carried on long enough to show Heathcliff at last an emptied man, burned out by his fever ragings, exhausted and will-less, his passion meaningless at last. And it goes even a little further, to Lockwood, the fop, in the graveyard, sententiously contemplating headstones. Thus in the end the triumph is all on the side of the cloddish world, which survives.

Perhaps not all on that side. For, like Densher at the end of *The Wings of the Dove*, we say, and surely Hareton and the second Cathy say,. "We shall never be again as we were!" But there is more point in observing that a certain body of materials, a girl's romantic daydreams, have, through the most conventional devices of fiction, been pushed beyond their inception in fancy to their meanings, their conception as a written book—that they, that is, are not at all as they were.

III

Technique alone objectifies the materials of art; hence technique alone evaluates those materials. This is the axiom which demonstrates itself so devastatingly whenever a writer declares, under the urgent sense of the importance of his materials—whether these are autobiography, or social ideas, or personal passions—whenever such a writer declares that he cannot linger with technical refinements. That art will not tolerate such a writer H. G. Wells handsomely proves. His enormous literary energy included no respect for the techniques of his medium, and his medium takes its revenge upon his bumptiousness. "I have never taken any very great pains about writing. I am outside the hierarchy of conscious and deliberate writers altogether. I am the absolute antithesis of Mr. James Joyce. . . . Long ago, living in close conversational proximity to Henry James, Joseph Conrad, and Mr. Ford Madox Hueffer, I escaped from under their immense artistic preoccupations by calling myself a journalist." Precisely. And he escaped—he disappeared—from literature into the annals of an era.

Yet what confidence! "Literature," Wells said, "is not jewelry, it has quite other aims than perfection, and the more one thinks of 'how it is done' the less one gets it done. These critical indulgences lead along a fatal path, away from every natural interest towards a preposterous emptiness of technical effort, a monstrous egotism of artistry, of which the later work of Henry James is the monumental warning. 'It,' the subject, the thing or the thought, has long since disappeared in these amazing works; nothing remains but the way it has been manipulated." Seldom has a literary theorist been so totally wrong; for what we learn as

James grows for us and Wells disappears is that without what he calls "manipulation," there *is* no "it," no "subject" in art. There is again only social history.

The virtue of the modern novelist—from James and Conrad down—is not only that he pays so much attention to his medium, but that, when he pays most, he discovers through it a new subject matter, and a greater one. Under the "immense artistic preoccupations" of James and Conrad and Joyce, the form of the novel changed, and with the technical change, analogous changes took place in substance, in point of view, in the whole conception of fiction. And the final lesson of the modern novel is that technique is not the secondary thing that it seemed to Wells, some external machination, a mechanical affair, but a deep and primary operation; not only that technique *contains* intellectual and moral implications, but that it *discovers* them. For a writer like Wells, who wished to give us the intellectual and the moral history of our times, the lesson is a hard one; it tells us that the order of intellect and the order of morality do not exist at all, in art, except as they are organized in the order of art.

Wells' ambitions were very large. "Before we have done, we will have all life within the scope of the novel." But that is where life already is, within the scope of the novel; where it needs to be brought is into novels. In Wells we have all the important topics in life, but no good novels. He was not asking too much of art, or asking that it include more than it happily can; he was not asking anything of it—as art, which is all that it can give, and that is everything.

A novel like *Tono Bungay*, generally thought to be Wells' best, is therefore instructive. "I want to tell—*myself*," says George, the hero, "and my impressions of the thing as a whole"—the thing as a whole being the collapse of traditional British institutions in the twentieth century. George "tells himself" in terms of three stages in his life which have rough equivalents in modern British social history, and this is, to be sure, a plan, a framework; but it is the framework of Wells' abstract thinking, not of his craftsmanship, and the primary demand which one makes of such a book as this—that means be discovered whereby the dimensions of the hero contain the experiences he recounts—is never met. The novelist flounders through a series of literary imitations —from an early Dickensian episode, through a kind of Shavian interlude, through a Conradian episode, to a Jules Verne vision at the end. The significant failure is in that end, and in the way that it defeats not only the entire social analysis of the bulk of the novel, but Wells' own ends as a thinker. For at last George finds a purpose in science. "I decided that in power and knowledge lay the salvation of my life; the secret that would fill my need; that to these things I would give myself."

But science, power, and knowledge are summed up at last in a destroyer. As far as one can tell Wells intends no irony, although he may here have come upon the essence of the major irony in modern history. The novel ends in a kind of meditative rhapsody which denies every value that the book had been aiming toward. For of all the kinds of social waste which Wells has been describing, this is the most inclusive, the final waste. Thus he gives us in the end not a novel, but a hypothesis; not an individual destiny, but a theory of the future; and not his theory of the future, but a nihilistic vision quite opposite from everything that he meant to represent. With a minimum of attention to the virtues of technique, Wells might still not have written a good novel; but he would at any rate have established a point of view and a tone which would have told us what he meant.

To say what one means in art is never easy, and the more intimately one is implicated in one's material, the more difficult it is. If, besides, one commits fiction to a therapeutic function which is to be operative not on the audience but on the author, declaring, as D. H. Lawrence did, that "One sheds one's sicknesses in books, repeats and presents again one's emotions to be master of them," the difficulty is vast. It is an acceptable theory only with the qualification that technique, which objectifies, is under no other circumstances so imperative. For merely to repeat one's emotions, merely to look into one's heart and write, is also merely to repeat the round of emotional bondage. If our books are to be exercises in self-analysis, then technique must—and alone can— take the place of the absent analyst.

Lawrence, in the relatively late Introduction to his *Collected Poems,* made that distinction of the amateur between his "real" poems and his "composed" poems, between the poems which expressed his demon directly and created their own form "willy-nilly," and the poems which, through the hocus-pocus of technique, he spuriously put together and could, if necessary, revise. His belief in a "poetry of the immediate present," poetry in which nothing is fixed, static, or final, where all is shimmeriness and impermanence and vitalistic essence, arose from this mistaken notion of technique. And from this notion, an unsympathetic critic like D. S. Savage can construct a case which shows Lawrence driven "concurrently to the dissolution of personality and the dissolution of art." The argument suggests that Lawrence's early, crucial novel, *Sons and Lovers,* is another example of meanings confused by an impatience with technical resources.

The novel has two themes: the crippling effects of a mother's love on the emotional development of her son; and the "split" between kinds of love, physical and spiritual, which the son develops, the kinds represented by two young women, Clara and Miriam. The two themes should, of course, work together, the second being, actually, the result of the first: this "split" is the "crippling." So one would expect to see the novel developed, and so Lawrence, in his famous letter to Edward Garnett, where he says that Paul is left at the end with the "drift towards death," apparently thought he had developed it. Yet in the last few sentences of the novel, Paul rejects his desire for extinction and turns toward "the faintly humming, glowing town," to life—as nothing in his previous history persuades us that he could unfalteringly do.

The discrepancy suggests that the book may reveal certain confusions between intention and performance.

One of these is the contradiction between Lawrence's explicit characterizations of the mother and father and his tonal evaluations of them. It is a problem not only of style (of the contradiction between expressed moral epithets and the more general texture of the prose which applies to them) but of point of view. Morel and Lawrence are never separated, which is a way of saying that Lawrence maintains for himself in this book the confused attitude of his character. The mother is a "proud, *honorable* soul," but the father has a "small, *mean* head." This is the sustained contrast; the epithets are characteristic of the whole, and they represent half of Lawrence's feelings. But what is the other half? Which of these characters is given his real sympathy — the hard, self-righteous, aggressive, demanding mother who comes through to us, or the simple, direct, gentle, downright, fumbling, ruined father? There are two attitudes here. Lawrence (and Morel) loves his mother, but he also hates her for compelling his love; and he hates his father with the true Freudian jealously, but he also loves him for what he is in himself, and he sympathizes more deeply with him because his wholeness has been destroyed by the mother's domination, just as his, Lawrence-Morel's, has been.

This is a psychological tension which disrupts the form of the novel and obscures its meaning, because neither the contradiction in style nor the confusion in point of view is made to right itself. Lawrence is merely repeating his emotions, and he avoids an austerer technical scrutiny of his material because it would compel him to master them. He would not let the artist be stronger than the man.

The result is that, at the same time that the book condemns the mother, it justifies her; at the same time that it shows Paul's failure, it offers rationalizations which place the failure elsewhere. The handling of the girl, Miriam, if viewed closely, is pathetic in what it signifies for Lawrence, both as man and artist. For Miriam is made the mother's scapegoat, and in a different way from the way that she was in life. The central section of the novel is shot through with alternate statements as to the source of the difficulty: Paul is unable to love Miriam wholly, and Miriam can love only his spirit. These contradictions appear sometimes within single paragraphs, and the point of view is never adequately objectified and sustained to tell us which is true. The material is never seen as material; the writer is caught in it exactly as firmly as he was caught in his experience of it. "That's how women are with me," said Paul. "They want me like mad, but they don't want to belong to me." So he might have said, and believed it; but at the end of the novel, Lawrence is still saying that, and himself believing it.

For the full history of this technical failure, one must read *Sons and Lovers* carefully and then learn the history of the manuscript from the book called *D. H. Lawrence: A Personal Record*, by one E. T., who was Miriam in life. The basic situation is clear enough. The first theme—the crippling effects of the mother's love—is developed right through to the end; and then suddenly, in the last few sentences, turns on itself, and Paul gives himself to life, not death. But all the way through, the insidious rationalizations of the second theme have crept in to destroy the artistic coherence of the work. A "split" would occur in Paul; but as the split is treated, it is superimposed upon rather than developed in support of the first theme. It is a rationalization made from it. If Miriam is made to insist on spiritual love, the meaning and the power of theme one are reduced; yet Paul's weakness is disguised. Lawrence could not separate the investigating analyst, who must be objective, from Lawrence, the subject of the book; and the sickness was not healed, the emotion not mastered, the novel not perfected. All this, and the character of a whole career, would have been altered if Lawrence had allowed his technique to discover the full meaning of his subject.

A Portrait of the Artist as a Young Man, like *Tono Bungay* and *Sons and Lovers*, is autobiographical, but unlike these it analyzes its material rigorously, and it defines the value and the quality of its experience not by appended comment or moral epithet, but by the texture of the style. The theme of *A Portrait*, a young artist's alienation from his environment, is explored and evaluated through three different styles and methods as Stephen Dedalus moves from childhood through boyhood into maturity. The opening pages are written in something like the Ulyssesean stream of consciousness, as the environment impinges directly on the consciousness of the infant and the child, a strange, opening world which the mind does not yet subject to questioning, selection, or judgment. But this style changes very soon, as the boy begins to explore his surroundings; and as his sensuous experience of the world is enlarged, it takes on heavier and heavier rhythms and a fuller and fuller body of sensuous detail, until it reaches a crescendo of romantic opulence in the emotional climaxes which mark Stephen's rejection of domestic and religious values. Then gradually the style subsides into the austere intellectuality of the final sections, as he defines to himself the outlines of the artistic task which is to usurp his maturity.

A highly self-conscious use of style and method defines the quality of experience in each of these sections, and, it is worth pointing out in connection with the third and concluding section, the style and method evaluate the experience. What has happened to Stephen is, of course, a progressive alienation from the life around him as he progressed in his initiation into it, and by the end of the novel, the alienation is complete. The final portion of the novel, fascinating as it may be for the developing esthetic creed of Stephen-Joyce, is peculiarly bare. The life experience was not bare, as we know from *Stephen Hero*; but Joyce is forcing technique to comment. In essence, Stephen's alienation is a denial of the human environment; it is a loss; and the austere discourse of the final section, abstract and almost wholly without sensuous detail or strong rhythm, tells us of that loss. It is a loss so great that the texture of the notation-like prose here suggests that the end is really all an illusion, that when Stephen tells us and himself that he is going forth to forge in the smithy of his soul the uncreated conscience of his race, we are to infer from the very quality of the icy, abstract void he now inhabits, the implausibility of his aim. For *Ulysses* does not create the conscience of the race; it creates our consciousness.

In the very last two or three paragraphs of the novel, the style changes once more, reverts from the bare, notative kind to the romantic prose of Stephen's adolescence. "Away! Away! The spell of arms and voices: the white arms of roads, their promise of close embraces and the black arms of tall ships that stand against the moon, their tale of distant nations. They are held out to say: We are alone—come." Might one not say that the austere ambition is founded on adolescent longing? That the excessive intellectual severity of one style is the counterpart of the excessive lyric relaxation of the other? And that the final passage of *A Portrait* punctuates the illusory nature of the whole ambition?

For *Ulysses* does not create a conscience. Stephen, in *Ulysses*, is a little older, and gripped now by guilt, but he is still the cold young man divorced from the human no less than the institutional environment. The environment of urban life finds a separate embodiment in the character of Bloom, and Bloom is as lost as Stephen, though touchingly groping for moorings. Each of the two is weakened by his inability to reach out, or to do more than reach out to the other. Here, then, is the theme again, more fully stated, as it were in counterpoint.

But if Stephen is not much older, Joyce is. He is older as an artist not only because he can create and lavish his godlike pity on a Leopold Bloom, but also because he knows now what both Stephen and Bloom mean, and *how much*, through the most brilliant technical operation ever made in fiction, they can be made to mean. Thus *Ulysses*, through the imaginative force which its techniques direct, is like a pattern of concentric circles, with the immediate human situation at its center, this passing on and out to the whole dilemma of modern life, this passing on and out beyond that to a vision of the cosmos, and this to the mythical limits of our experience. If we read *Ulysses* with more satisfaction than any other novel of this century, it is because its author held an attitude toward technique and the technical scrutiny of subject matter which enabled him to order, within a single work and with superb coherence, the greatest amount of our experience.

IV

In the United States during the last twenty-five years, we have had many big novels but few good ones. A writer like James T. Farrell apparently assumes that by endless redundancy in the description of the surface of American life, he will somehow write a book with the scope of *Ulysses*. Thomas Wolfe apparently assumed that by the mere disgorging of the raw material of his experience he would give us at last our epic. But except in a physical sense, these men have hardly written novels at all.

The books of Thomas Wolfe were, of course, journals, and the primary role of his publisher in transforming these journals into the semblance of novels is notorious. For the crucial act of the artist, the unique act which is composition, a sympathetic editorial blue pencil and scissors were substituted. The result has excited many people, especially the young, and the ostensibly critical have observed the prodigal talent with the wish that it might have been controlled. Talent there was, if one means by talent inexhaustible verbal energy, excessive response to personal experience, and a great capacity for auditory imitativeness, yet all of this has nothing to do with the novelistic quality of the written result; for until the talent is controlled, the material organized, the content achieved, there is simply the man and his life. It remains to be demonstrated that Wolfe's conversations were any less interesting as novels than his books, which is to say that his books are without interest as novels. As with Lawrence, our response to the books is determined, not by their qualities as novels, but by our response to him and his qualities as a temperament.

This is another way of saying that Thomas Wolfe never really knew what he was writing *about. Of Time and the River* is merely a euphemism for "Of a Man and his Ego." It is possible that had his conception of himself and of art included an adequate respect for technique and the capacity to pursue it, Wolfe would have written a great novel on his true subject—the dilemma of romantic genius; it was his true subject, but it remains his undiscovered subject, it is the subject which *we* must dig out for him, because he himself had neither the lamp nor the pick to find it in and mine it out of the labyrinths of his experience. Like Emily Brontë, Wolfe needed a point of view beyond his own which would separate his material and its effect.

With Farrell, the situation is opposite. He knows quite well what his subject is and what he wishes to tell us about it, but he hardly needs the novel to do so. It is significant that in sheer clumsiness of style no living writer exceeds him, for his prose is asked to perform no service beyond communication of the most rudimentary kind of fact. For his ambitions the style of the newspaper and the lens of the documentary camera would be quite adequate, yet consider the diminution which Leopold Bloom, for example, would suffer, if he were to be viewed from these, the technical perspectives of James Farrell. Under the eye of this technique, the material does not yield up enough; indeed, it shrinks.

More and more writers in this century have felt that naturalism as a method imposes on them strictures which prevent them from exploring through all the resources of technique the full amplifications of their subjects, and that thus it seriously limits the possible breadth of esthetic meaning and response. James Farrell is almost unique in the complacency with which he submits to the blunt techniques of naturalism; and his fiction is correspondingly repetitive and flat.

That naturalism had a sociological and disciplinary value in the nineteenth century is obvious; it enabled the novel to grasp materials and make analyses which had eluded it in the past, and to grasp them boldly; but even then it did not tell us enough of what, in Virginia Woolf's phrase, is "really real," nor did it provide the means to the maximum of reality coherently contained. Even the Flaubertian ideal of objectivity seems, today, an unnecessarily limited view of objectivity, for as almost every good writer of this century shows us, it is quite as possible to be objective about subjective states as it is to be objective about the circumstantial surfaces of life. Dublin, in *Ulysses,* is a moral setting: not only a city portrayed in the naturalistic fashion of Dickens' London, but also a map of the modern psyche with its oblique and baffled purposes. The second level of reality in no way invalidates the first, and a writer like Joyce shows us that, if the artist truly respects his medium, he can be objective about both at once. What we need in fiction is a devoted fidelity to every technique which will help us to discover and to evaluate our subject matter, and more than that, to discover the amplifications of meaning of which our subject matter is capable.

Most modern novelists have felt this demand upon them. André Gide allowed one of his artist-heroes to make an observation which considerably resembles an observation we have quoted from Wells. "My novel hasn't got a subject . . . Let's say, if you prefer it, it hasn't got *one* subject . . . 'A slice of life,' the naturalist school said. The great defect of that school is that it always cuts its slice in the same direction; in time, lengthwise. Why not in breadth? Or in depth? As for me I should like not to cut at all. Please understand; I should like to put everything into my novel." Wells, with his equally large blob of potential material, did not know how to cut it to the novel's taste; Gide cut, of course—in every possible direction. Gide and others. And those "cuts" are all the new techniques which modern fiction has given us. None, perhaps, is more important than that inheritance from French symbolism which Huxley, in the glittering wake of Gide, called "the musicalization of fiction." Conrad anticipated both when he wrote that the novel "must strenuously aspire to the plasticity of sculpture, to the colour of painting, and to the magic suggestiveness of music—which is the art of arts," and when he said of that early but wonderful piece of symbolist fiction, *The Heart of Darkness,* "It was like another art altogether. That sombre theme had to be given a sinister resonance, a tonality of its own, a continued vibration that, I hoped, would hang in the air and dwell on the ear after the last note had been struck."

The analogy with music, except as a metaphor, is inexact, and except as it points to techniques which fiction can employ as fiction, not very useful to our sense of craftsmanship. It has had an approximate exactness in only one work, Joyce's final effort, an effort unique in literary history, *Finnegans Wake,* and here, of course, those readers willing to make the effort Joyce demands, discovering an inexhaustible wealth and scope, are most forcibly reminded of the primary importance of technique to subject, and of their indivisibility.

The techniques of naturalism inevitably curtail subject and often leave it in its original area, that of undefined social experience. Those of our writers who, stemming from this tradition, yet, at their best, achieve a novelistic definition of social experience — writers like the occasional Sherwood Anderson, William Carlos Williams, the occasional Erskine Caldwell, Nathaniel West, and Ira Wolfert in *Tucker's People* — have done so by pressing naturalism far beyond itself, into positively Gothic distortions. The structural machinations of Dos Passos and the lyrical interruptions of Steinbeck are the desperate maneuvers of men committed to a method of whose limitations they despair. They are our symbolists *manqué*, who end as allegorists.

Our most accomplished novels leave no such impressions of desperate and intentional struggle, yet their precise technique and their determination to make their prose work in the service of their subjects have been the measure of their accomplishment. Hemingway's *The Sun Also Rises* and Wescott's *The Pilgrim Hawk* are consummate works of art not because they may be measured by some external, neoclassic notion of form, but because their forms are so exactly equivalent with their subjects, and because the evaluation of their subjects exists in their styles.

Hemingway has recently said that his contribution to younger writers lay in a certain necessary purification of the language; but the claim has doubtful value. The contribution of his prose was to his subject, and the terseness of style for which his early work is justly celebrated is no more valuable, as an end in itself, than the baroque involutedness of Faulkner's prose, or the cold elegance of Wescott's. Hemingway's early subject, the exhaustion of value, was perfectly investigated and invested by his bare style, and in story after story, no meaning at all is to be inferred from the fiction except as the style itself suggests that there is no meaning in life. This style, more than that, was the perfect technical substitute for the conventional commentator; it expresses and

26

it measures that peculiar morality of the stiff lip which Hemingway borrowed from athletes. It is an instructive lesson, furthermore, to observe how the style breaks down when Hemingway moves into the less congenial subject matter of social affirmation: how the style breaks down, the effect of verbal economy as mute suffering is lost, the personality of the writer, no longer protected by the objectification of an adequate technique, begins its offensive intrusion, and the entire structural integrity slackens. Inversely, in the stories and the early novels, the technique was the perfect embodiment of the subject and it gave that subject its astonishing largeness of effect and of meaning.

One should correct Buffon and say that style is the subject. In Wescott's *Pilgrim Hawk* — a novel which bewildered its many friendly critics by the apparent absence of subject — the subject, the story, is again in the style itself. This novel, which is a triumph of the sustained point of view, is only bewildering if we try to make a story out of the narrator's observations upon others; but if we read his observations as oblique and unrecognized observations upon himself the story emerges with perfect coherence, and it reverberates with meaning, is as suited to continuing reflection as the greatest lyrics.

The rewards of such respect for the medium as the early Hemingway and the occasional Wescott have shown may be observed in every good writer we have. The involutions of Faulkner's style are the perfect equivalent of his involved structures, and the two together are the perfect representation of the moral labyrinths he explores, and of the ruined world which his novels repeatedly invoke and in which these labyrinths exist. The cultivated sensuousity of Katherine Anne Porter's style — as of Eudora Welty's and Jean Stafford's — has charm in itself, of course, but no more than with these others does it have esthetic value in itself; its values lie in the subtle means by which sensuous details become symbols, and in the way the symbols provide a network which is the story, and which at the same time provides the writer and us with a refined moral insight by means of which to test it. When we put such writers against a writer like William Saroyan, whose respect is reserved for his own temperament, we are appalled by the stylistic irresponsibility we find in him, and by the almost total absence of theme, or defined subject matter, and the abundance of unwarranted feeling. Such a writer inevitably becomes a sentimentalist because he has no means by which to measure his emotion. Technique, at last, is measure.

These writers, from Defoe to Porter, are of unequal and very different talent, and technique and talent are, of course, after a point, two different things. What Joyce gives us in one direction, Lawrence, for all his imperfections as a technician, gives us in another, even though it is not usually the direction of art. Only in some of his stories and in a few of his poems, where the demands of technique are less sustained and the subject matter is not autobiographical, Lawrence, in a different way from Joyce, comes to the same esthetic fulfillment. Emily Brontë, with what was perhaps her intuitive grasp of the need to establish a tension between her subject matter and her perspective upon it, achieves a similar fulfillment; and, curiously, in the same way and certainly by intuition alone, Hemingway's early work makes a moving splendor from nothingness.

And yet, whatever one must allow to talent and forgive in technique, one risks no generalization in saying that modern fiction at its best has been peculiarly conscious of itself and of its tools. The technique of modern fiction, at once greedy and fastidious, achieves as its subject matter not some singleness, some topic or thesis, but the whole of the modern consciousness. It discovers the complexity of the modern spirit, the difficulty of personal morality, and the fact of evil — all the untractable elements under the surface which a technique of the surface alone cannot approach. It shows us — in Conrad's words, from *Victory* — that we all live in an "age in which we are camped like bewildered travellers in a garish, unrestful hotel," and while it puts its hard light on our environment, it penetrates, with its sharp weapons, the depths of our bewilderment. These are not two things, but only an adequate technique can show them as one. In a realist like Farrell, we have the environment only, which we know from the newspapers; in a subjectivist like Wolfe, we have the bewilderment only, which we record in our own diaries and letters. But the true novelist gives them to us together, and thereby increases the effect of each, and reveals each in its full significance.

Elizabeth Bowen, writing of Lawrence, said of modern fiction, "We want the naturalistic surface, but with a kind of internal burning. In Lawrence every bush burns." But the bush burns brighter in some places than in others, and it burns brightest when a passionate private vision finds its objectification in exacting technical search. If the vision finds no such objectification, as in Wolfe and Saroyan, there is a burning without a bush. In our committed realists, who deny the resources of art for the sake of life, whose technique forgives both innocence and slovenliness — in Defoe and Wells and Farrell — there is a bush but it does not burn. There, at first glance, the bush is only a bush; and then, when we look again, we see that, really, the thing is dead.

Techniques of Fiction

THERE must be many techniques of fiction, but how many? I suppose a great many more than there are techniques of poetry. Why this should be so, if it is, nobody quite knows, and if we knew, I do not know what use the knowledge would have. For the great disadvantage of all literary criticism is its radical ignorance, which in the very nature of its aims must be incurable. Even the aims of criticism are unknown, beyond very short views; for example, in the criticism of the novel, Mr. Percy Lubbock tells us that the secret of the art is the strategy of "point of view"; Mr. E. M. Forster that the novelist must simply give us "life," or the illusion of "bouncing" us through it—which looks like a broader view than Mr. Lubbock's, until we pause to examine it, when it turns out to be worse than narrow, since to look at everything is to see nothing; or again Mr. Edwin Muir holds that "structure" is the key to the novelist's success or failure. There is no need here to explain what these critics mean by "point of view," or "life," or "structure"; but they all mean something useful—in a short view, beyond which (I repeat) critics seem to know little or nothing.

What the novelists know may be another thing altogether, and

NOTE. Reprinted from the *Sewanee Review*, 1944, by permission of the author, the editor, and the Cummington Press.

it is that knowledge which ought to be our deepest concern. You will have to allow me the paradox of presuming to know what the novelists know—or some of them at any rate—while as a critic I profess to know nothing. The presumption might encourage us to predict from the very nature of the critic's ignorance the nature and quality of the knowledge possible to good writers of fiction. The novelist keeps before him constantly the structure and substance of his fiction as a whole, to a degree to which the critic can never apprehend it. For the first cause of critical ignorance is, of course, the limitations of our minds, about which we can do little, work at them as we will. It is the special ignorance by which we, as critics, are limited in the act of reading any extended work of the imagination. The imaginative work must always differ to such a great degree as almost to differ in kind from philosophical works, which our minds apprehend and retain almost as wholes through the logical and deductive structures which powerfully aid the memory. Who can remember, well enough to pronounce upon it critically, all of *War and Peace,* or *The Wings of the Dove,* or even *Death in Venice,* the small enclosed world of which ought at least to do something to aid our memories? I have reread all three of these books in the past year; yet for the life of me I could not pretend to know them as wholes, and without that knowledge I lack the materials of criticism.

Because Mr. Lubbock seems to know more than anybody else about this necessary ignorance of the critic, and for other important reasons, I believe him to be the best critic who has ever written about the novel. His book, *The Craft of Fiction,* is very nearly a model of critical procedure. Even in so fine a study as Albert Thibaudet's *Gustave Flaubert* there is nothing like the actual, as opposed to the merely professed, critical modesty of numerous statements like this by Lubbock: "Our critical faculty may be admirable; we may be thoroughly capable of judging a book justly, if only we could watch it at ease. But fine taste and keen perception are of no use to us if we cannot retain the image of the book; and the image escapes and evades us like a cloud."

Where, then, does Lubbock get the material of his criticism?

He gets as much of it as any critic ever gets by means of a bias
which he constantly pushes in the direction of extreme simplification of the novel in terms of "form," or "point of view" (after
James' more famous phrase, the "post of observation"), or more
generally in terms of the controlling intelligence which determines the range and quality of the scene and the action. It is the
only book on fiction which has earned unanimous dislike among
other critics (I do not know three novelists who have read it),
and the reason, I think, is that it is, in its limited terms, wholly
successful; or, if that is too great praise, it is successful in the
same sense, and to no less degree than the famous lecture notes
on the Greek drama taken down by an anonymous student at the
Lyceum in the fourth century B.C. The lecture notes and *The
Craft of Fiction* are studies of their respective arts in terms of
form; and I think that Lubbock had incomparably the more difficult job to do. The novel has at no time enjoyed anything like
the number and the intensity of objective conventions which the
drama, even in its comparatively formless periods, has offered to
the critic. The number of techniques possible in the novel are
probably as many as its conventions are few.

Having said so much in praise of Mr. Lubbock, I shall not, I
hope, seem to take it back if I say that even his intense awareness
of what the novelist knows fails somehow, or perhaps inevitably,
to get into his criticism. Anybody who has just read his account
of *Madame Bovary* comes away with a sense of loss, which is the
more intense if he has also just read that novel; though what the
loss is he no more than Mr. Lubbock will be able to say. Yet no
critic has ever turned so many different lights, from so many different directions, upon any other novel (except perhaps the
lights that are called today the social and the historical); and yet
what we get is not properly a revelation of the techniques of
Madame Bovary but rather what I should call a marvelously
astute chart of the operations of the central intelligence which
binds all the little pieces of drama together into the pictorial
biography of a silly, sad, and hysterical little woman, Emma
Bovary. It is this single interest, this undeviating pursuit of one

great clue, this sticking to the "short view" till the last horn blows and night settles upon the hunting field, which largely explains both the greatness of Mr. Lubbock's book and the necessary and radical ignorance of criticism. We cannot be both broad and critical, except in so far as knowledge of the world, of ideas, and of man generally is broadening; but then that knowledge has nothing to do specifically with the critical job; it only keeps it from being inhuman. That is something; but it is not criticism. To be critical is to be narrow in the crucial act or process of judgment.

But after we gather up all the short views of good critics, and have set the limits to their various ignorances, we are confronted with what is left out or, if you will, left over: I have a strong suspicion that this residue of the novel or the story is what the author knew as he wrote it. It is what makes the little scenes, or even the big ones, "come off." And while we no doubt learn a great deal about them when, with Mr. Muir, we study the general structure, or the relation of scenes, or, with Mr. Lubbock, follow the godlike control of the mind of Flaubert or of James through all the scenes to the climax—while this knowledge is indispensable, I should, myself, like to know more about the making of the single scene, and all the techniques that contribute to it; and I suspect that I am not asking the impossible, for this kind of knowledge is very likely the only kind that is actually within our range. It alone can be got at, definitely and at particular moments, even after we have failed, with Mr. Lubbock (honorable failure indeed), to "retain the image of the book."

It sounds very simple, as no doubt it is essentially a simple task to take a scene from a novel apart, and to see what makes it tick; but how to do it must baffle our best intentions. Suppose you want to understand by what arts Tolstoy, near the beginning of *War and Peace,* before the ground is laid, brings Peter, the bastard son of old Count Bezuhov, into the old Count's dying presence, and makes, of the atmosphere of the house and of the young man and the old man, both hitherto unknown to us, one of the great scenes of fiction: you would scarcely know better than I where to take hold of it, and I have only the merest clue. Suppose you feel, as I do, that after Rawdon Crawley comes home (I believe from gaol—it is hard to remember Thackeray) and finds Becky supping alone with Lord Steyne—suppose you feel that Thackeray should not have rung down the curtain the very moment Becky's exposure was achieved, but should have faced up to the tougher job of showing us Becky and Rawdon alone after Lord Steyne had departed: Is this a failure in a great novelist? If it is, why? The negative question, addressed to ourselves as persons interested in the techniques of an art, may also lead us to what the novelists know, or to much the same thing, what they should have known.

And, to come nearer home, what is the matter with Ty Ty Walden's philosophical meditations, towards the end of *God's Little Acre*, which freezes up our credulity and provokes our fiercest denial? It is surely not that Ty Ty is merely expressing as well as he can the doctrine of the innate goodness of man in the midst of depravity. That doctrine will do as well as any other in the mouth of a fictional character, provided his scene and his experience within the scene entitle him to utter it; but before we can believe that Ty Ty is actually thinking anything whatever, we have got in the first place to believe that Ty Ty is a man—which is precisely what Mr. Caldwell evidently did not think it important to make us do.

How shall we learn what to say about particular effects of the story, without which the great over-all structure and movement of the human experience which is the entire novel cannot be made credible to us? The professional critics pause only at intervals to descend to these minor effects which are of course the problems without which the other, more portentous problems which engage criticism could not exist. The fine artists of fiction, I repeat, because they produce these effects must understand them. And having produced them, they are silent about the ways they took to produce them, or paradoxical and mysterious like Flaubert, who told Maupassant to go to the station and look at the cab drivers until he understood the typical cab driver, and then to find the language to distinguish one cab driver from all others in the world. It is the sort of *obiter dicta* which can found schools and movements, and the schools and movements often come to some good, even though the slogan, like this one, means little.

I suppose only the better novelists, like Defoe, Madame de La Fayette, Turgenev, Dickens, Flaubert, many others as great as these, some greater, like Tolstoy and Dostoevski, knew the special secrets which I am trying, outside criticism, so to speak, to bring before you. There is almost a masonic tradition in the rise of any major art, from its undifferentiated social beginnings to the conscious aptitude which is the sign of a developed art form. Doubtless I ought to repeat once more that for some reason the moment the secrets of this aptitude come within the provenance of formal criticism, they vanish. They survive in the works themselves, and in the living confraternity of men of letters, who pass on by personal instruction to their successors the "tricks of the trade." The only man I have known in some twenty years of literary experience who was at once a great novelist and a great teacher, in this special sense, was the late Ford Madox Ford. His influence was immense, even upon writers who did not know him, even upon other writers, today, who have not read him. For it was through him more than any other man writing in English in our time that the great traditions of the novel came down to us. Joyce, a greater writer than Ford, represents by comparison a more restricted practice of the same literary tradition, a tradition that goes back to Stendhal in France, and to Jane Austen in England, coming down to us through Flaubert, James, Conrad, Joyce, Virginia Woolf, and Ernest Hemingway.

It is a tradition which has its own secrets to offer; yet in saying that, I am not claiming for it greater novelists than some other school can produce or novelists greater than those who just happen. There is Meredith (for those who, like Ramon Fernandez, can read him); there is Thomas Hardy, there is even the early H. G. Wells. But there is not Arnold Bennett; there is not Mr. Galsworthy; not Hugh Walpole nor Frank Swinnerton. This is prejudice, not criticism. And these are all Britons, not Americans.

35

FORMS OF MODERN FICTION

I have no desire to play possum on the American question. Yet I am convinced that among American novelists who have had large publics since the last war, only Dreiser, Faulkner, and Hemingway are of major importance. There are "good" popular novelists who have done much to make us at home physically in our own country; they have given us our scenes, our people, and above all our history; and these were necessary to the preliminary knowledge of ourselves which we have been a little late in getting and which must be got and assimilated if we are going to be a mature people. Possibly the American novel had to accomplish the task that in Europe had been done by primitive chronicle, mémoire, ballad, strolling player. The American novel has had to find a new experience, and only in our time has it been able to pause for the difficult task of finding out how to get itself written. That is an old story with us, yet beneath it lies a complexity of feeling that from Hawthorne down to our time has baffled our best understanding. The illustration is infinite in its variety. At this moment I think of my two favorite historians, Herodotus and Joinville, and I am embarrassed from time to time because Herodotus, the pagan, seems nearer to my experience than Joinville, the Christian chronicler of St. Louis. It is perhaps easier for us to feel comfortable with the remote and relatively neutral elements of our culture. Those experiences of Europe which just precede or overlap the American experience bemuse us, and introduce a sort of chemical ambivalence into our judgment. Joinville is both nearer to me than Herodotus, and less immediate. What American could not be brought to confess a similar paradox? To our European friends who are now beginning to know us, and who in all innocence may subscribe to the popular convention of The Simple American Mind, I would say, if it is not too impolite: Beware.

But the American novel is not my present subject, nor, thank heaven, the American mind. My subject is merely the techniques of fiction which now at last I feel that I am ready to talk about, not critically, you understand, but as a member of a guild. Ford used to say that he wrote his novels in the tone of one English gentleman whispering into the ear of another English gentleman: how much irony he intended I never knew; I hope a great deal. I intend none at all when I say that these remarks are set down by an artisan for other artisans.

Gustave Flaubert created the modern novel. Gustave Flaubert created the modern short story. He created both because he created modern fiction. I am not prepared to say that he created all our fictional forms and structures, the phases of the art of fiction that interest Mr. Lubbock and Mr. Muir. He did not originate all those features of the short story which interest historians and anthologists. These are other matters altogether. And I do not like to think that Flaubert created modern fiction because I do not like Flaubert. It was the fashion in France, I believe, until the Fall, to put Stendhal above Flaubert. I am not sure but I suspect that a very tired generation felt more at ease with a greater writer whose typical heroes are persons of mere energy and whose books achieve whatever clarity and form that they do achieve as an accident of the moral ferocity of the author. But without *Le Rouge et Le Noir,* or without what it put into circulation in the French literary milieu after 1830, Flaubert could not have written *Madame Bovary.* I do not like to think that Stendhal did this because I do not like Stendhal. Both Stendhal and Flaubert had the single dedication to art which makes the disagreeable man. Doubtless it would be pleasanter if the great literary discoveries could be made by gentlemen like Henry James, who did make his share, and who, of course, was a greater novelist than either of these Frenchmen; or by English squires; but we have got to take them, as Henry James would not do in the instance of Flaubert, as they come, and they often come a little rough.

A moment ago I introduced certain aspersions upon a few English novelists of the recent past, but it was with a purpose, for their limitations, sharply perceived by the late Virginia Woolf in her famous essay *Mr. Bennett and Mrs. Brown,* will make quite clear the difference between the novelist who, with Mr. Forster, merely bounces us along and the novelist who tries to do the whole job, the job that Flaubert first taught him to do. Mrs. Woolf is discussing Hilda Lessways, Arnold Bennett's heroine, and she says:

But we cannot hear her mother's voice, or Hilda's voice; we can only hear Mr. Bennett's voice telling us facts about rents and freeholds and copyholds and fines. What can Mr. Bennett be about? I have formed my own opinion of what Mr. Bennett is about—he is trying to make us imagine for him.

"Trying to make us imagine for him"—the phrase erects a Chinese wall between all that is easy, pleasant, and perhaps merely socially useful in modern fiction, and all that is rigorous, sober, and self-contained. Mrs. Woolf, again, in speaking of the novels of Galsworthy, Bennett, and Wells, says: "Yet what odd books they are! Sometimes I wonder if we are right to call them books at all. For they leave one with a strange feeling of incompleteness and dissatisfaction. In order to complete them it seems necessary to do something—to join a society, or, more desperately, to write a cheque."

That is very nearly the whole story: the novelist who tries to make us imagine for him is perhaps trying to make us write a cheque—a very good thing to do, and I am not sure that even the socially unconscious Flaubert was deeply opposed to it, though I shall not attempt to speak for him on the question of joining societies. Let us see this matter as reasonably as we can. All literature has a social or moral or religious purpose: the writer has something that he has got to say to the largest public possible. In spite of Flaubert's belief that he wrote only for himself, this is as true of *Madame Bovary* as of *Uncle Tom's Cabin*. Is there a real difference between these books that might justify us in setting apart two orders of literature? Perhaps; for the difference is very great between getting it all inside the book and leaving some of it irresponsibly outside. For even though the cheque be written in a good cause it is the result of an irresponsible demand upon the part of the novelist. But the distinction is not, I think, absolute, nor should it be. And I am sure that Sainte-Beuve was right when he wrote in his review of *Madame Bovary* that not all young married women in Normandy were like Emma: was there not the case of the childless young matron of central France who, instead of taking lovers and then taking arsenic, "adopted children about her . . . and instructed them in moral culture?" Very good; for it is obvious that persons who join societies and write cheques for moral culture are proper characters of fiction, as indeed all human beings of all degrees of charity or misanthropy are. But that is not the point at issue.

That point is quite simply that Flaubert, for the first time consciously and systematically, but not for the first time in the history of fiction, and not certainly of poetry—Flaubert taught us how to put this overworked and allegorical cheque *into* the novel, into its complex texture of scene, character, and action: which, of course, is one way of saying that he did the complete imaginative job himself, and did not merely point to what was going on, leaving the imaginative specification to our good will or to our intellectual vanity. (I pause here to remark the existence of a perpetual type of critic who prefers inferior literature, because it permits him to complete it. Flaubert understood the critics who, committed to the public function of teacher, resent being taught.) This completeness of presentation in the art of fiction was not, I repeat, something new, but I gather that it had previously appeared only here and there, by the sheer accident of genius: I think of Petronius; a few incidents in Boccaccio; half a dozen scenes by the Duke of Saint-Simon (the memorialists shade imperceptibly into the novelists); the great scene in which the Prince de Clèves tells his wife that he has refrained from expressing his love for her because he wished to avoid conduct improper to a husband; Emma Woodhouse with Mr. Knightly at the parlor table looking at the picture album; countless other moments in early prose literature; but most of all that great forerunner, *Moll Flanders,* which is so much all of a piece in the Flaubertian canon that sometimes I think that Flaubert wrote it; or that nobody wrote either Defoe or Flaubert. For when literature reaches this stage of maturity, it is anonymous, and it matters little who writes it.

This is extravagant language. Or is it? It is no more than we are accustomed to when we talk about poetry, or music, or most of all the classical drama. The fourth-century lecture notes, to which I have already referred, some time ago licensed the most pretentious claims for the stage, and for poetry generally. I am only saying that fiction can be, has been, and *is* an art, as the various poetries are arts. Is this an extravagant claim? Only, I am convinced, in the minds of the more relaxed practitioners of this art, who excuse something less than the utmost talent and effort, and in the minds of critics who find the critical task more exacting than historical reporting, which reduces the novel to a news supplement. Was, as a matter of fact, Emma typical of young Norman womanhood? Are the Okies and Arkies just as Steinbeck represents them? What a triumph for the historians when it was found that there had actually been a young man whose end was like Julien Sorel's! And is it true what Mr. Faulkner says about Dixie? If it is, is what Mr. Stark Young says also true? This, I submit, is the temper of American criticism of fiction, with rare exceptions of little influence.

It is time now, toward the end of this causerie, to produce an image, an *exemplum,* something out of the art of fiction that underlies all the major problems of "picture and drama," symmetry, foreshortening, narrative pattern, pace and language—all those complexities of the novelist's art which Henry James, alone of the great fictionists, tried to explain (how much he coyly evaded!) in his famous Prefaces: problems that laid the ground for Mr. Lubbock's beautiful study. I am looking for something very simple and, in its direct impact, conclusive; a scene or an incident that achieves fullness of realization in terms of what it gives us to see and to hear. It must offer us fullness of rendition, not mere direction or statement. Don't state, says James, time and again— render! Don't tell us what is happening, let it happen! So I would translate James. For our purposes here it cannot be too great a scene, if we would see all round it: it must be a scene that will give us the most elementary instruction in that branch of the art of which the critics tell us little. What shall it be? Shall it be

Prince André lying wounded under the wide heavens? Shall it be Moll Flanders peeping out of the upstairs window of the inn at her vanishing fourth (or is it fifth?) and undivorced husband, slyly avoiding him because she is in the room with her fifth or is it sixth? I could find perfect *exempla* in James himself. What could be better than Milly Theale's last soirée before she becomes too ill to appear again? Then there are James' fine "sitting-room scenes," the man and the woman talking out the destiny of one or both of them: Lambert Strether and Maria Gostrey, John Marcher and May Bartram, Merton Densher and Milly Theale. Or there is Strether looking down upon the boat in which Chad Newsome and Madame de Vionnet, unaware of Strether's scrutiny, betray that air of intimacy which discloses them for the first time to Strether as lovers.

Yet about these excellent scenes there is something outside our purpose, a clue that would sidetrack us into the terms of form and structure which I have virtually promised to neglect. Let us select an easy and perhaps even quite vulgar scene, a stock scene, in fact, that we should expect to find in a common romantic novel, or even in a Gothic story provided the setting were reduced to the bourgeois scale. Let the situation be something like this: A pretty young married woman, bored with her husband, a small-town doctor, has had an affair of sentiment with a young man, who has by this time left town. Growing more desperate, she permits herself to be seduced by a neighboring landowner, a coarse Lothario, who soon tires of her. Our scene opens with the receipt of his letter of desertion. He is going away and will not see her again. The young woman receives the letter with agitation and runs upstairs to the attic, where having read the letter she gives way to hysteria. She looks out the window down into the street, and decides to jump and end it all. But she grows dizzy and recoils. After a moment she hears her husband's voice; the servant touches her arm; she comes to and recovers.

It is distinctly unpromising: James would not have touched it; Balzac, going the whole hog, might have let her jump, or perhaps left her poised for the jump while he resumed the adventures of Vautrin. But in any case there she stands, and as I have reported the scene you have got to take my word for it that she is there at all: you do not see her, you do not hear the rapid breathing and the beating heart, and you have, again, only my word for it that she is dizzy. What I have done here, in fact, is precisely what Mrs. Woolf accused the Georgian novelists of doing: I am trying to make you imagine for me, perhaps even covertly trying to make you write a cheque for the Society for the Improvement of Provincial Culture, or the Society for the Relief of Small Town Boredom, or for a subscription to the Book-of-the-Month Club which would no doubt keep the young woman at improving her mind, and her mind off undesirable lovers. I hope that we shall do all these good things. But you must bear in mind that the Book-of-the-Month Club would probably send her the kind of literature that I have just written for you, so that she too might take to writing cheques. Is there any guarantee that they would be good cheques? The question brings us up short against certain permanent disabilities of human nature, which we should do well to see as objectively as possible, in the language of a greater artist; which is just what we shall now proceed to do:

Charles was there; she saw him; he spoke to her; she heard nothing, and she went on quickly up the stairs, breathless, distraught, dumb, and ever holding this horrible piece of paper, that crackled between her fingers like a plate of sheet-iron. On the second floor she stopped before the attic-door, that was closed.

Then she tried to calm herself; she recalled the letter; she must finish it; she did not dare to. And where? How? She would be seen! "Ah, no! here," she thought, "I shall be all right."

Emma pushed open the door and went in.

The slates threw straight down a heavy heat that gripped her temples, stifled her; she dragged herself to the closed garret-window. She drew back the bolt, and the dazzling light burst in with a leap.

Opposite, beyond the roofs, stretched the open country till it was lost to sight. Down below, underneath her, the village square was empty; the stones of the pavement glittered, the weather-cocks on the houses were motionless. At the corner of the street from a lower story, rose a kind of humming with strident modulations. It was Binet turning.

She leant against the embrasure of the window, and re-read the letter with angry sneers. But the more she fixed her attention upon it, the more confused were her ideas. She saw him again, heard him, encircled him with her arms, and the throbs of her heart, that beat against her breast like blows of a sledge-hammer, grew faster and faster, with uneven intervals. She looked about her with the wish that the earth might crumble into pieces. Why not end it all? What restrained her? She was free. She advanced, looked at the paving-stones, saying to herself, "Come! Come!"

The luminous ray that came straight up from below drew the weight of her body towards the abyss. It seemed to her that the floor dipped on end like a tossing boat. She was right at the edge, almost hanging, surrounded by vast space. The blue of the heavens suffused her, the air was whirling in her hollow head; she had but to yield, to let herself be taken; and the humming of the lathe never ceased, like an angry voice calling her.

"Emma! Emma!" cried Charles.

She stopped.

"Wherever are you? Come!"

The thought that she had just escaped from death made her faint with terror. She closed her eyes; then she shivered at the touch of a hand on her sleeve; it was Félicité.

"Master is waiting for you, madame; the soup is on the table."

And she had to go down to sit at table.*

The English translation is not good; its failure to convey the very slight elevation of tone is a fundamental failure. It is not a rhetorical elevation, but rather one of perfect formality and sobriety. We are not looking at this scene through Emma's eyes. We occupy a position slightly above and to one side, where we see her against the full setting; yet observe that at the same time we see nothing that she does not see, hear nothing that she does not hear. It is one of the amazing paradoxes of the modern novel, whose great subject is a man alone in society or even against society, almost never with society, that out of this view of man isolated we see developed to the highest possible point of virtuosity and power a technique of putting man wholly into his physi-

* *Madame Bovary,* Modern Library edition, pp. 235–36.

cal setting. The action is not stated from the point of view of the author; it is rendered in terms of situation and scene. To have made this the viable property of the art of fiction was to have virtually made the art of fiction. And that, I think, is our debt to Flaubert.

But we should linger over this scene if only to try our hands at what I shall now, for the first time, call sub-criticism, or the animal tact which permits us occasionally to see connections and correspondences which our rational powers, unaided, cannot detect. What capital feature of the scene seems (if it does) to render the actuality more than any other? The great fact, I think, is the actuality, and your sense of it is all that is necessary. Yet I like to linger over the whirring lathe of old Binet, a lay figure or "flat character" who has done little in the novel and will never do much, and whose lathe we merely noted from the beginning as a common feature of a small town like Yonville. I should like to know when Flaubert gave him the lathe, whether just to tag him for us; whether, writing the present scene, he went back and gave it to him as a "plant" for use here later; or whether, having given him the lathe, he decided it would be useful in this scene.

What is its use? James said that the work of fiction must be "a direct impression of life," a very general requirement; but in the perspective of nearly ninety years since the publication of *Madame Bovary* and the rise of the Impressionist novel through Henry James, James Joyce, and Virginia Woolf, the phrase takes on a more specific sense. Mind you the phrase is not "direct representation," which only the stage can give us. But here, using this mechanic's tool, Flaubert gives us a direct *impression* of Emma's sensation at a particular moment (which not even the drama could accomplish), and thus by rendering audible to us what Emma alone could hear he charged the entire scene with actuality. As Emma goes to the window she merely notes that Binet's lathe is turning—"C'était Binet qui tournait." Then she looks down at the street which seems to rise towards her—"Allons! Allons!" she whispers, because she cannot find the will to jump. We have had rendered to us visually the shock of violent suicide. Now comes the subtle fusion of the reaction and of the pull towards self-destruction, which is the humming in her head: how can Flaubert *render* it for us? Shall we not have to take his word for it? Shall we not have to imagine for him? No: "l'air circulait dans sa tête creuse," he says; and then: "le ronflement du tour ne discontinuait pas, comme une voix furieuse qui l'appelait"—"the whirring of the lathe never stopped, like a voice of fury calling her." The humming vertigo that draws the street towards her is rendered audible to us by the correlative sound of the lathe.

That is all, or nearly all, there is to it; but I think it is enough to set up our image, our *exemplum.* I leave to you, as I constantly reserve for myself, the inexhaustible pleasure of tracing out the infinite strands of interconnection in this and other novels, complexities as deep as life itself but ordered, fixed, and dramatized into arrested action. If I have made too much of Flaubert, or too much of too little of Flaubert, I can only say that I have not willfully ignored men as great, or greater. It is proper to honor France, and to honor the *trouvère,* the discoverer; for it has been through Flaubert that the novel has at last caught up with poetry.

The Witness of the Notebooks

FOR a certain class of reader, larger in numbers now than at any
time in the last hundred years, the most notable literary event of
the decade is likely to be *The Notebooks of Henry James*, now at
length in print.* The reader in question is one who loves to follow
up the simple enjoyment of a book with a serious analysis of its
artistry, one whose preference in fiction is for work inviting to
such analysis by the lavish and unremitting care bestowed by the
author on every minutest point of fitness and beauty—always
providing that the author is of an intelligence and sensibility
promising well for such an undertaking and that his subject matter is of human interest and solidity capable of bearing so great
pressure of thought. It is of the highest interest, in such a case,
to have records from the author's own pen of his artistic intentions and of the process by which he has endeavored to realize
them in his work, as in the priceless correspondence of Flaubert.
Among novelists in English, it has long been recognized that
Henry James is the one who best fulfills all the conditions for providing this supremest gratification of critical connoisseurship.

With his prefaces to the New York edition of his collected

NOTE. Reprinted from *Furioso*, 1948, by permission of the editors and the author.
   * Edited with an introduction and commentary by F. O. Matthiessen and
Kenneth B. Murdock. New York: Oxford University Press, 1947. 425 pp.

works (1907–9), this enchanting game could begin in earnest, or
—for those without access to these precious volumes—with the
collection of these prefaces under a single cover, *The Art of the
Novel* (1934). The original prefaces were followed in 1917 by the
publication, along with his unfinished novels, *The Ivory Tower*
and *The Sense of the Past*, of the "scenarios" for these stories dictated by James to his secretary. And now, with the publication of
nine of his notebooks, and of three preliminary sketches for novels
published or unpublished (including *The Ambassadors*), we have
the largest body of material ever made available for study of the
imaginative process by which the dim first hint of a story is
elaborated, modified, and carried through infinite readjustments
of detail to its triumphant objectification in the finished work.
In addition, we have a record of James' agonized and ill-fated
struggle, through years, to make himself a successful writer for
the stage; and a record, too, of how, in compensation for his failure in this line, he tried to apply in short story and novel the
technical lessons derived from his experience as a playwright. And
finally we have bits of autobiography more intimate and unstudied than anything in *Notes of a Son and Brother* and *The
Middle Years*. There are numerous references to the litmus-paper
reaction of his temperament to European subjects in preference
to American which has brought upon him such a flood of censorious criticism. And there are more obscure hints in regard to
his private emotional life which, undocumented as this life still
remains, cannot fail to have a bearing on the essential character
of his product.

Psychologists would give much to know precisely what was the
physical disability from which James suffered following an accident in his eighteenth year, preventing his enlistment as a soldier
in the Civil War, and quite probably having something to do
with his never being married. It is argued by Saul Rosenzweig*
that this accident was for James' psychology but the culmination
of a long series of circumstances, largely having to do with the
personal prestige of his father and his elder brother, contributing

* "The Ghost of Henry James," *Partisan Review*, 11:436–55, Fall 1944.

in him to the development of a "castration complex," or to the psychological "death" which corresponded to the actual or spiritual death of characters in several of his stories. Whatever we may think of this particular formula, we cannot but be impressed with the essential loneliness of James, his comparative want of commitment to intimate personal relations of the kind that require an absolute surrender of one's self to the demands of "life." To the pieties of kinship he paid adequate tribute. He had many close friendships, literary and social, with both men and women, and we cannot suppose him to have failed in any of the obligations of friendship. He was a deeply and finely feeling man, but one does not see him as the sort of man for whom feeling is never complete till it is expressed in action, and who, for the sake of this objectification of feeling in experience, will take the great crude risks and—if necessary—lose in life itself the mastery over himself.

No one touched life at more points, but he seems to have touched it with the imagination, at a distance, with a steady maintenance of esthetic detachment. Perhaps this makes him the artist in essence; but we have few records anywhere of the artist so reduced to essence and uninvolved with the urgencies and appetites of the man. There is something pathetic in James' references to his own intensities of "living" in the seclusion of his workshop—living, that is, in the passionate reconstruction of the lives of imaginary beings. The famous outburst of Lambert Strether to Little Bilham in *The Ambassadors,* in which he urges the young man not to fail to live as he has failed, suggested by a similar earnest demonstration of William Dean Howells under like circumstances, always makes one wonder whether James' own case may not have been obscurely present in his mind.

The matter is rather complicated as we may see from the following notebook entry: "Something in reference to man who, like W. D. H. (say), has never known *at all* any woman BUT his wife —and at 'time of life' somehow sees it, is face to face with it: little situation *on* it. *Ca rentre,* however, rather, into the idea (is a small side of it) of *The Ambassadors.* But *never,* NEVER—in any

48

degree to call a relation at all: *and on American lines.* x x x x x"
Well! James had himself many relations with women that might
well be called relations—like Strether's relation with Mrs. Newsome, or better, as not "on American lines," with Maria Gostrey.
But had he never thought of what a man's relation with his wife
might involve for one who had "never known at all any woman
BUT" her—for depth, intensity, for finesse and "drama"? James'
stories testify to the fact of his knowledge here. And somewhere
in the deeper reaches of his consciousness he must have suspected
that Howells' relation to his wife, all by itself, might have been
worth a dozen of Strether's with Maria Gostrey. James' intense
concern with very special and esoteric "relations," relations with
a *difference,* might be seen as an effort at compensation for what
he had missed in the way of the old standard shopworn relations
into which the ordinary man plunges so recklessly and with so
little thought of making them special. The ideal (or sentimental)
essence of living experience which he so steadily pursued would
be, in this view, a substitute for the gross stuff of experience
which he may have felt obscurely as having passed him by. His
losses, at any rate, were amply balanced by his gains. One special
gain that he had made in passing from the gross substance to
the refined essence of human experience was his vastly greater
freedom in invention and in manipulation of the elements of story.

James records in his notebooks the germination of his "pretty
idea for a short tale to which I should give the name of *The Altar
of the Dead.*" In this story he presents a man who made a special
cult of friends whom he had lost and burned candles in their
memory on a special altar in a suburban church. But at a certain
point in the writing he broke off, asking himself whether it was
worth while going on with. For "the thing is a 'conceit,' after all,
a little fancy which doesn't hold a great deal. Such things betray
one—that I more and more (if possible) feel. *Plus je vais,* the
more intensely it comes home to me that solidity of subject, importance, emotional capacity of subject, is the only thing on
which, henceforth, it is of the slightest use for me to expend myself. . . . Only the fine, the large, the human, the fundamental,

49

the passionate things." James did finish *The Altar of the Dead,* managing to elicit from his shadowy subject some of the "importance, emotional capacity" which would make it worthy of his serious treatment. But we can well understand why, as it first came to him, he considered it a mere conceit; and why to many other ideas for stories he applied the same term or called them "thin little things."

He gathered his ideas from many diverse sources. From the lady he took down to dinner, who told him of the scandalous quarrel between a Scotch woman and her son over the precious things she had taken away with her from the dower house, carried to such a pitch of acrimony that the mother did not hesitate to denounce her son as illegitimate (*The Spoils of Poynton*); from a story told of the Vanderbilt divorce, "his engaging the *demi-mondaine,* in Paris, to *s'afficher* with him in order to force his virago of a wife to divorce him" (*The Special Type*); from Edmund Gosse's account of the J. A. Symonds ménage, the wife's complete want of sympathy with what he wrote and with his entire outlook on life (*The Author of Beltraffio*). Certainly none of these subjects were "conceits"; they were life in the raw as it might have been seen by Balzac or Zola, with fullest provision for "the human, the fundamental, the passionate things." By the time James was through with them the crudities of motive and action had been eliminated or alembicated. They were still human and fundamental in all conscience; but it was the refined humanity of idealizing sentiment, and not the gross animality of greed, hatred, and sensual passion. To *The Author of Beltraffio* James added "horrors" of his own necessary to dramatize the theme; but these were psychological horrors, perversions of feeling which only a Freud would be able to trace back through all their subtle disguises to their obscure origin.

More often the germs of story in James were much more tenuous, abstract, and depersonalized. "What is there to the idea of *Too late*—of some friendship or passion or bond—some affection long desired and waited for, that is formed too late?" Or this: "*L'honnête femme n'a pas de roman*—beautiful little 'literary

(?)' subject to work out in a short tale. The trial, the exhibition, the proof: —either it's not a *'roman,'* or it's not *honnête.* When it becomes the thing it's guilty, when it doesn't become guilty it doesn't become the thing." Somewhat less abstract but still far from anything like a constituted character or situation are the first dim hints for *The Sense of the Past* and *The Ambassadors* — the first developed from Howells' suggestion of an "international ghost," the second from the "five words" spoken by Howells to Jonathan Sturges in Whistler's garden. None of these germs is greater than the biblical grain of mustard seed, "which is indeed the least of all seeds: but when it is grown, it is the greatest of all herbs, and becometh a tree, so that the birds of the air come and lodge in the branches thereof." And the same parable applies to the only slightly more concrete situations which formed the starting point for *The Golden Bowl, The Awkward Age, The Wings of the Dove.* He was forever grasping at "the tip of the tail" of some elusive idea. Sometimes an idea would lie dormant for many years, and a considerable number were never seriously taken up.

But once his imagination had been quite caught by an idea, he began working on it with all his powers of invention and manipulation. He turned it in every light; altered the sex and nationality of his characters; revised their marital status—single, married, lovers, widows; provided them with confidants, with foils, with fathers, with money, determined their occupation. He reversed the situation or in some way doubled it, trying for new "values" and points of reference, for some "turn of the screw" that would raise the situation to a higher pitch of intensity or rarity and squeeze out the last drop of "precious" meaning. He complicated the relations of his characters, gave them double and triple functions in reference to the theme and issue. He "squared" them, paired them off, set them in new and elaborate combinations. He arranged the material circumstances of his story so as to give the freest play to his characters' penchant for spiritual intrigue. He always had something up his sleeve. He was as full of devices as a French exponent of the well-made play. His matter was as plastic to his hand as the matter of the cosmos to the Platonic demiurge.

And his matter was thus plastic because what he is primarily concerned with is not the gross substance so much as the ideal essence of life. In American scholarship there is a disposition to classify James as a realist, and that for reasons to which I will later refer. But if the realist is one who aims to tell the plain truth about human nature under ordinary or typical circumstances, then James will hardly qualify. For his aim is ever to tell the special truth about highly selected types under circumstances carefully arranged to give free play to their exceptionally refined sentimental reactions. The point is not that he does not tell the truth, and highly significant and illuminating truth, about human nature. But his stage is so set, his issues so drawn, his primary assumptions so determined, that the truth he tells is normative rather than descriptive and statistical. And that is surely not what is meant by realism when we are considering its main direction and intention.

In every major story of James some of the principals, at least one of them, is devoted before all else to what we may call the fine art of living on the ethical plane. And this means that what they are after primarily is not the gross substance of life, with its instinctive and more or less material satisfactions, but whatever will satisfy the demands of their ideal nature. This should be enough in itself to make us hesitate to apply the term *realism* without qualification to the stories in which they figure. One thinks at once of Lambert Strether in *The Ambassadors* and of Maisie in *What Maisie Knew*. In *The Ambassadors* the central situation, so far as active living and moral problem are concerned, is that of the young man, Chad Newsome, whom Strether has undertaken to "save" from the toils of some woman in Paris. Strether has nothing to do with this directly, and yet he is given the center of the stage, which is transferred from the action itself, the problem itself, as it concerns the principals, Chad and Mme de Vionnet, to the mind of the middle-aged Strether, whose mission, as he sees it, requires that he should appraise the situation and take a stand in regard to it. And so, for James, the story proper, the "adventure" itself, is that of Lambert Strether, who is making up in appreciation of Chad's case for the "life" which he has somehow missed himself. This exciting experience *is* indeed Strether's tardy and vicarious form of living.

In *What Maisie Knew* James provides a rather complicated plot, in which the parents of a little girl, after being divorced, are each remarried, and then the two step-parents form a tie with one another. Since the ruling of the court is that Maisie shall live alternately with her two divorced parents, she comes to know in turn the persons they marry, one of whom is more attached to her than either of her proper parents. She is also in a position to follow, with a child's mind of angelic innocence and uncanny knowingness, all the windings of this sordid intrigue, of which the keynotes are selfishness, sensuality, and social irresponsibility. But it is not the intrigue that holds the stage — as would normally be the case in realistic fiction — it is the child's mind, and (ironically) the part played by her innocence in the development of the intrigue. "The child seen as creating by the fact of its forlornness a relation between its step-parents, the more intimate the better, dramatically speaking; the child by the mere appeal of neglectedness . . . weaving about, with the best faith in the world, the close web of sophistication; the child becoming the center and pretext for a fresh system of misbehaviour . . . there would be the 'full' irony, there the promising theme into which the hint I had originally picked up would logically flower."

Two points of particular interest strike one in connection with *Maisie*. One is the illustration it gives of James' faculty for manipulation, elaboration, and combination of the story elements. Given the first germ of the story he has to determine the sex of the child, and he seems immediately to have felt that its being a girl would enable him to squeeze out more of irony and general interest from the situation. It is not clear whether, in the first hint, it was one or both of the parents who had remarried; for his account in the preface does not agree in this matter with that in the notebooks. It seems not unlikely that, as the incident came to him from his informant, it was only *one* of them, but that by the time he came to write down his note, two days later, he already realized the infinitely greater possibilities involved in making it both. Without this he would not have had the new tie formed by the step-parents, and the sense of responsibility and love which they felt for Maisie greater than that of her real parents, and the way in which this brought them into their unhallowed relation. The remarriage of both parents provided one of those symmetries of which James was so fond; and in what followed he performed one of his characteristic tricks of reversing the natural situation and turning everything upside down. All of this prodigious flowering of the germ had taken place within two days. But innumerable further points remained to be clarified and entirely new items to be added. It was still to be determined what should be the tie between the step-parents, whether to have them marry one another after the death of the parents, or, better still, "to make the child a fresh bone of contention, a fresh source of dramatic situations *du vivant* of the original parents." Names and conditions and peculiarities of character remained to be provided later. And much later were to be provided the governesses, and especially the incomparable Mrs. Wix, with whom Maisie was destined to carry on the astonishing conversations in which the child and the scandalized adult were to shadow forth by ingenious and decorous indirections all the crude and indecorous turnings of the intrigue.

Mrs. Wix was absolutely necessary in order to displace the center of interest—divert the main interest from the four elders and their gross story to Maisie and her refined interpretation of it all. And this brings us to the second point in connection with James' method. Mrs. Wix is one of innumerable examples of the confidant, a necessary device for implementing his favorite technique of the limited point of view. As in *The Ambassadors* everything is presented to us from the point of view of Lambert Strether, so in *Maisie* everything is presented from that of the little girl. There are many things to be said in favor of the limited point of view. It is a means of giving to the picture focus, perspective, scale, intensity, intimacy, and many other highly desirable artistic values. But one cannot miss the infallible connection in James between the limited point of view and the indirect presentation. And one cannot fail to associate this preference for indirection with the fact that so many of his characters seem, like James himself, to touch life with the imagination, by "appreciation," rather than with the common emotions, by participation, so that what they experience is not the direct contact with life but life at one remove.

Somehow related to this is the frequency with which James' characters find their satisfaction in renunciation rather than possession of the object of desire. We know, of course, that a lower satisfaction has often to be given up for the sake of a higher. We know that self-sacrifice may be, under the right circumstances, a religious or a patriotic virtue. We know, too, that many people are afflicted with the psychological malady known as masochism. But with James' characters self-sacrifice is not religious or patriotic; and he is not thinking of it as a symptom of abnormal psychology. It is clearly offered as an example of a refined and superior reaction to certain situations. And we cannot but feel that the examples are too numerous for ordinary reality; and that, even where, as with Fleda Vetch and Isabel Archer, there is something like a point of honor involved, the point of honor is somewhat over-strained for normal human nature. We feel that in such cases again we have to do with spirits who are content with life at one remove.

Even with a character like Maggie Verver, whose dealings with life are calculated to recover what she has lost rather than to let it go, we feel that the whole tone and manner of her approach to the situation are those of a spirit more capable of "appreciation" than of passionate emotional involvement. Otherwise she would have been unable to maintain such cool self-possession and such perfect control over the emotional forces represented by her husband, her father, and the woman who had become her father's wife and her husband's mistress. The husband and the mother-in-law fall in the same category. And as for the Prince Amerigo, the facility with which he lends himself to Maggie's desire to keep up her intimacy with her father, even to the point of starting a liaison with the father's wife, and the equal facility with which he is brought back to his wife when that is what is called for by her strategy, is evidence of his extraordinary capacity for appreciation, his extraordinary faculty for taking the affairs of the heart on the high level of abstract sentiment.

It is characters like these that lend themselves most readily to James' passion for sentimental mathematics, in which each of the Pythagorean numbers is susceptible of being used in every conceivable relation to all the others—in which the possible combinations and recombinations are practically unlimited, and the most interesting and edifying solutions may be arrived at by the most unexceptionable of processes. It is largely this which gives him his surprising facility in manipulating the phenomena of life. For the realist the phenomena are much more refractory, with limits set on every hand to what is humanly possible.

But there is a sense in which the word realist may properly be applied to James. (And this apart from the fact that, in the supporting framework of his story, he was much more daring than earlier American novelists in the use of situations generally considered taboo—such as that between Charlotte Stant and the Prince Amerigo.) He was much more concerned to give convincing particularity to all the circumstances of the story than was the case with the common run of American novelists before his time. He was deeply immersed in the great French and Russian realists; and was it not Maupassant himself, in the preface to *Pierre et Jean,* who pointed out that the primary aim of the realist is to assemble facts in such a way as to produce the *illusion of reality?* It is true that James did not rely, especially in his later work, on the piling up of detail in the manner of Zola. His reliance was rather on *selection* of detail, with emphasis on what was characteristic and individualizing. Here he was in the tradition of Flaubert and Maupassant, with their insistence on the *mot juste*; for the *mot juste* in fiction is the word that most precisely evokes the particular essence of the particular cab horse or whatever it is that is being given the spotlight.

The disposition of most American novelists had been to deal in the general or broadly typical and content themselves with the most literary, the most conventional, and the least concretely characterizing term. And the general effect was pretty pale and thin. James had an abhorrence for the cliché, the phrase worn thin with constant using and vaguely applicable to any of the innumerable members of the same species. He had a passion for giving uniqueness to any place, any occasion, any character, and he had a passion for discovering altogether new species of place, occasion, and character — species not new in nature, but never before identified by a writer of fiction; and not necessarily out of the way except in the sense that they do not fall under any of the half-dozen long exploited types. The new species is the species freshly seen, independently realized in the imagination, not taken on faith, and so for all psychological purposes more *real* than the old hand-me-down. This passion he had naturally; it was developed by his reading; and it was a valuable asset, if not a positive prerequisite, for one, like him, who was dealing with super-subtle essences, which if not objectified with more than usual preciseness would remain merely sentimental and romantic.

You can see James forever working on this problem in his notebooks and scenarios. You see him patiently evolving and giving sharper definition to the character of Strether, of Mrs. Newsome, Maria Gostrey, Little Bilham, Mona Brigstock. You see him trying out various alternatives for Strether as to profession, career, and earlier domestic involvements. You see him trying to suggest "the kind of *monde*" the de Vionnets belong to, of which Maria Gostrey gives to Strether "all due, all manageable or communicable, notion, putting the presumptions before him vividly and interestingly enough." You see him imagining, of Jeanne de Vionnet, how different she is, "in her way and degree, from pretty little girls of seventeen as hitherto known to him."

But most of the concrete details of characterization and the words themselves are to be left till the moment of writing the story proper. It is on another type of detail that James bestows the greatest pains in the notebooks. In order to make his narrative truthful and right in effect, he must work out in advance and play by play the intricate game of chess in which his characters are engaged. He must see that every move is plausibly motivated, that every change of position is "inevitable" in terms of the given forces, that every individual scene is firmly grounded, vividly imagined, and attached to those that go before and after by threads as frail as gossamer and as binding as steel. It is for *The Spoils of Poynton* and *What Maisie Knew* that we have the most detailed of these outlines as from day to day they were being patiently and laboriously drawn up, with James perpetually admonishing himself to look closer at his subject and give it the utmost rightness of presentation in detail.

Fleda Vetch is down at Ricks—has come down to find Mrs. Gereth installed and in possession of most of the treasures of Poynton. I did what I could yesterday to handle her arrival, but I *must thresh out finely every inch of the action** from that point to the end. The sense of what her friend has done quite appals the girl, and what has now passed between her and Owen prepares her for a great stir of feeling on his behalf and pitying sense of his spoliations. *I am here dealing with very delicate elements, and I must make the operation, the presentation, of each thoroughly sharp and clear.** . . . (the situation as to Owen's marriage) The light on Mrs. Gereth's action . . . that she encounters at Ricks changes the whole situation: causes her to hold her breath . . . Now, *voyons un peu, mon bon;*† the whole idea of my thing is that Fleda becomes rather fine, DOES something, distinguishes herself (to the reader), and that this is really almost all that has made the little anecdote worth telling at all. . . . But *I am confronted with a little difficulty which requires my looking it as coolly and calmly as I can in the face and figuring it out.** What I have seen Fleda do is operate successfully (to state it as broadly as possible), to the end that the things be mainly sent back to Poynton. But there are 2 necessary facts in regard to this. One is that a certain event, or certain events, certain forces, *lead up*†

* My italics.   † James' italics.

to it, with their irresistible pressure on the girl. The other resides in *the particular way in which she responds to that pressure.** She gets the things back. *How* does she get them back? My idea has been that she successfully persuades Mrs. Gereth to send them. . . . *Let me make out first, however, exactly what precedes, and then I shall see my way a little more into what follows.**

This is the sort of thing that James was wrestling with at the time when he had come to realize his failure as a playwright, and was hoping, at least, to take advantage in fictional narrative of the lessons learned in his apprenticeship to drama. He was coming to realize, what was worse, that there was virtually no demand for his novels and short stories. He never could seem to keep his tales down to the measure of the magazines. He was destined to see his project for *The Ambassadors* cold-shouldered by *Harper's* ("I do not advise acceptance. We ought to do better"). And while this novel was eventually serialized in the *North American Review,* neither *The Wings of the Dove* nor *The Golden Bowl* was given the honor of magazine publication. And yet this was the period (from 1895 to 1904) in which he produced what has now come to be regarded as his best, certainly his most characteristic, work. It was in this period that he called into being his own peculiar world—his firmly textured, consistently toned, shimmering, and unchallengeable world of the imagination. In Fleda and Maisie, in Strether and Marie de Vionnet, in Milly Theale and Maggie Verver (not to speak of the inimitable minor figures, Sir Claude and Waymarsh and Miss Barrace), he had fathered characters which, for individuality and persistent life, have for many readers taken their place alongside of Uncle Toby and Becky Sharp, Wilkins Micawber and Archdeacon Grantly, Arthur Dimmesdale and Tess Durbeyfield.

He had accomplished this in the monastic seclusion of Lamb House or his London lodgings, in strenuous sessions of creative labor, grueling and intensely pleasurable, and by the studious methods recorded in his notebooks. Numerous passages of almost

* My italics.

religious fervor testify to the profound satisfaction, the "sacred" joy, taken by the artist in the devoted exercise of his craft. For anyone engaged in a similar labor of imaginative creation, there is endless profit and encouragement to be derived from these packed and glowing pages. And even one who must take his pleasures vicariously, by sympathetic vibration to the artist's touch, will find in this record cause for delight and exultation.

Many of James' notebooks were destroyed when they had served their purpose, and none of them were meant for the public eye. The survival of so many of them is a rare piece of luck. The finished work of art comes first in interest. But for the connoisseur the next greatest privilege is to be able to follow the stages of that mysterious process by which, out of the untidy, ambiguous, and unpromising stuff of life, is fashioned, by infinite patient strokes of art, the ordered cosmos, the brave new world of the imagination.

ᴇ᳜ DAVID DAICHES

James Joyce: The Artist as Exile

JAMES JOYCE was born in 1882 in a Dublin whose main characteristic was a shabby gentility displayed against a rather dreary
background of politics, religion, and drink. His shiftless and sociable father, his patient and passive mother, and the bitter and
fanatical governess, Mrs. Conway, were the three characters who
presided over the young Joyce's home life as the family descended
from comparative prosperity to ever-increasing poverty, striving
desperately but with lessening success to maintain some appearance of respectability and continually moving to smaller and
shabbier residences as the family income diminished. It was not
an encouraging environment for a potential artist. And after the
death of the Irish national leader, Parnell, in 1892, the confused
ebb of post-Parnell Irish politics added to the prevailing atmosphere of decay a note of muddled hopelessness that all the heroics
of the Irish literary revival were unable to hide. It was in this
mess that James Joyce grew up. The only aspect of Dublin that
he could accept wholeheartedly was its love of song, with the
result that he almost became a professional tenor singer himself.
For the rest, growing up in Ireland meant for Joyce the gradual
realization of the necessity for leaving his native land.

NOTE. Reprinted from *College English*, 1940, by permission of the editors and the
author.

Joyce was educated at the Jesuit colleges of Clongowes and Belvedere, entering the former at the age of six and a half and leaving the latter in 1898 at the age of sixteen. In the autumn of that year he entered the Catholic University of Dublin (University College, a partial revival of the Catholic University founded earlier in the century by Cardinal Newman) where he specialized in modern languages, leaving with his B.A. degree in 1902 to go immediately into voluntary exile in Paris. Though he returned to Dublin a year later, from necessity and not from choice, it was for a comparatively brief time. In 1904 he left Ireland again, this time for an exile which, except for two brief visits to his native land in 1909 and in 1912, lasted until his death.

It was during the years of his education at the three Catholic institutions that he discovered what he deemed to be the necessity for his exile. The background of his home life, with its religious and political quarrels so vividly symbolized in the Christmas dinner scene in *A Portrait of the Artist as a Young Man* and its shabby gentility growing ever shabbier, was something from which he felt with increasing urgency that he must escape, while the political and artistic life of Dublin came to seem to him as narrow, as petty, and as restricting as his own domestic background. At first he found compensating values in religion, and while at Belvedere he passed through a period of intense religious devotion which he later came to see as the sublimation of certain feverish adolescent desires. Before he left Belvedere he had rejected his religion, respecting the intellectual quality of its theology (a respect he always retained) while dismissing its values as sterile and frustrating. But the Catholic religion represented only one of the forces tugging at him throughout his youth; the other was patriotism, both political and cultural, and this too he eventually dismissed, resisting the claims of the "new" Irish literature of Lady Gregory, W. B. Yeats, and others.

Why, we may ask, was Joyce driven to such extreme nonconformity? Why was he driven, by the time he was twenty years old, to see in exile his only possible way of life? In the answer to this question lies the key to the understanding both of Joyce the man and of Joyce the artist.

The answer is given by Joyce himself in his autobiographical work, *A Portrait of the Artist as a Young Man.* Here, in the story of the development of Stephen Dedalus, he records his own progressive rejection of his environment which is at the same time the story of his emergence as an artist. We see the inhibiting home background, the cold oppressive atmosphere of school, the chattering triviality of the university. We see Stephen (who is Joyce) rejecting one by one his home, his religion, his country, growing ever more aloof and proud, exclaiming *"Non serviam"* to all the representatives of orthodoxy and convention. And the more aloof he becomes, the more he removes himself from his fellow men, the closer he comes to the objective vision of the artist. Stephen the artist begins to be born at the moment when he has successfully resisted the temptation to enter the Jesuit order: he suddenly realizes that he is born to dwell apart, to look objectively on the world of men and record their doings with the disinterested craftsmanship of the artist:

He would never swing the thurible before the tabernacle as priest. His destiny was to be elusive of social or religious orders. . . . He was destined to learn his own wisdom apart from others or to learn the wisdom of others himself wandering among the snares of the world.

His destiny as artist demands his choice of exile.

A Portrait of the Artist as a Young Man is thus the record of the parallel development of the artist and the exile. The book closes with Stephen's development of a philosophy of art — and with his decision to leave Ireland. From the moment when the scales fall from his eyes and he looks out on the world with the eye of the artist — not of the Catholic, or the Irishman, but as a "naked sensibility," a pure esthetic eye — he has renounced the normal life of compromise and adjustment. From now on his "artistic integrity" is all that matters to him; he has become aloof and intransigent. Joyce might well have become a priest, but the choice lay only between priest and artist. That type of uncompromising mind, combining asceticism with lust for power, could have satisfied itself only with "the power of the keys, the power to bind and loose from sin," or with the artist's godlike power to re-create the world with the word. That is why Stephen's rejection of the call to join the Jesuit order is the climax of *A Portrait of the Artist as a Young Man*; henceforth the choice of the artist is the only one left, and the remainder of the book is naturally taken up with the formulation of an esthetic and, on its completion, his plans for exile.

The esthetic which Joyce developed—the one which Stephen discusses at length in the *Portrait*—was of a kind one might expect from a writer for whom art implies exile. Art is regarded as moving from the lyrical form, which is the simplest, the personal expression of an instant of emotion, through the narrative form, no longer purely personal, to the dramatic, the highest and most perfect form, where "the artist, like the God of creation, remains within or behind or beyond or above his handiwork, invisible, refined out of existence, indifferent, paring his fingernails." The function of the highest type of artist is thus to cultivate a wholly objective, wholly indifferent and impersonal point of view, to re-create in language the world of men to which the artist must not regard himself as belonging any more than God regards himself as belonging to the world that he has created. The artist must become an exile in order that he may become like God.

In the concluding part of the *Portrait* two main themes emerge: the development of Stephen's esthetic and his progressive rejection of his environment. Somehow these two processes imply each other, and the devices that Joyce employs in order to make this implication clear are worth noting. First, we note that the working out of the hero's esthetic view is done either by himself alone, in complete isolation, or in direct opposition to his friends. Second, from this point in the book to the conclusion Stephen looks on his friends and acquaintances with the aloof eye of the artist, not with the eye of a normal human being, with the result that he is constantly presented as being *alone* and *different*. And, third, the esthetic view which he is shown as developing—Joyce's own view, of course—is one which implies distance and objectivity on the part of the artist: the world is something to be re-created from a distance, not imitated from within. Thus Joyce tries to show the development of the artist and the exile as part of a single process.

If we look carefully at the manner in which the conception of artist as a private rather than as a public figure emerged in the late nineteenth century, we can understand more clearly what was happening. With Oscar Wilde, with the "decadents" of the nineties, we find the renunciation both of the function of art ("All art is perfectly useless," said Wilde) and of the social interests of the artist. And from isolation to exile is but a step.

The fact is—and literary history provides abundant illustration of this—that when the social value framework begins to disintegrate the artist's function becomes in doubt. He ceases to possess any defined status in society, and he responds by retreat or exile. This was a general European movement that developed as the stability of the Victorian world gave way to increasing confusion. It is not simply—as some literary historians have seen it—the rejection of the middle classes by the artist: it is the rejection by the artist of all implication in society.

Thus the birth of Stephen Dedalus (who is James Joyce) as an artist does not mean his recruitment into any specific profession; it does not mean that he has found his place in the social hierarchy and that henceforth his task is smooth. On the contrary, it means that he has discovered that he has no place, no recognized function. As the nineteenth century drew to a close, the status of serious literature as a profession became more and more ambiguous. Methods of recruitment into any of the artistic professions were confused. Arbiters of taste ceased to exist. It is against such a background that the artist in self-defense regards himself as an exile and evolves a view of artistic integrity that implies complete disinterestedness. Joyce's dissatisfaction with Dublin was the occasion, not the real cause, of his retreat.

So Joyce, responding to conditions of which he was perhaps but dimly aware, left Ireland for the Continent to practice his art in "silence, exile, and cunning." His first work was a collection of short stories, thumbnail sketches of typical aspects of that Dublin which he had rejected, entitled simply enough *Dubliners.* Beginning with sketches of a Dublin childhood, told in the first person, the book moves on to more objective studies, in which the author epitomizes with conscious aloofness characteristic situations in Dublin life. We see the development from "lyrical" to "dramatic" art as Joyce understood these terms. Sketches such as "Ivy Day in the Committee Room" bring together in a single picture all the main preoccupations of the average Dubliner and suggest in addition the mood and atmosphere — a gray mood of dreariness mixed with recklessness — which surrounded them. There is a quiet Flemish realism here, yet the stories are more than realistic portraits; they are symbolic, for each character and each image stands as a symbol of Dublin and its people.

The last story in *Dubliners,* "The Dead," stands apart from the others. It is less a picture of a typical Dublin situation than a fable designed to illustrate a point. Joyce is attempting to show the change from a wholly egocentric point of view, where you regard the world as revolving round yourself, to a point of view where your own personality is eliminated and you can stand back and look disinterestedly on yourself and on the world. The hero of this story starts off in a mood of pompous egotism and, as a result of the events of the story, emerges with his personality eliminated in a mood of indifferent acceptance of all things. Written after the other stories of *Dubliners* and no part of the original collection, "The Dead" is a kind of afterthought expressing indirectly Joyce's preoccupation with the question of the proper esthetic attitude. Actually, what is happening to Gabriel is that, like Stephen in the *Portrait,* he is moving from the "lyrical" point of view, the egocentric approach which Joyce regarded as the most immature, to the "dramatic" approach, which for Joyce was the proper esthetic approach.

The *Portrait* followed *Dubliners.* In this autobiographical novel — autobiographical, yet, significantly, written in the third person — Joyce attempts to stand back from himself and his environment and write of his development as an artist with perfect objectivity. It is, as we have seen, a record of the parallel development of the artist and the exile. With this work accomplished, Joyce could now settle down to the writing of his first great opus.

Joyce's view of the artist as exile, closely related as it is to his ideal of artistic indifference and objectivity, naturally determined his choice of subject and of technique in his first great work. Thus *Ulysses* is an attempt to portray the activities of men with complete and utter aloofness—this being the requirement of the "dramatic" mode and the necessary attitude of the artist as exile. Dublin is the world, from which Joyce as artist has retired. In his work, then, Dublin must be made into a symbol of the world in general and the activity of men in Dublin must be shown as a microcosm of all human activity. If the duty of the true artist is, as Joyce claimed, to be "invisible, refined out of existence, indifferent, paring his fingernails," then Joyce could be the true artist in respect to Dublin, which he had renounced, to which he had made himself indifferent. Writing of Dublin from Switzerland or Paris, he was "like the God of creation" contemplating his handiwork from the remote heavens.

Ulysses is the description of a limited number of events concerning a limited number of people in a limited environment—Dublin. Yet Joyce must make Dublin into a microcosm of the world so that he can raise his distance from that city into an esthetic attitude. So the events of the story are not told on a single level; the story is narrated in such a complex manner that depth and implication are given to the events and they become symbolic of the activity of man in the world, not simply descriptive of a group of individual men in Dublin. The most obvious of the devices which Joyce employs in order to make clear the microcosmic aspect of his story is the parallel with Homer's *Odyssey*. Because Joyce regarded Homer's Ulysses as the most complete man in literature—a man who is shown in all his aspects, being both coward and hero, cautious and reckless, weak and strong, husband and lover, generous and mean, revengeful and forgiving, sublime and ridiculous—he endeavored to model the adventures of his hero, Leopold Bloom, an Irish Jew, on those of his Homeric prototype Ulysses. Thus every incident in Bloom's activity during that one day of his in Dublin has some kind of parallel with an adventure of Ulysses in the *Odyssey*. Bloom becomes Everyman and Dublin becomes the world, while the other characters represent incomplete men—Stephen, for example, reappears in *Ulysses* to play an important part as "man as artist," exclusively artist, whereas Bloom is part artist and part scientist, both his artistic and his scientific faculties being of course on a much lower level than they would be in the "pure" artist or scientist.

The book opens at eight o'clock on the morning of June 16, 1904. Stephen Dedalus, summoned back to Ireland by his mother's death after a year in Paris (just as Joyce was), is living in an old military tower on the shore, with Buck Mulligan, a rollicking medical student, and an English visitor. During these early episodes Stephen's character is built up very carefully. He is the aloof, uncompromising artist, rejecting all advances by representatives of the normal world, the incomplete man, to be contrasted later with the complete Leopold Bloom, who is the representative of compromise and conciliation. After following Stephen through his early-morning activities and learning, through the presentation of his "stream of consciousness," all the main currents of his mind, we are taken to the home of Leopold Bloom, whom we subsequently follow through the day's activities. Bloom at home, attending a funeral, transacting his business, eating his lunch, walking through the Dublin streets—we follow closely his every activity, while at each point the contents of his mind, including retrospect and anticipation, are presented to the reader, until all his past history is revealed.

Finally, Bloom and Stephen, who have been just missing each other all day, get together. By this time it is late, and Stephen, who has been drinking with some medical students, is rather the worse for liquor. Bloom, moved by a paternal feeling toward Stephen—his own son had died in infancy, and in a symbolic way Stephen takes his place—follows him during subsequent adventures in the role of protector. The climax of the book comes when Stephen, far gone in drink, and Bloom, worn out with fatigue, succumb to a series of hallucinations where their subconscious and unconscious come to the surface in dramatic form and their whole personalities are revealed with a completeness and a frankness unique in literature. Then Bloom takes Stephen to his home and gives him a meal. After Stephen's departure Bloom retires to bed — it is now two o'clock in the morning on June 17 — while his wife, representing the principles of sex and reproduction on which all human life is based, closes the book with a long monologue in which her experiences as woman are remembered.

In *Ulysses* Joyce wishes to express everything, to make his account of the adventures of one small group of people during one day symbolic of the sum total of human activity — with no point of view expressed, no preference shown, no standard of values applied. For the artist, according to Joyce, must be aloof and indifferent; he must have no point of view. Thus the numerous technical devices employed in *Ulysses* serve a double function — to expand the implications of the story so that it includes all human activity and to prevent any attitude, any point of view, from emerging. The characters are shown as having multiple and subtle relations with each other, their relationship being symbolic as well as realistic. And each character is given a Homeric prototype which serves the function of expanding the implications of his actions. The events of the story are carefully patterned so as to form a closely interrelated unit. The events, too, are given Homeric prototypes which have both relations with each other and with their realistic, Dublin aspects. Further, the events are given meaning on yet a third level, a mystical or philosophical level, utilized by Joyce in order to introduce in the course of the book all the main types of speculation which the human mind has engaged in since the beginning of time. Thus the Homeric level of the story is designed to emphasize the "completeness" of Leopold Bloom, the hero, while the third level has for its function the linking of the story to dominant motifs in human thought, thus enlarging its general implications. This third level also helps to establish Joyce's indifference: if an action is on the realistic level trivial and unimpressive yet on the mystical level profound and weighty, the implication is that the trivial and the profound are really the same thing and no real distinction between more or less valuable human activities is possible. Mr. Bloom raising his hat and Mr. Bloom defending the cause of justice are equally important — or equally unimportant. The heroic and the trivial, the ludicrous and the profound, the transient and the permanent, are identified by Joyce's method of telling the story on several levels at once. His "integrity" as an artist — his indifference, his exile from the world — is thus maintained.

There are many other devices employed by Joyce to emphasize the microcosmic aspect of *Ulysses,* some of them extremely ingenious and subtle, but space forbids any discussion of these. Suffice it to say that through style and technique an otherwise trivial story becomes significant in the sense of inclusive, but in no other sense. It is by the careful patterning and writing on several levels at once that Joyce is able to turn his picture of a few events in Dublin into an undifferentiated panorama of life. For Joyce, esthetic activity meant the re-creation of the human scene by means of language, without the expression of any point of view, without the intrusion of any non-esthetic value standard. He patterns his story in such a way as to identify all aspects of human experience with each other.

This is even clearer in *Finnegans Wake,* his last work. Here the surface level of the story concerns the dream of a Dubliner of Norwegian descent, H. C. Earwicker — like Bloom, a sort of Everyman whose experience is expanded into a symbol of all human experience. (His initials, it will be noted, stand for "Here Comes Everybody.") Earwicker's dream — which is far too complicated to summarize — is told in a language which is scarcely English; for in his endeavor to make the mind of one sleeping man during a few hours symbolize all human life and history Joyce has to write on about a dozen levels at once, making each word have a series of multiple meanings, one on each of the dozen or so levels on which the story is told. Yet these levels are not kept distinct, any more than the different meanings of each word are kept distinct, but keep fading into each other, combining constantly into new patterns. The complex puns and "portmanteau words" which Joyce employs in this work are probably unique in the history of language and show an incredible degree of ingenuity. The whole story is patterned with a subtlety that defies explanation in a short article.

In *Finnegans Wake* Joyce takes an even shorter space of time than that which formed the basis of the plot in *Ulysses* and patterns it with much greater complexity in order to achieve the effect of microcosm — to make one word mean everything — that we have noted as the aim of *Ulysses*. It is the aim of the artist who, upset by the confusion and disintegration of values in the world in which he grows up, feels compelled to escape from that world, within which his function as an artist is not clear, and to evolve a view of art which makes that escape into a virtue. In order to avoid the problem of selection — and selection implies a point of view, while Joyce rejected all points of view, all standards of value — Joyce tries not to select at all, but to employ his technique so skillfully that in saying one thing he says everything. To make a choice, to admit that it is more important to show a character doing this than that, would be to involve himself in that world of values and standards which he had repudiated because it confused and inhibited him as an artist.

Thus escaping from the world, Joyce preferred loneliness and exile and a definition of art as that technical virtuosity which enables the artist to communicate, without preference or emphasis, everything at once. In doing so he has produced the most brilliant literary craftsmanship of the modern world — perhaps of all time. But craftsmanship is not all, and those who seek for a purpose or a value pattern to give significance and permanent "human interest" (the much-abused popular term is not an inaccurate one) to Joyce's work will be disappointed. There is a fundamental difference between art and craft, though the forces that conditioned Joyce caused him to think it a virtue to equate them.

D. H. Lawrence's Sensibility

"THE STYLE IS THE MAN"

Iᴛ ɪs tempting to assert that Lawrence would have been an artist pure and simple if he had been able to find a traditional belief, of the kind which in the past has given both content and stability to what an artist had to say. His sufferings may be regarded as those of a frustrated artist rather than those of a seer, if these distinctions have any meaning when applied to so Protean a spirit as Lawrence's. These points may be illustrated by a consideration of the order of his works.

He still considered himself a novelist while writing *Sons and Lovers*. He accepted the large, loose form of the nineteenth-century novel, as it was still being turned out in England by Arnold Bennett and others. For theme and subject matter he had his own history and the history of his family to write—all he had to say for the moment: the prophet is not yet born. But *The Rainbow* is already more ambitious. The form begins to seem stale to him, and he becomes bored with his characters, which come to seem so numerous and monotonous as to lose all meaning. "Human beings ultimately bore me, and you can't have fic-

ɴᴏᴛᴇ. Reprinted from *Hound and Horn*, 1933, by permission of the author. The sections of Mr. Fergusson's article reprinted here compose parts three and four of a considerably longer article.

tion without human beings," he says in one of his wartime letters. By the time he reached *Women in Love* he was sure that he was through with the traditional novel, that he no longer cared for individual character and circumstance. Mrs. Catherine Carswell writes as follows about this development of Lawrence's: "Those who say 'What a pity he did not care!' have a point of view with which it is difficult not to sympathize at times. With Lawrence, and perhaps with Lawrence alone, the dumb cottagers and inexpressive 'workers' of industrial England might for the first time have found a voice. Even as it is, we now see them *because* of Lawrence, as they have not been seen before. We are pierced by a passional knowledge of them never even suggested by any other writer. But he has given us, practically speaking, no characters."

This is a very good description of *Women in Love*. He will give you his people's feelings for the earth, the sky, and the ruins of industry, so sharply that it is like living in the Midlands yourself. He will render the essence of the emotional relations between them so well that you almost forget the parties to the relation are not realized. As for his minor characters, whom he studies more externally, he makes you feel their presence, their emotional effect, so surely, that if you happen to have known any of the real people that suggested them you can identify them with certainty, even after a period of years. But his main characters, from whose point of view he writes, and whom he designs to carry the chief burden of his meaning, disappear as characters, as he dives through them in search of what Mrs. Carswell calls the life stream. He was simply not interested in what they were in the objective world; he was interested only in the inner world of their emotional and spiritual life. And his trouble was that the people he found to study were not interested in it, or not aware of it, as he was.

Lawrence was not the first novelist to encounter this problem. Henry James met it in his way, by suggesting a vast structure of scruples and heroisms behind and above the little destinies he knew. Joyce elaborates a point-to-point correspondence between the spiritual movements of a little Dublin city-dweller and the mythical wanderings of Ulysses. The effect is all the stronger for Bloom's unconsciousness of the antique pattern he fits into. But Lawrence rejected both the moral nature of man as Henry James knew it and the mythical and cultural heritage of the race, searching, as he proclaimed, for new values and new symbols. Yet he was far too much of an artist to try to do without symbols; he knew better than anyone that our emotional or moral or religious sensibility is shared only by means of "objective equivalents." You might almost say that his imagination was so concrete that he failed to distinguish between the reality and the metaphor or symbol which makes it plain to us. Certainly he is always improvising with his metaphors, laying about him informally for things to body forth his meanings: endowing a landscape with human emotions, or seeing his agony in the wobblings of the moon's reflection in troubled water.

If you go to Lawrence with a great deal of free and undefined emotion, he will orchestrate it for you; he will provide sensuous molds for your emotion to flow into. Birkin's continual smashing of the moon's reflection in the pond is a good example of this. The scattering and the regathering of the sparkles of light will do to embody any sort of struggle for control, for the very reason that the image itself has no exact reference and the context does not provide it. It is like romantic music: it might be about anything, and only if you ask what it *is* all about do you feel that something has been put over on you.

Why not simply call Lawrence a pantheist and be done with it? He seems to perceive the "objective equivalents" at one glance, inextricably mixed with the reality they are to convey. It seems that they are themselves the new territory he is exploring. Certainly they are always part of his initial inspiration, never conscious technical devices. He can never see anything without feeling it as part of his own spiritual life. Besides, his most characteristic metaphors are interwoven with the whole sweep of his longer works, and receive their full development only as the whole work develops, so that it is very hard to quote examples with any fairness. In *Women in Love* Gerald is likened to the white moon, to the Alps, to the Arctic snow-wilderness. His place in history, his human relations, and his class are gradually involved in this figure. Even Lawrence's poems, especially the later ones in *Birds, Beasts and Flowers,* are developed figures of this kind, too long to quote entire. The object and the symbol or figure of the object are built up side by side, together.

Mr. Eliot's distinction between Shakespeare's use of simile and Dante's gives us, I think, the clue. "Whereas the simile of Dante is merely to make you see how the people looked, and is explanatory, the figure of Shakespeare is expansive rather than intensive; its purpose is to *add* to what you see." In Lawrence's poem "Figs" we read,

Folded upon itself, enclosed like any Mohammedan woman,
Its nakedness all within walls, its flowering forever unseen . . .

Lawrence is not trying to make you see the fig more closely, but through the fig to see something different and larger. When Lawrence's style is successful it is that he has found something which can stand exactly for some particular meaning; and he lets the image stand in all its roundness and suggestiveness.

But in "Figs" he puts as it were an intolerable burden on the poor fig. When his style fails it is because he himself feels — sooner than the reader, usually — that the image will not do for the meaning. Sometimes he has not quite found the meaning itself, but is only feeling for it with images. Sometimes the correspondence is not clear, and he will break off the fiction entirely and write a long explanatory philosophical essay. Sometimes, as in "Kangaroo," he will introduce a frankly personal narrative, as though to say that the work of art is only an improvisation, a makeshift, for some more direct means of communication. Dante takes the inner world for granted, and writes only for those who accept it as he does, and have some experience of it. All he expects his style to do is to record his impression of what is, was, and ever shall be. Even Hamlet, who was struggling with the archetype of Lawrence's problem, contents himself with telling Horatio that there are more things in heaven and earth than are dreamed of in his philosophy. But Lawrence in his longer works was trying to force a new experience upon us.

In Lawrence's case it is peculiarly true to say that the style is the man. True because of his unique candor, because of his life-long effort to respect the reality of every moment's feeling. He had, not one style, but several voices. In *The Plumed Serpent*, when the naturalistic narrative fades away, he speaks out through Ramon Carrasco in parables and apothegms, with a voice like that of Nietzsche's Zarathustra. It is a kind of synthetic modern biblical style. He has the voice of a bewildered, angry, and repetitious man when he loses his bearings; yet when he records his visits to Sicily or Mexico, or his interviews with the classic American authors, he speaks crisply, nimbly, and neatly. And when his other voices are exhausted, or disgusted, or have fallen silent for some other reason, his muse creeps out.

Lawrence's moments of pure artistry are scattered through all his works, and they dominate certain short stories, including "Smile," "Two Bluebirds," and "The Captain's Doll." It is not that his vision of reality is different at these times, it is rather as though he had accepted a vision that was there all the time, and as though with the acceptance had come the ability to render it objectively. For the moment he lets the fiction stand. Take "The Captain's Doll." It is laid in Germany and Austria after the War. Its subject is as usual the relation between a man and a woman, and as usual the characters interest him far less than the emotional states they share. The unity of the whole includes the geographical and historical setting, the crowds of pleasure-seekers, like weary Tristans and unbelieving Isoldes, and the end of the old Austrian Empire. The doll itself is an extraordinarily suggestive symbol; and though he explains it in various ways he never explains it away. The two lovers' mountain climbing, the Captain's scrambling absurdly up over the slippery ice while skeptical Hannele eyes him from below, is a dramatic or scenic device comparable to Paolo and Francesca's restless wind.

When Lawrence is in possession of his subject his style achieves another kind of triumph which is extremely rare, and very characteristic of Lawrence: it seems entirely limpid, natural, and effortless. This quality is the reward of serving always one's own sensibility, and Lawrence sought it very consciously. He never polished or fixed his writings: if he thought they needed polishing he rewrote them entire. So he stayed as close as possible to his source. When this source is impure it is Lawrence's own voice we hear yelling in its agony; when it is pure, the prose which flows from it is as clear and living as a trout stream.

"ART IS A QUESTION OF BEING ALIVE. GO IN PEACE."— HIM

Lawrence has been likened to Keats, Blake, Burns, and with less aptness to Dostoevski. Toward the end of his life especially he is very comparable to Nietzsche. Certainly he is in the tradition of romantic writers whose sensibility is more important than their works. Professor Borgese has said (in his lectures at the New School) that romantic writers identify art with its source or root in inspiration, while classical writers identify it with its realization or flowering in achieved form. Lawrence's sensibility, whether religious, moral, or poetic, was a root sensibility. The distinction is very good, because it does not attempt to say whether *root* in this sense is to mean rudimentary and primitive, or basic and profound. Was Lawrence religious? Yes; but whether Greek, Christian, or Hopi it would be hard to say. He was a moralist, but sometimes his ethics seem hardly more than a psychological therapy analogous to M. Fernandez' training of the personality, while at other times he gives us to understand that nothing matters but faith. And he was an artist who seldom produced a work of art. Yet with his very live, very acute, and very courageous sensibility he performed for our day the root function of the poet or the seer, at a level where the two functions are hardly distinguishable. One might say that "the conscience of a blackened street impatient to assume the world" could never quite assume the world while Lawrence was in it.

For some readers, perhaps especially women, this sensibility is enough. They find Lawrence a touchstone for vitality, integrity, or faith, and are satisfied. His influence on other writers is different. Whether they agree with him or not, they find him a source or a beginning, fertile in problems and nearly devoid of solutions; and they tend to try to elaborate or crystallize the raw materials of pure perception he gives them. Mr. Wyndham Lewis and Mr. Aldous Huxley are examples. Most of the important contemporary writers live in the same world as Lawrence did, a world which he did as much as anyone to make us aware of. So in *The Rainbow,* when Ursula is struggling with her first experience of love in the industrial chaos of the Midlands, she has the following reverie:

. . . It was a place of Kings for her—Richard and Henry and Wolsey and Queen Elizabeth. She divined great lawns with noble trees, and terraces whose steps the water washed softly, where the swans sometimes came to earth. Still she must see the stately, gorgeous barge of the Queen float down, the crimson carpet put upon the landing stairs, the gentlemen in their purple velvet cloaks, bare-headed, standing in the sunshine grouped on either side waiting.

"Sweet Thames run softly till I end my song."

And in *The Wasteland* the following passages occur:

. . . The nymphs are departed.
And their friends, the loitering heirs of
  city directors;
Departed, have left no addresses.
By the waters of Leman I sat down and wept . . .
Sweet Thames run softly till I end my song,

. . . .

Elizabeth and Leicester
Beating oars
The stern was formed
A gilded shell
The brisk swell
Rippled both shores . . .

It is evident that the inspiration or primary poetic idea is similar in the two episodes, with their startling juxtapositions of images from the past with an awareness of the present, and the quotation from Spenser to bring it home to us. It is not necessary to my point to assume that Mr. Eliot had been reading *The Rainbow*; it is enough to point out that in their feeling of where we are, nowadays, the two writers are very close together. And a study of *The Wasteland* would reveal the difference between Lawrence's inspirations and a poetic idea realized. What Lawrence gets partially, as a flash of intuition, Eliot is able to see as part of a much larger and more highly developed pattern — as round, solid, and independent of the observer or recorder. Lawrence's works are all invitations to try to realize something. That is why it is so difficult to write about him without trying to realize him, in necessarily alien terms, better than he bothered to realize himself.

Scott Fitzgerald:
The Authority of Failure

OF COURSE, in any absolute sense, Scott Fitzgerald was not a
failure at all; he has left one short novel, passages in several
others, and a handful of short stories which stand as much chance
of survival as anything of their kind produced in this country
during the same period. If the tag is so often attached to his
name, it has been largely his own fault. It is true that he was the
victim, among a great number of other influences in American
life, of that paralyzing high pressure by which the conscientious
American writer is hastened to premature extinction as artist
or as man. Upon the appearance of *The Crack-Up*, a selection by
Edmund Wilson of Fitzgerald's letters, notebooks, and fugitive
pieces, it was notable that all the emptiest and most venal elements in New York journalism united to crow amiably about his
literary corpse to this same tune of insufficient production. Actually their reproaches betrayed more of their own failure to estimate
what was good and enduring in his writing than his acknowledge-
able limitations as an artist. If Fitzgerald had turned out as much
as X or Y or Z, he would have been a different kind of writer,
undoubtedly more admirable from the standpoint of the quasi-
moral American ethos of production at any cost, but possibly less
worth talking about five years after his death. And it might be

NOTE. Reprinted from *Accent*, 1945, by permission of the editors.

said that Fitzgerald never hovered so close to real failure as when he listened from time to time, with too willing an ear, to these same reproaches.

But Fitzgerald brought most of it on himself by daring to make failure the consistent theme of his work from first to last. (Similarly Virginia Woolf used to be accused by the reviewers of being a sterile writer because she made sterility her principal theme.) It is perhaps only adumbrated in *This Side of Paradise*; for the discovery of its hero Amory Blaine that the world is not altogether his oyster is hardly the stuff of high tragedy. The book is interesting today as a document of the early twenties; nobody who would know what it was like to be young and privileged and self-centered in that bizarre epoch can afford to neglect it. But it can also be read as a preliminary study in the kind of tortured narcissism that was to plague its author to the end of his days. (See the article called "Early Success" in the Wilson collection.)

The Beautiful and Damned is a more frayed and pretentious museum piece, and the muddiest in conception of all the longer books. It is not so much a study in failure as in the *atmosphere* of failure—that is to say, of a world in which no moral decisions can be made because there are no values in terms of which they may be measured. Hardly is it a world suited to the purposes of the novelist, and the characters float around in it as in some aquamarine region comfortably shot through with the soft colors of self-pity and romantic irony. Not until *The Great Gatsby* did Fitzgerald hit upon something like Mr. Eliot's "objective correlative" for the intermingled feeling of personal insufficiency and disillusionment with the world out of which he had unsuccessfully tried to write a novel.

Here is a remarkable instance of the manner in which adoption of a special form or technique can profoundly modify and define a writer's whole attitude toward his world. In the earlier books author and hero tended to melt into one because there was no internal principle of differentiation by which they might be separated; they respired in the same climate, emotional and moral; they were tarred with the same brush. But in *Gatsby* is achieved a dissociation, by which Fitzgerald was able to isolate one part of himself, the spectatorial or esthetic, and also the more intelligent and responsible, in the person of the ordinary but quite sensible narrator, from another part of himself, the dream-ridden romantic adolescent from St. Paul and Princeton, in the person of the legendary Jay Gatsby. It is this which makes the latter one of the few truly mythological creations in our recent literature—for what is mythology but this same process of projected wish fulfillment carried out on a larger scale and by the whole consciousness of a race? Indeed, before we are quite through with him, Gatsby becomes much more than a mere exorcising of whatever false elements of the American dream Fitzgerald felt within himself: he becomes a symbol of America itself, dedicated to "the service of a vast, vulgar and meretricious beauty."

Not mythology, however, but a technical device which had been brought to high development by James and Conrad before him, made this dissociation possible for Fitzgerald. The device of the intelligent but sympathetic observer situated at the center of the tale, as James never ceases to demonstrate in the prefaces, makes for some of the most priceless values in fiction—economy, suspense, intensity. And these values *The Great Gatsby* possesses to a rare degree. But the same device imposes on the novelist the necessity of tracing through in the observer or narrator himself some sort of growth in general moral perception, which will constitute in effect *his* story. Here, for example, in so far as the book is Gatsby's story it is a story of failure—the prolongation of the adolescent incapacity to distinguish between dream and reality, between the terms demanded of life and the terms offered. But in so far as it is the narrator's story it is a successful transcendence of a particularly bitter and harrowing set of experiences, localized in the sinister, distorted, El Greco-like Long Island atmosphere of the later twenties, into a world of restored sanity and calm, symbolized by the bracing winter nights of the Middle Western prairies. "Conduct may be founded on the hard rock or the wet marshes," he writes, "but after a certain point I don't care what it's founded on. When I came back from the East last autumn I felt that I wanted the world to be in uniform and at a sort of moral attention forever; I wanted no more riotous excursions with privileged glimpses into the human heart ever recurring."

By reason of its enforced perspective the book takes on the pattern and the meaning of a Grail-romance—or of the initiation ritual on which it is based. Perhaps this will seem a far-fetched suggestion to make about a work so obviously modern in every respect; and it is unlikely that Fitzgerald had any such model in mind. But like *Billy Budd, The Red Badge of Courage,* or *A Lost Lady*—to mention only a few American stories of similar length with which it may be compared—it is a record of the strenuous passage from deluded youth to maturity.

Never again was Fitzgerald to repeat the performance. *Tender Is the Night* promises much in the way of scope but it soon turns out to be a backsliding into the old ambiguities. Love and money, fame and youth, youth and money—however one shuffles the antitheses they have a habit of melting into each other like the blue Mediterranean sky and sea of the opening background. To Dick Diver, with a mere change of pronoun, may be applied Flaubert's analysis of Emma Bovary: "Elle confondait, dans son désir, les sensualités du luxe avec les joies du coeur, l'élégance des habitudes et les délicatesses du sentiment." And it is this Bovaryism on the part of the hero, who as a psychiatrist should conceivably know more about himself, which in rendering his character so suspect prevents his meticulously graded deterioration from assuming any real significance. Moreover, there is an ambiguous treatment of the problem of guilt. We are never certain whether Diver's predicament is the result of his own weak judgment or of the behavior of his neurotic wife. At the end we are strangely unmoved by his downfall because it has been less a tragedy of will than of circumstance.

Of *The Last Tycoon* we have only the unrevised hundred and thirty-three pages, supported by a loose collection of notes and synopses. In an unguarded admission Fitzgerald describes the book as "an escape into a lavish, romantic past that perhaps will not come again into our time." Its hero, suggested by a well-known Hollywood prodigy of a few years ago, is another one of those poor boys betrayed by "a heightened sensitivity to the promises of life." When we first meet him he is already a sick and disillusioned man, clutching for survival at what is advertised in the notes as "an immediate, dynamic, unusual, physical love affair." This is nothing less than "the meat of the book." But as much of it as is rendered includes some of the most unfortunate writing which Fitzgerald has left; he had never been at his best in the approach to the physical. Nor is it clear in what way the affair is related to the other last febrile gesture of Stahr—his championship of the Hollywood underdog in a struggle with the racketeers and big producers.

Fortuitously the sense of social guilt of the mid-thirties creeps into the fugue, although in truth this had been a strong undertone in early short stories like "May Day" and "The Rich Boy." It is evident that Stahr is supposed to be some kind of symbol—but of what it would be hard to determine. From the synopses he is more like a receptacle for all the more familiar contradictions of his author's own sensibility—his arrogance and generosity, his fondness for money and his need for integrity, his attraction toward the fabulous in American life and his repulsion by its waste and terror. "Stahr is miserable and embittered toward the end," Fitzgerald writes, in one of his own last notes for the book. "Before death, thoughts from *Crack-Up*." Apparently it was all to end in a flare-up of sensational and not too meaningful irony: Stahr, on his way to New York to call off a murder which he had ordered for the best of motives, is himself killed in an airplane crash, and his possessions are rifled by a group of school children on a mountain. If there is anything symbolic in this situation, could it be the image of the modern Icarus soaring to disaster in that "universe of ineffable gaudiness" which was Fitzgerald's vision of the America of his time?

Inquiry into what was the real basis of Fitzgerald's long preoccupation with failure will not be helped too much by the autobiographical sketches in *The Crack-Up*. The reasons there offered

WILLIAM TROY

are at once too simple and too complicated. No psychologist is likely to take very seriously the two early frustrations described —inability to make a Princeton football team and to go overseas in the last war. In the etiology of the Fitzgerald case, as the psychologists would say, the roots run much deeper, and nobody cares to disturb them at this early date. His unconscionable good looks were indeed a public phenomenon, and their effect on his total personality was something which he himself would not decline to admit. The imago of the physical self had a way of eclipsing at times the more important imago of the artist. But even this is a delicate enough matter. Besides, there were at work elements of a quite different order—racial and religious. For some reason he could never accept the large and positive influence of his Celtic inheritance, especially in his feeling for language, and his hearkening back to the South has a little too nostalgic a ring to be convincing. Closely related to this was the never resolved attitude toward money and social position in relation to individual worth. But least explored of all by his critics were the permanent effects of his early exposure to Catholicism, which are no less potent because rarely on the surface of his work. (The great exception is "Absolution," perhaps the finest of the short stories.) Indeed, it may have been the old habit of the confession which drove him, pathetically, at the end, to the public *examen de conscience* in the garish pages of *Esquire* magazine.

To add to his sense of failure there was also his awareness of distinct intellectual limitations, which he shared with the majority of American novelists of his time. "I had done very little thinking," he admits, "save within the problems of my craft." Whatever he received at Princeton was scarcely to be called an education; in later years he read little, shrank from abstract ideas, and was hardly conscious of the historical events that were shaping up around him. Perhaps it is not well for the novelist to encumber himself with too much knowledge, although one cannot help recalling the vast cultural apparatus of a Tolstoy or a Joyce, or the dialectical intrepidity of a Dostoevski or a Mann. And recalling these Europeans, none of whom foundered on the way, one wonders whether a certain coyness toward the things of the mind is not one reason for the lack of development in most American writers. Art is not intellect alone; but without intellect art is not likely to emerge beyond the plane of perpetual immaturity.

Lastly, there was Fitzgerald's exasperation with the *multiplicity* of modern human existence—especially in his own country. "It's under you, over you, and all around you," he protested, in the hearing of the present writer, to a young woman who had connived at the slow progress of his work. "And the problem is to get hold of it somehow." It was exasperating because for the writer, whose business is to extract the unique quality of his time, what Baudelaire calls the quality of *modernité*, there was too much to be sensed, to be discarded, to be reconciled into some kind of order. Yet for the writer this was the first of obligations, without it he was nothing—"Our passion is our task, and our task is our passion." What was the common problem of the American novelist was intensified for him by his unusually high sense of vocation.

In the last analysis, if Fitzgerald failed, it was because the only standard which he could recognize, like the Platonic conception of himself forged by young Jay Gatsby in the shabby bedroom in North Dakota, was too much for him to realize. His failure was the defect of his virtues. And this is perhaps the greatest meaning of his career to the younger generation of writers.

"I talk with the authority of failure," he writes in the notebooks, "Ernest with the authority of success. We could never sit across the same table again." It is a great phrase. And the statement as a whole is one neither of abject self-abasement nor of false humility. What Fitzgerald implies is that the stakes for which he played were of a kind more difficult and more unattainable than "Ernest" or any of his contemporaries could even have imagined. And his only strength is in the consciousness of this fact.

⊷§ RAY B. WEST, JR.

Ernest Hemingway:
The Failure of Sensibility

Too often critics have been content to accept Ernest Hemingway's attitudes at their face value. Thus, when he writes that all
men die like animals, he is put down as a materialist or a naturalist. When he says, as he does through the character of Jake
Barnes in *The Sun Also Rises*, that all love becomes finally a
matter of sex, or through Frederick Henry in *A Farewell to Arms*
that the life of man is no more than the struggle of ants on the
burning log of a campfire, the inference is only too plain: he is
indeed the spokesman for the lost generation. When he says that
morals are what you feel good after, he is put down as an impressionist and a pragmatist.

Just recently, however, his critics have begun to suspect something quite different. Malcolm Cowley, for instance, in referring
to his first novel states that "It is a less despairing book than the
critics like to think, with their moral conviction that drinkers
and fornicators are necessarily unhappy." What Mr. Cowley fails
to recognize, apparently, is that this is not alone the dilemma of
the critics. It has all along represented the dilemma of the author
himself. Mr. Hemingway explains in a short and curious little
essay entitled "A Natural History of the Dead" that "The first

NOTE. Reprinted from the *Sewanee Review*, 1945 (copyright 1944), by permission of the editor and the author.

thing you found out about the dead was that, hit badly enough, they died like animals. Some quickly from a little wound you would not think would kill a rabbit. . . . Others would die like cats . . . that crawl into the coal bin with a bullet in the brain and will not die until you cut their heads off." This certainly represents an ideology of despair in Hemingway, yet there are innumerable examples in his books to contradict this view. Perhaps the most notable is the death of Catherine Barkley in *A Farewell to Arms,* notable because in this case the author is attempting to portray the futility of her death. There is Manuel, the old bullfighter in "The Undefeated." There is Ole Andreson in "The Killers," and there is the stoical Indian who commits suicide because he cannot bear his wife's suffering in "Indian Camp." Though these stories all preceded or were roughly contemporary with "A Natural History of the Dead," these characters do not die like animals. They are all fair examples of human decorum in the face of death.

The first apparently conscious attempt of Mr. Hemingway to reconcile ideology and sensibility appeared in the third novel, *To Have and Have Not,* but the importance of the change was generally overlooked at the time, because the critics' chief concern was for what the Marxists were calling "social consciousness" in fiction. What no one seemed to realize was that this book was a re-examination of the problem presented eight years earlier in *A Farewell to Arms,* with the principal character affirming a kind of lukewarm socialism in place of the nihilism of Frederick Henry. It was a failure on almost every other count. It was badly organized and weak in characterization, and it substituted the rough hero—Harry Morgan—for the sensitive Jake and Frederick of the earlier books. The chief female character, Marie, Harry's wife, is a parallel with, almost a parody of, Frederick Henry's position in the preceding novel. Marie finds no consolation in her husband's death, because she is too old to remarry and certainly unable to find a second husband with a "talent for the bed" as great as Harry's.

The most important point concerning *To Have and Have Not*

is that in it the author was struggling for an acceptable form of affirmation for the first time. The attempt was repeated in the play *The Fifth Column*, with Hemingway obviously unable to come to terms with Marxism.

A more satisfactory solution, however, is achieved in the later novel, *For Whom the Bell Tolls*. In it, Robert Jordan is made to say:

He fought now in this war because it had started in a country that he loved and he believed in the republic and that if it were destroyed life would be unbearable for all those people who believed in it. He was under Communist discipline for the duration of the war. Here in Spain the Communists offered the best discipline and the soundest and sanest for the prosecution of the war. He accepted their discipline for the duration of the war because, in the conduct of the war, they were the only party whose program and discipline he could accept.

This is, in fact, a rejection of Marxism as well as defeatism, an admission that the conflict of *The Fifth Column*—between personal love and political duty—has been resolved. Communism is merely an expedient for the winning of the war. More important, however, is the suggestion of some greater affirmative value: He fought in this war because it had started *in a country that he loved* and he *believed in the republic*. If after this statement anyone can still doubt that Mr. Hemingway has reversed himself since *A Farewell to Arms*, let him compare the above statement with the remarks given to Frederick Henry ten years earlier:

I was always embarrassed by the words sacred, glorious, and sacrifice and the expression in vain. We had heard them . . . and had read them, on proclamations, now for a long time, and I had seen nothing sacred, and the things that were glorious had no glory and the sacrifices were like the stockyards at Chicago if nothing was done with the meat except to bury it.

It is not only that the explicit statement indicates a changed point of view on the part of the author. The shift from a negative to an affirmative philosophy demands a shift in the resultant action. Thus, while Frederick Henry deserts the Italian army, Robert Jordan continues a mission which he knows to be hopeless. He continues despite the knowledge, uncertain though it is, that he is to die as a result of that mission. He continues despite the confusion in command, which was almost as disorganized as the retreat at Caporetto and which was one of the motives for Frederick's desertion. He continues despite a love affair in every way similar to the attachment of Frederick to Catherine, and just as in the first affair, the philosophical change is even clearer when we are directly concerned with the relationship between Robert Jordan and Maria. "Is it all right for me to love Maria?" Hemingway has Robert ask.

Yes, himself said.
Even if there isn't supposed to be any such thing as love in a purely materialistic conception of society?
Since when did you ever have any such conception? himself asked. Never. And you never could have. You're not a real Marxist and you know it. You believe in Liberty, Equality, and Fraternity. You believe in Life, Liberty, and the Pursuit of Happiness. . . . You have put many things in abeyance to win a war. If this war is lost all of those things are lost.

But we must realize that Ernest Hemingway has not been, from the beginning, primarily interested in political ideology. To deny the materialism is a long step toward answering the questions he had asked in the relationship of Jake and Brett Ashley, or Frederick and Catherine, but it is again simply a denial, not a solution. This is suggested by Maria, a Spanish girl raised in the Neo-Platonic tradition of Roman Catholicism. "But we will be one now and there will never be a separate one," she is made to say early in the book. "I will be thee when thou art not there." Robert Jordan apparently accepts this, for at the end of the book, when he is wounded and when the only possibility of the party's escaping lies in their leaving him behind, he talks with her:

"*Guapa*," he said to Maria and took hold of her two hands. "Listen. We will not be going to Madrid—"
Then she started to cry.
"No, *guapa*, don't," he said. "Listen. We will not go to Madrid now but I go with thee wherever thou goest. Understand?"

She said nothing and pushed her head against his cheek with her arms around him.

"Listen to this well, rabbit," he said. He knew there was a great hurry and he was sweating very much, but this had to be said and understood. "Thou wilt go now, rabbit. But I go with thee. As long as there is one of us there is both of us. Do you understand?"

This is the end of despair and futility—the end of the "lost generation." It was no accident that Ernest Hemingway took the title for this novel from a seventeenth-century devotion of John Donne or that he quoted a section of the devotion in his preface, for there is more of Donne in *For Whom the Bell Tolls* than the critics have imagined. Both authors were gifted with a highly developed sensitivity, making them doubly aware of the diversity of nature and of human experience. Both were conscious of the breakdown of institutional humanism—the conflict of science and the church—and both were particularly concerned with those mysteries for which an expanding knowledge of natural science was unable to supply the answer. As though to erase any doubt as to his final solution, the twentieth-century author has Robert Jordan consider the problem again while he is awaiting death at the hands of the fascists:

Try to believe what you told her. That is the best. And who says it is not true? Not you. You didn't say it, anymore than you would say the things did not happen that happened. Stay with what you believe now. Don't get cynical. The time is too short and you have just sent her away. Each one does what he can. You can do nothing for yourself but perhaps you can do something for another.

Mr. Hemingway might very well have been talking to himself as he wrote those lines.

II

Upon the appearance of *For Whom the Bell Tolls* in 1940, the reviewers, with their customary enthusiasm, hailed it as a masterpiece. Mr. Howard Mumford Jones, writing in the *Saturday Re-*

view of Literature, went so far as to state that "Manner has been replaced by style, and the mere author has died out in the artist." More considered evaluations since then have either evaded the comparison or have come out strongly for the view that it is inferior to *The Sun Also Rises* and *A Farewell to Arms.* Alfred Kazin is most perceptive when he states, in his critical volume *On Native Grounds:* "Yet *For Whom the Bell Tolls* is among the least of Hemingway's works. . . . And if one compares this work of his ambitious conversion, with its eloquence, its calculation, and its romantic inflation with the extraordinarily brilliant story of this period, 'The Snows of Kilimanjaro,' it is clear that the attempted affirmation of life in the novel, while passionate enough, is moving only in itself, while the concentrated study of wastes and death in the story is perfectly dramatic, perfectly Hemingway's own."

Mr. Jones' statement is most curious because it states the superiority of the novel on the grounds that most critics have used to condemn it, namely upon the basis of style. Most critics would agree, I suppose, that Hemingway's early style represents the triumph of his work, and that the final novel is unsuccessful because it attempts to go beyond the sparse understatement, the "premeditated casualness," as one critic has called it, of the earlier works.

The argument goes something like this: The Hemingway style, with its short, crisp sentences, its ironic contrast between understatement and violent action, is perfectly suited to bear the weight of brutal action in the bull ring, the big-game hunt. and the prize ring, but is incapable of sustaining the long passages of description and meditation to be found in *For Whom the Bell Tolls.* While there is some truth in this argument, it represents a superficial attitude toward the problem of style. If we examine the passages already quoted from *A Farewell to Arms* and the later novel, we will discover that the failure of the passage from *For Whom the Bell Tolls* does not come as a result of an attempt to wrestle with ideology in terms of simplicity or complexity of language. It is true that the quotation from the later book does have a slightly more complicated structure, but we could revise the selection from *A Farewell to Arms* to approximate the later passage, thus:

I was always embarrassed by the words sacred, glorious, and sacrifice and the expression in vain, *because* I had heard them . . . and had read them, on proclamations, now for a long time, and *because* I had seen nothing sacred, and the things that were glorious had no glory and the sacrifices were like the stockyards at Chicago if nothing was done with the meat except to bury it.

It will be seen that the insertion of the italicized subordinating conjunctions do little to weaken this passage. Its strength lies in the shocking force of its imagery. Yet there are few sentences more complicated than this in *For Whom the Bell Tolls*. Even in the passages of meditation, Hemingway adopts a rhetorical device already familiar from the earlier works: he has the speaker cross-examine himself, and if this manner seems stilted and sometimes artificial it is more noticeable in the later book only because it is slightly more common. *For Whom the Bell Tolls* is a longer book than its predecessors. It is a more pretentious work. True, its pages seem more crowded, and its paragraphs are longer, and the picture is obscured slightly by the device which the author uses in an attempt to catch the idiom of its Spanish dialogue. I do not feel, however, that this feature represents the failure of Ernest Hemingway's style. The same charge could be made against the style of his two latest short stories, at least one of which represents the high point in Mr. Hemingway's method. His failure in the novels is, indeed, a stylistic failure, but not superficially. It is a failure of that insight—that sensitivity— which is part and parcel of his style.

The reader may well ask what is meant by insight or sensitivity. I mean that perceptivity or natural awareness of the artist for the variety and range of sense objects surrounding him in nature and which he consciously or unconsciously organizes or synthesizes into an artful pattern or form. Thus the creation of a *meaningful* (ideological) image or the formation of a *meaningful* order of events from the raw material of nature is the result of the artist's sensibility in operation. Speaking of Hemingway's sensibility, Cleanth Brooks and Robert Penn Warren, in their book *Understanding Fiction,* say:

The short simple rhythms, the succession of co-ordinate clauses, and the general lack of subordination—all suggest a dislocated, an ununified world. Hemingway is apparently trying to suggest in his style the direct experience—things as seen and felt, one after another, and not as the mind arranges and analyzes them.

The weakness of Hemingway, from the beginning, has been that he has attempted—at some place or another in every novel —to pause and comment upon the material—to force it to his own ideological end—to moralize. That this tendency has not been noticed and condemned is due primarily to the manner in which it has been done, through a series of sharp—often shocking —images that were successful in themselves though not integrated with the work: life as a baseball game where each error is punished by death or compared to the struggle of ants on a burning log, condemned because the "Messiah" is too lazy or too insensible to do anything about it, the comparison of a hero's death with the slaughter of animals at the stockyard. Hemingway's sensibility, like John Donne's, has always worked upon an immediate, objective level, which translates ideas into terms of concrete things. Donne's imagery is, upon a superficial glance, even more impious and shocking: the flea becomes the Godhead, the church is depicted as a prostitute, or man's sick body is likened to a flat map. To choose an example near to one facet of Hemingway's subject in *For Whom the Bell Tolls,* we can point to the use of the compass in "A Valediction: Forbidding Mourning." Speaking of the separate souls of the two lovers who must part, Donne says:

> If they be two, they are two so
> As stiff twin compasses are two.

This is exactly the point Hemingway wishes to make in the problem confronting Robert and Maria:

> Dull sublunary lovers' love,
> Whose soul is sense, cannot admit

> Absence, because it doth remove
> Those things which elemented it.
>
> But we by a love so much refined
> That ourselves know not what it is
> Inter-assurèd of the mind,
> Care less eyes, lips, hands to miss.

But it is a point so completely foreign to the explicit statement in the early Hemingway, that when he comes to stating it, his muse (to make use of a conception still valid except in terminology) fails him. Robert can only assure Maria that "I will go with thee." He cannot rise above the simple statement: "As long as there is one of us there is both of us."

This is illustrated even better in the passage where Robert Jordan is attempting to justify the affirmative value which he has discovered in the continuation of his mission. The objectification is on so simple and so conventional a level that it lacks conviction, and perhaps this is the reason so few critics have even admitted its presence. He fought in a war because *it had started in a country that he loved* and *he believed in the Republic*. This argument might have come from the platform of any patriotic orator, and it is a failure, not because it is an affirmative value, not because it is a patriotic sentiment, but because it is conventional and trite. When he says, "You believe in Liberty, Equality, and Fraternity. You believe in Life, Liberty, and the Pursuit of Happiness," the author is attempting to rely only upon generalities which, admirable as they may be as a statement or even as symbols of democracy, are not sharp enough to carry the emotional weight put upon them. And rather than summing up with a striking image, as he does in the passage cited from the early novel, he ends with the puerile statement: "You have put many things in abeyance to win a war."

I do not mean to suggest that Ernest Hemingway's failure is entirely a matter of imagery. I have mentioned his well-known use of understatement. Its effectiveness is still evident in the final novel in such passages as the one where Robert Jordan is awaiting the arrival of the fascists at the end of the book. Robert has sent Maria, Pilar, and the others on, and he has lain in ambush, hoping to delay the enemy, hoping to get himself killed quickly. The tension of the scene is held in the casual manner in which the author soliloquizes about their coming. "Robert Jordan's luck held very good because he saw, just then, the cavalry ride out of the timber and cross the road." The fact that Hemingway can state the arrival of the enemy as an example of Robert Jordan's luck holding is an illustration of the effectiveness of the use of understatement in moments of crisis. But the irony operates within a small frame. It refers, perhaps, as far back as Jordan's separation from Maria, but it does not, as it is capable of doing in the short stories, pick up and charge the whole narrative with meaning, as it does, for instance, in the case of Manuel, the bull-fighter, at the end of "The Undefeated."

"I was going good," Manuel insists just as he is about to die, and the reader agrees with him. He was indeed "going good," but not in the ordinary sense. The spectators had not thought he was "going good." They had thrown cushions into the bull ring, and one of these cushions was, indirectly, the cause of his death. In "The Killers" it is the constant interplay between the world of normality and the "unreal" world of the gangsters that is high-lighted by the irony of understatement. Mrs. Bell, the maid at Mrs. Hirsh's boardinghouse, represents the normal world on its simplest level. She it is who, in talking about Ole Andreson, the man who is awaiting the arrival of the killers, says: "He's been in his room all day. . . . I guess he don't feel well. I said to him: 'Mr. Andreson, you ought to go out and take a walk on a nice day like this,' but he didn't feel like it." This speech elucidates the whole relationship between Nick and the world of the Killers; it suggests all the relationships in the story—the various levels between Mrs. Bell's unconscious normality and Ole's complete awareness and acceptance—all of which have their representations in other characters.

But these short stories are focused upon relatively small, iso-lated worlds with clearly defined codes. Though the interpreta-tion is complex, the references are simple. The reader is left with two primary objections: (1) Too much dependence upon the method of understatement leaves him with a feeling of having been tricked or cheated. This accounts for those readers who have complained that Ernest Hemingway's style was "forced" or "unreal." (2) Too limited a background gives the impression that the author is concerned only with the sensibilities of simple people, which accounts for the accusation that Hemingway is interested only in the values of a primitive society.

On the other hand, there is at least one example of an almost perfect integration. In the story "The Short and Happy Life of Francis Macomber" these objections are overcome by the use of a third, and more common, type of irony—that which is inherent in the action itself. To use an expression of T. S. Eliot, Ernest Hemingway has, in this story, found the "objective correlative" for the conveyance of emotion and theme. The scene is laid in Africa, where an American sportsman has just shown himself to be a coward on the hunt. The body of the story is concerned with the subtle relationships between Francis Macomber and his wife which are thrown out of balance by the act of cowardice. Margot, the wife, feels herself freed of restraint by his violation of their unspoken code, and she is untrue to him. When he redeems himself by standing up to a charging water buffalo, she, under a pretense of shooting the animal, sends a bullet into his brain.

But a simple statement of the action does not suggest the careful and intricate weaving of it by the author, the subtle ironies which combine and reinforce the final irony of Francis Macomber's death—another example of victory in the face of death. "That was a pretty thing to do," the guide said in a toneless voice. "He would have left you too." Ernest Hemingway has not only found the objective correlative, he has allowed it to carry its proper burden in the story even though it contradicted the views expressed in "A Natural History of the Dead." This is true also of "The Snows of Kilimanjaro" where the author not only does not refute the obvious theme of his story, but where he uses a highly self-conscious symbolism to reinforce it. While I consider this story one of Hemingway's best, I do not share Mr. Kazin's enthusiasm for it. The story is technically more complex than most, but it is spoiled for me by the conventionality of its leading symbol: the White-capped mountain as the House of God.

Which brings us again to the problem presented in *For Whom the Bell Tolls*: whether Ernest Hemingway has succeeded finally in freeing himself from a conception which he was unable to integrate with the material supplied him by his sensitivity, and if he has, why has he not succeeded in writing his masterpiece in this final novel? The first half of the problem has, I believe, been solved. The answer to the second lies inherent in the comparison with John Donne. While the seventeenth-century poet began with a doubt similar to Hemingway's and while his work exhibits a similar self-searching, he ended with a recognition that the mystery was real and absolute and could be expressed as an art object:

> Betray, kind husband, thy spouse to our sights,
> And let mine amorous soul court thy mild dove,
> Who is most true and pleasing to thee then
> When she is embraced and open to most men.

The paradoxical image he recognized as the most that could be said concerning divine mystery. Also, his sensitivity seemed to be functioning at its highest point of awareness when confronted by such a mystery. We get the shocking, almost irreverent, image of the church, the bride of Christ, becoming a mild, innocent prostitute courted by all men. The crowded imagery of the lines, the paradoxical resolution suggest a certainty-within-uncertainty, a conclusion tinged with irony, which is the objectification of the emotion Donne obviously wished to convey. It is not merely that he, like Plato's poet, is singing hymns of praise to God. He is suggesting the subtle relationship between the poet—between man and God.

Hemingway's sensitivity, too, has presented him with such paradoxes. Mr. Cowley has suggested one of them in his discussion of *The Sun Also Rises*: There are some positive values suggested in the novel, despite Jake Barnes' belief (as stated) that

RAY B. WEST, JR.

his impotency is the final, degrading blow. "It always gets around to that," he tells Brett Ashley, who apparently accepts this judgment, for almost the entire novel is concerned with her experimentation with sex. Yet her final act is one of restraint. "You know it feels rather good deciding not to be a bitch," she tells Jake after giving up the young bullfighter.

The familiar theme of death is, similarly, a kind of paradox—even Catherine's statement of it: "I'm not afraid," she tells Frederick, "I just hate it." But the chiefly paradoxical nature of the incident lies in the fact that Catherine does not die like an animal. She hates it, but she is not afraid to talk about it, and she seems almost more concerned for Frederick than for herself. Likewise, though more completely, the death of Francis Macomber is an exemplification of the paradoxical idea that man achieves his greatest success through death.

I do not mean to say that, except in the instance of "The Short and Happy Life," Ernest Hemingway was consciously attempting to portray death as anything other than what he explicitly says it is in "A Natural History of the Dead." The paradox is not conscious, as it was with Donne, but results, rather, from the conflict between his ideology, on the one hand, and his sensitivity, which, on the other, could not force his materials into the mold prepared for them. The early novels are successful partly because of this conflict and partly despite it. They are not completely successful, and Ernest Hemingway himself must have been aware of this by the time he came to write *To Have and Have Not*.

I have suggested that part of this failure lay in the inability of the author's style to encompass a form so large and inclusive as that of the novel. His greatest successes, particularly in the early works, were with the short story. This is as true of the later novel as it was of the first two, but it is not the whole story. In *For Whom the Bell Tolls* there is, in addition, a failure of that sensibility which had served him so well in the early books. At that time he was more or less certain in his point of view, though it did, as we have seen, conflict with the objective portrayal of natural experience. By the time we come to the later novel, the

99

solution is pat. Robert Jordan did not believe in Marxism; he believed in democracy. But what is democracy? It is life, liberty, and the pursuit of happiness. This is the answer of the rhetorician, the public orator, or the moralist; it is not the method of the artist. What about religion? He did not believe in materialism; he accepted a form of mysticism similar to that of John Donne. Notice:

Listen, one thing. Do you remember? Pilar and the hand? Do you believe that crap? No, he said. Not with everything that's happened? No, I don't believe it. She was nice about it early this morning before the show started. She was afraid maybe I believed it. I don't though. But she does. They see something. Or they feel something. Like a bird-dog. What about extra-sensory perception?

Ernest Hemingway's conversion seems to have been a struggle, not so much against doubt as a struggle for complete acceptance of the affirmative aspects of democracy and Christianity, and this seems somehow to have made him susceptible to general phrases of belief rather than to the striking objective portrayal of which he is capable. There is but a single figure of speech in the above passage. It refers to Pilar's claim for supernaturalism, and it could be restated something like this: She sees something or feels something, like a bird dog. Contrast this with the striking example already cited from *A Farewell to Arms*: The death of a hero in war is like the stockyards at Chicago if nothing was done with the meat except to bury it.

It is the difference between the expression of those two ideas which I would term the failure of sensibility in Ernest Hemingway. It illustrates, I believe, the fallacy of a more or less popular theory today that to clothe oneself in an affirmative ideology is enough to assure the "responsibility" of the artist. Rather, if we examine the evidence of novelists from Tolstoy to Aldous Huxley, I believe we can convince ourselves of the opposite. The artist has a greater responsibility to his sensibility in relation to his materials than he nas to any body of abstract knowledge. The ideology is not imposed upon the material, it grows out of it, and any attempt to impose it results in artistic failure.

This is not to say that Ernest Hemingway is a failure in the usual sense of the word. The measure of his failure lies only in comparison with the very best writers in the genre—perhaps with Dostoevski and Henry James. He has written a few of the best short stories of our age. His present limitations would incline me to prefer that his future work would be done in the field of the short story, but these are limitations no greater than have been overcome by other artists. Our greatest hope lies in the fact that he has never, despite appearances to the contrary, relaxed his self-searching. But this is not ground for hope alone. It is a test of the "responsibility" of a writer who has become the chief target for all charges of "irresponsibility."

The Brontës, or, Myth Domesticated

WHEN *Jane Eyre* and *Wuthering Heights* appeared in 1847, they were denounced as coarse, immoral, and subversive. Later Mrs. Humphrey Ward and the Brontë Society came to cherish the Brontës—"these dear women," one member called them—as romantic rebels against repressive conventions and as writers who had made "passion" a part of the novelistic tradition. The Society was safe in this attitude, for neither Jane Eyre nor Catherine Earnshaw had violated the marriage law—and Wordsworth had after all spoken of passion. The nineteenth-century vocabulary, which depended so heavily on words like "rebellion," "passion," and "imagination," was often inaccurate; and Victorian criticism of the Brontës remains nebulous—nebulously rhapsodic as in Swinburne's *A Note on Charlotte Brontë* or nebulously ethical as, say, in the writing of A. C. Benson, from whom the following passage is taken:

Charlotte Brontë's new philosophy of love . . . was not a revolt against tame and formal conventions so much as a new sense of right and dignity, a manifesto, so to speak, of the equality of noble love. Compare the conception of love, from the woman's standpoint, in the novels of Dickens and Thackeray, with Charlotte Brontë's conception. In Dickens and Thackeray love is at

NOTE. Reprinted from the *Kenyon Review,* 1947, by permission of the editor and the author.

best a reward, a privilege, graciously tendered and rapturously accepted; and the highest conception of wifely love is one of fidelity and patience and unselfish tendance gently rendered by a domestic angel, whose glory is self-repression, and whose highest praise is to afford an uncritical haven of repose to an undisputed master.

The truth of these sentences is superficial. The reader of *Jane Eyre* has every reason to feel that the coy badinage of the closing pages none too subtly transforms Jane into the "domestic angel" herself.

The new century brought the Brontës into better perspective, and in such an attack as Rosamond Langbridge's *Charlotte Brontë: A Psychological Study* we see Charlotte pictured as a kind of scribbling Florence Nightingale, an intensely neurotic woman whose early family life had filled her with unquenchable urges to succeed, and, if not to succeed, then to expire under the burden of a masochistic "duty." I call this a better perspective because it makes us think of the Brontës as true-blue Victorians rather than as romantic rebels. The purpose of Brontë criticism at present is to proceed from that point. Why do *Jane Eyre* and *Wuthering Heights* now seem the most exciting of Victorian novels? Because, I think, these novels translated the social customs of the time into the form of mythical art, whereas many other Victorian novels were translated by the social customs into more or less tiresome canting.

II

The familiar stories about the Brontës' home life may or may not be true in detail. But there is no doubt that it was harrowing. The horrendous Puritanism of the Reverend Patrick Brontë, who catechized his children on the differences between the male and female bodies and on the advisability of preparing for Eternity, pervaded the isolated Yorkshire parsonage. Mr. Brontë may or may not have fired pistols out of the back door, burned up the pretty new shoes of his small daughters, and torn to bits the only silk dress of his wife as she lay dying of cancer after bearing her sixth child in seven years. But there is no doubt that Haworth Parsonage was a man's society, brooded over by the usually invisible poetry-scribbling patriarch who lived in his room, as one writer says, "in a fiery and impotent seclusion." He was the living symbol of the nineteenth-century patriarch: the Romantic Man of Mystery, alternately maudlin and fanatical, his brilliant eye bespeaking the libidinal potential of Sex and War, his gloomy brow displaying the emblems of ancient guilt, his stern jaw advertising the tenacity of his self-repression. And if this scribbling patriarch began to lose his luster as the sisters grew older, there was their theatrical brother Bramwell to admire when he soliloquized or painted pictures or to behold with awe when, dying of alcohol and opium, he sank down among the tombstones of Haworth Churchyard, armed with a kitchen knife in case he should meet the Devil. Small wonder that Emily Brontë should have burned herself with a red hot iron and beaten her dog Keeper into insensibility or that Charlotte developed an agonizing sense of inferiority which she never overcame. The wonder is that Emily should have written a first-rate novel about the violent forces of human nature and that Charlotte produced, as Rebecca West says, the subtle and complete analysis of inferiority which constitutes her novels.

Swinburne, whose God was a Great Mother, thought it was an "insoluble riddle" that Charlotte Brontë "came first to conceive and finally to fashion that perfect study of noble and faultful and suffering manhood," Edward Rochester. Our debunking Freudian, Miss Langbridge, finds no riddle: All the Brontë men characters "have the pettifogging tyranny of the Victorian father, and the Victorian only son. As Mr. Rochester is transcendental Bramwell, with his 'coarse' bygone amours and theatrical remorses, his Olympian damns and virile thunderings, so St. John Rivers in his tyrannical evangelism, his cold, harsh dominance, his torpid Christian love-making is Mr. Brontë *père*." It is all too simple, but again we have been put on the right track.

"If he were a *clever* man and loved me, the whole world weighed in the balance against his slightest wish should be light as air," writes Charlotte to a friend. This indicates what, in their intellectual parsonage, the sisters came to admire and fear most: sexual and intellectual energy. In *Jane Eyre* and *Wuthering Heights* the universe is conceived as the embodiment of this energy or *élan*. In *Jane Eyre* the wondrous Helen Burns, as she is dying, places her faith in "the impalpable principle of life and thought, pure as when it left the Creator to inspire the creature: whence it came it will return; perhaps again to be communicated to some being higher than man—perhaps to pass through gradations of glory, from the pale human soul to brighten to the seraph! Surely it will never on the contrary be suffered to degenerate from man to fiend?" The "principle" of life and thought in the Brontë novels is sexual energy; the universe is the stone and flesh which make the energy palpable; it is a masculine universe. Art is the representation of the "principle" as the Brontë heroines perceived it embodied in nature, in man, in seraph, and in fiend.

Charlotte, always given to imagining concrete situations, however unlikely, pictures herself in her poems as the wife of Pilate, who "sought my presence dyed in blood," who exercised a "cold and crushing sway," who crushed "my mind and did my freedom slay." Or she imagines "Gilbert," who gloats over the abjectness of the wife to whom he had descended "like a God." Or she pictures the enslavement of a woman with an "endowed and youthful frame" by a tyrannical husband who finally kills himself with an axe. Or she feels a "perfect energy" within her and when this energy burns in harmony with her lover's soul, she achieves "identity" in a newly meaningful universe which was once "dumb/ Stone-deaf, and blank, and wholly blind." "Point not to thy Madonna, Priest—/ Thy sightless saint of stone," she writes in another poem; rather will she worship the burning image of her lover-lord.

Emily writes of a daughter who longs to be with her father in "the eternal home":

> From suffering and corruption free,
> Restored into the Deity.

Elsewhere she speaks of "selfish-hearted men," but her first impulse is always away from the concrete situation and toward the symbolization of principles. Whereas Charlotte seeks "identity," Emily longs to sleep in an eternal ocean of mild light "without identity." In the fine poem which begins "Ah! why because the dazzling sun," after a nightlong peaceful watch, the "glorious eyes" of the stars "gazing down in mine" with "one sweet influence," the sun bounds over the hills—"Blood-red, he rose, and arrow-straight/ His fierce beams struck my brow." She buries her face in her pillow to escape the intolerable force, but

> It would not do—the pillow glowed,
> And glowed both roof and floor;
> And birds sang loudly in the wood,
> And fresh winds shook the door.

The energy, when it kindles the universe, is intolerable to the sensibility which revolts against its own identity, since identity implies being part of the palpable universe and thus being subject to the agony of the intense illumination. The world is moved to exquisite vibrancy:

> The curtains waved, the wakened flies
> Were murmuring round my room,
> Imprisoned there till I should rise,
> And give them leave to roam.

And the poem ends with a prayer that the poet may "sleep through" the "blinding reign" of the hostile light and awake among the gentle stars.

Sometimes Emily Brontë says that the illuminating energy is the only reason for bearing the burden of existence and that she wishes for death because the illumination will not come. Addressing "that spirit," she writes,

> Had I but seen his glorious eye
> *Once* light the clouds that wilder me,
> I ne'er had raised this coward cry . . .

Again, and this is the typical note, she speaks of death as a return to the Light she once knew in Eternity.

RICHARD CHASE

In that somewhat fantastic Gothic-Byronic character Edward
Rochester we have Charlotte Brontë's symbolic embodiment of
the masculine *élan*. Jane Eyre's feelings toward Rochester are
ambivalent. He draws her to him with a strange fascination; yet
she is repelled by his animalism and his demonism. She wishes to
submit herself to him; yet she cannot. She is nearly enthralled
by the "tenderness and passion in every lineament" of his
"kindled" face; yet she shrinks from the flashing of his "falcon
eye" and from the glamor of his self-proclaimed guilt and his
many exploits among women of other countries (in France,
Céline; in Italy, Giacinta; in Germany, Clara—"these poor girls"
Jane calls them). She cannot permit the proffered intimacies of
this man who keeps a mad wife locked up in his attic. And if her
moral scruples would allow his embrace, still she could not endure the intensity of his passion. The noble, free companionship
of man and woman does not present itself to her as a possibility.
She sees only two possible modes of behavior; meek submission
or a flirtatious, gently sadistic skirmishing designed to keep her
lover at bay. Finally her sense of "duty" compels Jane to run
away. The inevitable parting of the lovers had been forecast
when the lightning, summoned from the sky by their first declaration of love, had split the garden chestnut tree asunder.

The splitting of the tree, however, may also symbolize two
alternate images of Jane Eyre's soul, two possible extremes which,
as she believes, her behavior may take. At one extreme is Bertha,
Rochester's mad wife; at the other is St. John Rivers, the clergyman cousin whom Jane meets after she flees Rochester and who
wants to marry her. Before the story can end, Jane must purge
these extreme images of herself. Bertha represents the woman
who has given herself blindly and uncompromisingly to the principle of sex and intellect. As Fanny E. Ratchford (the expert in
the voluminous juvenile romances written by the Brontës) has
shown, the character of Bertha was evolved from a certain Lady
Zenobia Ellrington, a heroine of Charlotte Brontë's childish
fantasy-kingdom of Angria. Miss Ratchford describes Lady
Zenobia thus: She was a "noble woman of strong mind and lofty

thought. On the other hand, she is given to fits of rage in which she shrieks like a wild beast and falls upon her victim hand and foot. On one occasion she kicked Lord Charles [a juvenile version of Rochester] down the stairs." Always she is depicted as tall of stature and strong of body. Lord Charles once declared that she could spar on equal terms with her husband, "one of the best boxers on record." She was, furthermore, a learned and intellectual woman, a bluestocking in fact. Like Bertha, she was a Creole and came from a family notorious for mad crimes and passions. May not Bertha, Jane seems to ask herself, be a living example of what happens to the woman who gives herself to the Romantic Hero, who in her insane suffragettism tries herself to play the Hero, to be the fleshly vessel of the *élan*?

We may think that fear drives Jane away from Rochester; *she,* however, says that it is "duty." In St. John Rivers she meets duty incarnate. In a poem Charlotte Brontë had imagined herself as a missionary to the pagans. No "coward love of life," she says, has made "me shrink from the righteous strife." Rivers has given up Rosamond Oliver, a charming and life-loving girl, and wants to marry Jane and take her to India, where he plans to devote himself to missionary work. Plainly, it would be a sexless marriage. Rivers wants a wife to "influence." He is cold, selfish, fanatical — a narrow bigot, who shakes Jane's confidence in "duty." She cannot marry Rivers; she must purge her soul of the image of "duty" as she has of the image of Bertha.

How to resolve the plot? It must be done as Charlotte, the leader of her sisters in all practical matters, was accustomed to do things: by positive action. The universe conspiring against Jane Eyre, like the circumstances which so often conspired against the sisters, must be chastened by an assertion of will, catastrophic if necessary. And so Charlotte sends Rochester's house up in flames and makes him lose his eyesight and his left hand in a vain attempt to save Bertha. Rochester's injuries are, I should think, a symbolic castration. The faculty of vision, the analysts have shown, is often identified in the unconscious with the energy of sex. When Rochester had tried to make love to Jane, she felt a "fiery hand grasp at her vitals"; the hand, then, must be cut off. The universe, not previously amenable to supernatural communication between the parted lovers, now allows them to hear each other though they are leagues apart. It is as if the masterless universe had been subdued by being lopped, blinded, and burned. Jane Eyre now comes into her own. She returns to Rochester. She baits him coyly about her relations with Rivers; he exhibits manly jealousy. They settle down to a mild married life; they have a child; Rochester partly, but only partly, regains his eyesight. The tempo and energy of the universe can be quelled, we see, by a patient, practical woman.

In the fantasy of Jane Eyre she is able to answer Rochester's question whether she is entirely his by saying, "to the finest fibre of my nature, sir." In *Wuthering Heights* we remember Cathy's passionate declaration of oneness with her lover: "I *am* Heathcliff." Heathcliff is Emily Brontë's symbol of "the impalpable principle of life and thought." He is the very spirit of the wild Yorkshire moors, an "unreclaimed creature," as Cathy knows, but the only creature who can "reconcile her to God and humanity." Like Rochester, he is flamboyant, mysterious, morose, and sadistic. Cathy *is* Heathcliff, yet even as she admits this she rejects him for reasons which she herself cannot enunciate and takes Edgar Linton, who, though a good gentleman, disgusts her with his effeteness. She is, apparently, afraid of Heathcliff. And unlike Rochester, he can never be domesticated. He is less human and more of the essence of the universal *élan*. We realize that with a few adjustments of the plot he need not have entered the story as a human being at all. His part might have been played by fate, or nature, or God, or the Devil. He is sheer dazzling sexual and intellectual force. As Heathcliff expires at the end of the book, we feel, not so much that a man is dying, as that an intolerable energy is flagging. And we see that Heathcliff without energy cannot possibly survive in human form. His "termination" is "absurd," as he himself says. The titan is now reduced to a buffoon who tries clumsily to leap out of the flesh into the spirit, to beat down invisible walls; he is a tumbler trying to transfigure himself into the Other World; he is, as he says, a "sport" of "intolerable torture." Heathcliff and Cathy die without making a fact of the oneness they both feel is theirs. To Emily Brontë, their marriage is unthinkable. It can happen only as a distant parody: the marriage of Hareton Earnshaw and Cathy the younger at the end of the book. Hareton is watered-down Heathcliff; Cathy is a pale, though still vivacious, replica of her mother. The two novels end similarly: a relatively mild and ordinary marriage is made after the spirit of the masculine universe is controlled or extinguished.

III

We have so far maintained that the Brontë novels are concerned with the neuroses of women in a man's society. But surely this theme alone cannot account for the wonder and interest we feel in *Jane Eyre* and *Wuthering Heights*. The personalist theme involves a societal theme; the sexual involves the utopian. What is the large moral upshot of the relation between Jane and Cathy and their lovers? What is the ultimate significance of these heroines? Well, obviously *Jane Eyre* is a feminist tract, an argument for the social betterment of governesses and equal rights for women. But we have to see this propaganda and other explicit elements of the Brontë novels in comprehensive mythical images before we can begin to understand their full significance.

A serving woman sings these disheartening verses to little Jane:

My feet they are sore, and my limbs they are weary;
    Long is the way, and the mountains are wild;
Soon will the twilight close moonless and dreary
    Over the path of the poor orphan child.

Why did they send me so far and so lonely,
    Up where the moors spread and the grey rocks are piled?
Men are hard hearted, and the kind angels only
    Watched o'er the steps of a poor orphan child.

This poor orphan child with a mission in a hostile world is like Cinderella certainly. Also she is like Joan of Arc and, as Chesterton observes, the solitary virgin of the folk tales who goes to the castle of the ogre. I suggest that to the Brontës this pilgrim virgin is a culture heroine. The culture heroes of mythology are those figures who, like Hercules, Prometheus, or the animal deities of the American Indians, slay the monsters or overcome natural or human obstacles or bring intelligence to men so that civilization can be born out of savagery and chaos—"transformers," the anthropologists call these culture heroes. It was the Victorian period which supposed that the primeval social order consisted of a murderous old man and his company of females and weaker males and which bequeathed the idea to Freud. We may almost say that the Brontë household *was* this primeval social order. The purpose of the Brontë culture heroine as a mythical being is to transform primeval society into a humane and noble order of civilization. But this idea requires another excursus.

There are many methods of describing the transformation of primitive society into civilization. But the method most applicable to the problem as creative writers conceive it in novels and poems is that of A. J. Toynbee (*A Study of History,* 1933–38). Briefly, Toynbee's method is mythological: primitive society is a stasis presided over by a once-creative Father-God, Whose perfection is also a stasis. God must be forced into the motion of further creativity by a wager flung to Him by the Devil. The human protagonist of the cultural tragedy (Toynbee follows the theme of Goethe's *Faust*) must perform a dynamic act, which will set God and the Devil at war. In the path of the culture hero there stands an Obstacle. The dynamic act of the hero hurls him against the Obstacle—if he is overcome by it, the Devil has won the wager and society fails to advance along the path of civilization; but if he overcomes it, God has won; the Devil, who sought to perpetuate the death-like stasis, is routed; and God, the creative *Élan* or "the impalpable principle of life and thought," as Helen Burns calls Him, reasserts Himself in the soul of man.

Our Brontë culture heroine, then, is the human protagonist of the cosmic drama. Rochester and Heathcliff are portrayed as being at once godlike and satanic. In them the universal enemies

111

may be set at war by a culture heroine. Then if the Devil is over-come, a higher state of society will have been achieved. The tyrannical Father-God will have been displaced. The stasis will have been smashed by the creative *élan* of sex and intelligence. The Brontë heroines fail in their missions; they refuse to venture so much; they will not accept the challenge of the God-Devil. They will not accept the challenge, for fear the Devil should win. Yet when we understand these heroines in some such terms as the foregoing, they acquire a new significance: it had not occurred to us that the stakes were so great.

Charlotte Brontë, whose many practical predicaments, as we have noted, forced her to solve problems by forthright acts of will, made the plot of *Jane Eyre* proceed in a rhythm of stasis and activity. Thus we find Jane on a hillside near Rochester's estate after she has been hired as governess but before she has met Rochester. She has forced herself out of her inert existence at Lowood School, having a great desire for "liberty" and adventure. As yet she has not found the driving force of the new life for which she hopes. The universe is frozen in the cold of winter; the world is silent, in "leafless repose." The pale moon presides over the scene. Then suddenly the stasis is shattered by a vigorous animal invasion; Rochester with horse and dog comes upon the scene. Not knowing it to be her "master," Jane returns to the house reluctantly: "to pass its threshold was to return to stagnation . . . to slip again over my faculties the viewless fetters of an uniform and too still existence." But she is soon in love with her master. He "eclipses God." As the time comes for the abortive wedding (interrupted by the announcement that Rochester has a lunatic wife), Jane Eyre is "an ardent and expectant woman." Apparently, she is on the point of rescuing herself definitively from the "leafless repose." But when the wedding fails to come off, she is again "desolate" in a frozen world; her "blooming and glowing" wishes are "stark, dull, livid corpses." She flees Rochester and turns to St. John Rivers.

If in the soul of Rochester the Devil might meaningfully fight with God, there can be no such struggle in the soul of Rivers.

"God" has become, not the creative principle, but a prim task-master, and there is no doubt that the Devil will easily defeat Him. "If I were to marry you," says Jane, "you would kill me. You are killing me now." She has now renounced two men; an obviously devilish man and a possibly devilish man. Disgusted with Rivers, she sets out to find Rochester. She does not yet know that his wife has died and that he has been maimed. Have her spiritual adventures now prepared her to give herself un-equivocally to Rochester? Charlotte Brontë leaves the question unanswered and we can only discuss what Jane actually does. (There is a hint that the culture heroine was prepared for her noble mission: "It was *my* time to assume ascendancy. *My* powers were in play, and in force.")

The esthetic procedure of Charlotte Brontë makes her novel a series of set pieces, tableaux, or great scenes which periodically resolve themselves out of the interspersed areas of formless activity (like the charades staged by Rochester and Blanche Ingram for his aristocratic guests). Emily Brontë's work lacks this differentiation and consequently is harder to discuss, which is why most discussions of *Wuthering Heights* take refuge in such superlatives as "passion," "purity," and "powerful." Charlotte constantly lays violent hands on the progress of her story. Emily simply stands in the midst of things and records what goes on. There is an "amazing quality of innocence" in the Brontës, especially Emily, writes Herbert Read. And it is true that they do not always seem to be fully aware of what is going on in their own novels. In *Jane Eyre* this produces some remarkably naïve and inapposite dialogue. Emily Brontë's "innocence," however, is akin to what Keats called "negative capability"— the ability of the tragic writer to retain an unbaffled, even uninquiring, per-ception of elementals in the midst of awful and confusing events. Charlotte perpetually inquires, analyzes, and moralizes; Emily watches the terrific interplay of events with no comment except that they are terrifying or beautiful. She does not moralize: in a poem she recalls how she once raged at fools and fiercely defended "truth, right, liberty," but she has learned that

113

> however I frown,
> The same world will go rolling on.

"The world is going," she exclaims elsewhere, and we realize that her detachment is not only a moral one. It is an immediate sense impression of being set apart from the material world, a truly frightening homelessness.

> The very grey rocks, looking on,
> Asked, "What do you here?"

Herbert Read cannot be right to say that Emily Brontë "is forever perplexed by the problem of evil." She does not allow herself to be perplexed; if she did she would no longer be "innocent" and she would no longer be a tragic writer, if we are to stick to Keats' stringent prescription. She has little of the grandly humane moral sense of Sophocles; she is Aeschylean. Heathcliff is a creature whose beginning and end remain, in the purely mundane moral sense, meaningless. He does not, like Oedipus, finally recognize himself as a man whose hidden deeds have bound him up with certain moral consequences. There is no such recognition of the hero's moral self anywhere in *Wuthering Heights*.

But though Emily Brontë cannot be said to be "perplexed" by evil, there is a central moral assertion in *Wuthering Heights*. This we come upon in the scene where both Heathcliff and Cathy realize the appalling consequences of Cathy's failure to fulfill her mission; which was, clearly, to marry Heathcliff. The terrible recriminations which pass between the two lovers are the anguished utterances of human beings who are finally, because of the moral failure of Cathy, being dragged down into the flux of the dehumanized universe. Cathy dissolves into pure matter and force almost before our eyes (as Heathcliff is to do later) and while she yet retains enough of sensibility to make the experience articulate. Yet though this is the single moral assertion, the whole action of the book depends upon it.

As in *Jane Eyre*, the culture heroine of *Wuthering Heights* fails. Heathcliff relentlessly charges her with her failure: "You teach me now how cruel you've been—cruel and false. *Why* did you despise me? *Why* did you betray your own heart, Cathy? I have

not one word of comfort. You deserve this. You have killed yourself. Yes, you may kiss me, and cry; and wring out my kisses
and tears; they'll blight you—they'll damn you. You loved me—
then what *right* had you to leave me? What right—answer me—
for the poor fancy you felt for Linton? Because misery and degradation, and death, and nothing that God or Satan could inflict
would have parted us, *you*, of your own free will did it." Like
Jane Eyre, Cathy has refused the act which would have set Satan
at war with God in the soul of Heathcliff. The penalty for not
throwing herself into the agony of the spiritual struggle and
birth is certainly unequivocal: she must die. This spiritual
struggle Emily Brontë pictures in a poem:

> So stood I, in Heaven's glorious sun
> And in the glare of Hell
> My spirit drank a mingled tone
> Of seraph's song and demon's moan—
> What my soul bore my soul alone
> Within itself may tell.

If, then, we are to call *Wuthering Heights* a tragedy, we must
leave room in our definition of the word for the following circumstances: a heroine comes to grasp the significance of her spiritual
mission too late; the hero degenerates into "absurdity" and dies,
since the God-Devil figure is absurd without the human protagonist on whom he depends.

Emily Brontë's "innocence" is partly due to her almost absolute devotion to death. Surely no first-rate writer has ever been
more of the Other World. She was

> Weaned from life and torn away
> In the morning of [her] day.

She is also, as one would expect, devoted to her own childhood
(she seems to have taken some of her images from Wordsworth;
notice her habit of referring to infancy as a "glory," a "lost vision," a "light," and so forth). Cathy dies, as she hopes, into a
wonderful world of light; she dies "like a child reviving." The
poem beginning "The soft unclouded blue of air" unites the theme
of childhood with the theme of the Lover-Lord. The poem con-

cerns the thoughts of an unnamed "I" on a day "as bright as Eden's used to be":

> Laid on the grass I lapsed away,
> Sank back again to childhood's day;
> All harsh thoughts perished, memory mild
> Subdued both grief and passion wild.

But, she asks, does the sunshine that bathes the "stern and swarthy brow" of "that iron man" elicit in his memory a sweet dream of childhood, or is

> Remembrance of his early home
> So lost that not a gleam may come?

He sits in silence.

> That stormy breast
> At length, I said, has deigned to rest;
> At length above that spirit flows
> The waveless ocean of repose . . .
> Perhaps this is the destined hour
> When hell shall lose its fatal power
> And heaven itself shall bend above
> To hail the soul redeemed by love.

But all in vain. One glance at the "iron man" reveals

> how little care
> He felt for all the beauty there

and how soon her own breast can grow as cold "as winter wind or polar snow." Her futile desire has been to drag the hero back into infancy—perhaps into that "Unique Society" of childish heroes and heroines who perform romantic deeds among the islands of the Pacific in Emily Brontë's juvenile writings. She has wanted to transform the universal energy of the "iron man" into the mild light of the Other World, or "home." She has thought that by detachment from this world she could deprive Hell of "its fatal power" and make Heaven "hail the soul." But detachment cannot solve the conflict between the Devil and God; that is work which must be done in This World. Cathy, too, tries to take Heathcliff into "that glorious world" which she sees "dimly through tears" and yearns for "through the walls of an aching

heart." But this is only an imaginary Heathcliff, "*my* Heathcliff,"
she says, not the relentless inquisitor who stands before her.
"*My* Heathcliff" is a child returning to what Wordsworth called
the "imperial palace" and what Emily Brontë described thus:

> I saw her stand in the gallery long,
> Watching the little children there,
> As they were playing the pillars among
> And bounding down the marble stair.

Virginia Woolf writes that Emily Brontë "looked out upon a
world cleft into gigantic disorder and felt within her the power
to unite it into a book." *Wuthering Heights* displays the schisms
between the forces of the universe; we have a sense of great mo-
tions taking place without immediately recognizable relation.
Things do not fit together and we are left to contemplate the
estrangement of parts. The book is meaningful because it portrays human beings caught in the schisms — caught between the
Other World and This World, between Childhood and Adulthood,
between Savagery and Civilization, between the Devil and God,
between Matter and Spirit, between Stasis and Motion.

IV

We are asked to consider three pairs of lovers in *Wuthering
Heights*: Heathcliff and the elder Cathy, Linton Heathcliff and
the younger Cathy, Hareton Earnshaw and the younger Cathy.
Nothing could be more Victorian than the child-lovers, Linton
and the younger Cathy, both aged seventeen, under the baleful
influence of Heathcliff. They are sweet, innocent children; they
are persecuted and forced into a morbid sex relationship. They
are both spoiled — Linton is an invalid who sucks sugar candy
and asks Cathy not to kiss him, because it takes his breath away;
he is pettish, willful, and mortally afraid of his father. Cathy has
some of the vivacity of her mother; she is pretty; but she too is
pettish and spoiled. "I should never love anyone better than
papa," she says.

In my family there is an illustrated Victorian autograph album,
inherited from elder generations. It contains — along with many

117

elaborately scrolled signatures, pictures of doves, and a recipe for smelling salts — an engraving of a smiling and cherubic girl sucking a stick of candy. At first glance she seems perfectly innocent; yet there is an almost wicked knowingness in her expression. Behind her is a dark, bestial face carved heavily in wood; the leg of the table on which she leans is carved in the shape of a menacing griffon or gargoyle. It is exactly the relation of Linton and Cathy to Heathcliff in those appalling love scenes on the moors. The theme of childhood, voiced by the elder Cathy on her deathbed, is thus continued in the main action of the second half of the book. We begin to see that, in one way or another, childhood is in fact the central theme of Emily Brontë's writing.

There is a childishness too about the love relationship of Hareton and the younger Cathy. They marry when Hareton is twenty-five and Cathy is nineteen, but Hareton is still a primitive waif, having been deliberately kept untaught by Heathcliff. Cathy is still a spoiled child. Their marriage promises to be a happy one, however. Hareton, though in many ways the image of Heathcliff, has little of Heathcliff's force. He can be domesticated. Cathy promises to mature into a responsible woman. As in the marriage of Jane and Rochester, the woman has a strong advantage over her lover; for Cathy is educated and intelligent and she will teach Hareton, who desperately desires to be educated. In *Jane Eyre* the principal lovers finally come together, though in a compromised relationship. *Wuthering Heights* is a more uncompromising book. Heathcliff and the elder Cathy come together only at several removes: Hareton and the younger Cathy are but pale replicas of their elders.

v

I have said that the Brontës were essentially Victorian. The happy marriages at the end of *Jane Eyre* and *Wuthering Heights* represent the ostensible triumph of the secular, moderate-liberal, sentimental point of view over the mythical, tragic point of view. The moral texture of these novels is woven whole cloth out of the social customs of the day. To the marriage of free and godlike souls, to humane utopias of sexual society, the Brontës plainly

RICHARD CHASE

preferred domesticity—and this despite the fact that no one knew better the readiness with which the Victorian family reverted to the primitive horde. The Brontës' tremendous displacement of the domestic values toward the tragic and mythical, though it falls short of ultimate achievement, gives their work a margin of superiority over that of other Victorian novelists. The Brontës were more fully committed to art than most of their contemporaries. They "rebelled" only in the sense that they translated the Victorian social situation into mythical forms. And this reminds us that the fault of much of our "new criticism" of the best nineteenth-century literature is to mistake art for rebellion.

T. S. ELIOT

Ulysses, Order, and Myth

Mr. Joyce's book has been out long enough for no more general expression of praise, or expostulation with its detractors, to be necessary; and it has not been out long enough for any attempt at a complete measurement of its place and significance to be possible. All that one can usefully do at this time, and it is a great deal to do, for such a book, is to elucidate any aspect of the book —and the number of aspects is indefinite—which has not yet been fixed. I hold this book to be the most important expression which the present age has found; it is a book to which we are all indebted, and from which none of us can escape. These are postulates for anything that I have to say about it, and I have no wish to waste the reader's time by elaborating my eulogies; it has given me all the surprise, delight, and terror that I can require, and I will leave it at that.

Amongst all the criticisms I have seen of the book, I have seen nothing—unless we except, in its way, M. Valery Larbaud's valuable paper which is rather an Introduction than a criticism— which seemed to me to appreciate the significance of the method employed—the parallel to the *Odyssey*, and the use of appropriate styles and symbols to each division. Yet one might expect this to be the first peculiarity to attract attention; but it has

NOTE. Reprinted from the *Dial*, 1923, by permission of the editors and the author.

T. S. ELIOT

been treated as an amusing dodge, or scaffolding erected by the
author for the purpose of disposing his realistic tale, of no interest
in the completed structure. The criticism which Mr. Aldington
directed upon *Ulysses* several years ago seems to me to fail by this
oversight—but, as Mr. Aldington wrote before the complete work
had appeared, fails more honorably than the attempts of those
who had the whole book before them. Mr. Aldington treated Mr.
Joyce as a prophet of chaos; and wailed at the flood of Dadaism
which his prescient eye saw bursting forth at the tap of the
magician's rod. Of course, the influence which Mr. Joyce's book
may have is from my point of view an irrelevance. A very great
book may have a very bad influence indeed; and a mediocre book
may be in the event most salutary. The next generation is responsible for its own soul; a man of genius is responsible to his
peers, not to a studio-full of uneducated and undisciplined cox-
combs. Still, Mr. Aldington's pathetic solicitude for the half-
witted seems to me to carry certain implications about the nature
of the book itself to which I cannot assent; and this is the important issue. He finds the book, if I understand him, to be an invitation to chaos, and an expression of feelings which are perverse,
partial, and a distortion of reality. But unless I quote Mr. Aldington's words I am likely to falsify. "I say, moreover," he says,
"that when Mr. Joyce, with his marvellous gifts, uses them to
disgust us with mankind, he is doing something which is false
and a libel on humanity."* It is somewhat similar to the opinion
of the urbane Thackeray upon Swift. "As for the moral, I think
it horrible, shameful, unmanly, blasphemous: and giant and
great as this Dean is, I say we should hoot him." (This, of the
conclusion of the Voyage to the Houyhnhnms—which seems to
me one of the greatest triumphs that the human soul has ever
achieved. It is true that Thackeray later pays Swift one of the
finest tributes that a man has ever given or received: "So great
a man he seems to me that thinking of him is like thinking of an
empire falling." And Mr. Aldington, in his time, is almost equally
generous.)

* *English Review,* April 1921.

Whether it is possible to libel humanity (in distinction to libel in the usual sense, which is libeling an individual or a group in contrast with the rest of humanity) is a question for philosophical societies to discuss; but of course if *Ulysses* were a "libel" it would simply be a forged document, a powerless fraud, which would never have extracted from Mr. Aldington a moment's attention. I do not wish to linger over this point: the interesting question is that begged by Mr. Aldington when he refers to Mr. Joyce's "great *undisciplined* talent."

I think that Mr. Aldington and I are more or less agreed as to what we want in principle, and agreed to call it classicism. It is because of this agreement that I have chosen Mr. Aldington to attack on the present issue. We are agreed as to what we want, but not as to how to get it, or as to what contemporary writing exhibits a tendency in that direction. We agree, I hope, that "classicism" is not an alternative to "romanticism," as of political parties, Conservative and Liberal, Republican and Democrat, on a "turn-the-rascals-out" platform. It is a goal toward which all good literature strives, so far as it is good, according to the possibilities of its place and time. One can be "classical," in a sense, by turning away from nine tenths of the material which lies at hand, and selecting only mummified stuff from a museum—like some contemporary writers, about whom one could say some nasty things in this connection, if it were worth while (Mr. Aldington is not one of them). Or one can be classical in tendency by doing the best one can with the material at hand.

The confusion springs from the fact that the term is applied to literature and to the whole complex of interests and modes of behavior and society of which literature is a part; and it has not the same bearing in both applications. It is much easier to be a classicist in literary criticism than in creative art—because in criticism you are responsible only for what you want, and in creation you are responsible for what you can do with material which you must simply accept. And in this material I include the emotions and feelings of the writer himself, which, for that writer, are simply material which he must accept—not virtues to be enlarged or vices to be diminished. The question, then, about Mr. Joyce, is: how much living material does he deal with, and how does he deal with it: deal with, not as a legislator or exhorter, but as an artist?

It is here that Mr. Joyce's parallel use of the *Odyssey* has a great importance. It has the importance of a scientific discovery. No one else has built a novel upon such a foundation before: it has never before been necessary. I am not begging the question in calling *Ulysses* a "novel"; and if you call it an epic it will not matter. If it is not a novel, that is simply because the novel is a form which will no longer serve; it is because the novel, instead of being a form, was simply the expression of an age which had not sufficiently lost all form to feel the need of something stricter. Mr. Joyce has written one novel — the *Portrait*; Mr. Wyndham Lewis has written one novel — *Tarr*. I do not suppose that either of them will ever write another "novel." The novel ended with Flaubert and with James. It is, I think, because Mr. Joyce and Mr. Lewis, being "in advance" of their time, felt a conscious or probably unconscious dissatisfaction with the form, that their novels are more formless than those of a dozen clever writers who are unaware of its obsolescence.

In using the myth, in manipulating a continuous parallel between contemporaneity and antiquity, Mr. Joyce is pursuing a method which others must pursue after him. They will not be imitators, any more than the scientist who uses the discoveries of an Einstein in pursuing his own, independent, further investigations. It is simply a way of controlling, of ordering, of giving a shape and a significance to the immense panorama of futility and anarchy which is contemporary history. It is a method already adumbrated by Mr. Yeats, and of the need for which I believe Mr. Yeats to have been the first contemporary to be conscious. It is a method for which the horoscope is auspicious. Psychology (such as it is, and whether our reaction to it be comic or serious), ethnology, and *The Golden Bough* have concurred to make possible what was impossible even a few years ago. Instead of narrative method, we may now use the mythical method. It is, I seriously believe, a step toward making the modern world possible for art, toward that order and form which Mr. Aldington so earnestly desires. And only those who have won their own discipline in secret and without aid, in a world which offers very little assistance to that end, can be of any use in furthering this advance.

William Faulkner

Malcolm Cowley's editing of *The Portable Faulkner** is remarkable on two counts. First, the selection from Faulkner's
work is made not merely to give a cross section or a group of
good examples but to demonstrate one of the principles of integration in the work. Second, the introductory essay is one of the
few things ever written on Faulkner which is not hagridden by
prejudice or preconception and which really sheds some light on
the subject.

The selections here are made to describe the place, Yoknapatawpha County, Mississippi, which is, as Cowley puts it, "Faulkner's mythical kingdom," and to give the history of that kingdom.
The place is the locale of most of Faulkner's work. Its 2400 square
miles lie between the hills of north Mississippi and the rich, black
bottom lands. It has a population of 15,611 persons, composing a
society with characters as different as the Bundrens, the Snopeses,
Ike McCaslin, Percy Grimm, Temple Drake, the Compsons,
Christmas, Dilsey, and the tall convict of *The Wild Palms.* No
land in all fiction lives more vividly in its physical presence than
this mythical county—the "pine-winey" afternoons, the nights
with "a thin sickle of moon like the heel print of a boot in wet

note. Reprinted from the *New Republic,* 1946, by permission of the editors and
the author.
    * *The Portable Faulkner,* edited by Malcolm Cowley. New York : Viking Press.

sand," the tremendous reach of the big river in flood, "yellow and sleepy in the afternoon," and the "little piddling creeks, that run backward one day and forward the next and come busting down on a man full of dead mules and hen houses," the ruined plantation which was Popeye's hangout, the swamps and fields and hot, dusty roads of the Frenchman's Bend section, and the remnants of the great original forests, "green with gloom" in summer, "if anything actually dimmer than they had been in November's gray dissolution, where even at noon the sun fell only in windless dappling upon the earth which never completely dried."

And no land in all fiction is more painstakingly analyzed from the sociological standpoint. The descendants of the old families, the descendants of bushwhackers and carpetbaggers, the swamp rats, the Negro cooks and farm hands, bootleggers and gangsters, peddlers, college boys, tenant farmers, country store-keepers, county-seat lawyers are all here. The marks of class, occupation, and history are fully rendered and we know completely their speech, dress, food, houses, manners, and attitudes. Nature and sociology, geography and human geography, are scrupulously though effortlessly presented in Faulkner's work, and their significance for his work is very great; but the significance is of a conditioning order. They are, as it were, aspects of man's "doom" —a word of which Faulkner is very fond—but his manhood in the face of that doom is what is important.

Cowley's selections are made to give the description of the mythical kingdom, but more important, they are made to give its history. Most critics, even those who have most naïvely or deliberately misread the meaning of the fact, have been aware that the sense of the past is crucial in Faulkner's work. Cowley has here set up selections running in date of action from 1820 to 1940. The first, "A Justice," is a story about Ikkemotubbe, the nephew of a Chickasaw chief who went to New Orleans, where he received the name of *du Homme,* which became Doom; who came back to the tribe to poison his way to the Man-ship; and who, in the end (in Faulkner's "history" though not in "A Justice" itself), swaps a mile square of "virgin north Mississippi dirt" for a racing mare owned by Jason Lycurgus Compson, the founder of the Compson family in Mississippi. The last selection, "Delta Autumn," shows us Isaac McCaslin, the man who brings the best of the old order, philosopher, aristocrat, woodsman, into the modern world and who gives the silver-mounted horn which General Compson had left him to a mulatto woman for her bastard son by a relative of McCaslin's. In between "A Justice" and "Delta Autumn" fall such pieces as the magnificent "Red Leaves," the profoundly symbolic story called "The Bear," the Civil War and Reconstruction stories, "Rain" (from *The Unvanquished*) and "Wash," "Old Man" (the story of the tall convict from *The Wild Palms*), and the often anthologized "That Evening Sun" and "A Rose for Emily," and the brilliant episode of "Percy Grimm" (from *Light in August*). There are other pieces included, but these are the best, and the best for showing the high points in the history of Yoknapatawpha County.

Cowley's introduction undertakes to define the significance of place and history in Faulkner's work, that "labor of imagination that has not been equaled in our time." That labor is, as he points out, a double labor: "first, to invent a Mississippi county that was like a mythical kingdom, but was complete and living in all its details; second, to make his story of Yoknapatawpha County stand as a parable or legend of all the Deep South." The legend — called a legend "because it is obviously no more intended as a historical account of the country south of the Ohio than *The Scarlet Letter* was intended as a history of Massachusetts"—is, as Cowley defines it, this:

The South was settled by Sartorises (aristocrats) and Sutpens (nameless, ambitious men) who, seizing the land from the Indians, were determined to found an enduring and stable order. But despite their strength and integrity their project was, to use Faulkner's word, "accursed" by slavery, which, with the Civil War as instrument, frustrated their design. Their attempt to rebuild according to the old plan and old values was defeated by a combination of forces—the carpetbaggers and Snopeses ("a new exploiting class descended from the landless whites"). Most of the descendants of the old order are in various ways incompetent: They are prevented by their code from competing with the codeless Snopeses, they cling to the letter and forget the spirit of their tradition, they lose contact with the realities of the present and escape into a dream world of alcohol or rhetoric or gentility or madness, they fall in love with defeat or death, they lose nerve and become cowards, or they, like the last Jason in *The Sound and the Fury*, adopt Snopesism and become worse than any Snopes. Figures like Popeye (eyes like "rubber knobs," a creature having "that vicious depthless quality of stamped tin," the man "who made money and had nothing he could do with it, spend it for, since he knew that alcohol would kill him like poison, who had no friends and had never known a woman") are in their dehumanized quality symbols of modernism, for the society of finance capitalism. The violence of some of Faulkner's work is, according to Cowley, "an example of the Freudian method turned backward, being full of sexual nightmares that are in reality social symbols. It is somehow connected in the author's mind with what he regards as the rape and corruption of the South."

This is, in brief, Cowley's interpretation of the legend, and it provides an excellent way into Faulkner; it exactly serves the purpose which an introduction should serve. The interpretation is indebted, no doubt, to that of George Marion O'Donnell (the first and still an indispensable study of Faulkner's theme), but it modifies O'Donnell's tendency to read Faulkner with an allegorical rigidity and with a kind of doctrinal single-mindedness.

It is possible that the present view, however, should be somewhat modified, at least in emphasis. Although no writer is more deeply committed to a locality than Faulkner, the emphasis on the Southern elements may blind us to other elements, or at least other applications, of deep significance. And this is especially true in so far as the work is interpreted merely as Southern apologetics or, as it is by Maxwell Geismar, as the "extreme hallucinations" of a "cultural psychosis."

ROBERT PENN WARREN

It is important, I think, that Faulkner's work be regarded not in terms of the South against the North, but in terms of issues which are common to our modern world. The legend is not merely a legend of the South, but is also a legend of our general plight and problem. The modern world is in moral confusion. It does suffer from a lack of discipline, of sanctions, of community of values, of a sense of a mission. It is a world in which self-interest, workableness, success, provide the standards. It is a world which is the victim of abstraction and of mechanism, or at least, at moments, feels itself to be. It can look back nostalgically upon the old world of traditional values and feel loss and perhaps despair—upon the world in which, as one of Faulkner's characters puts it, men "had the gift of living once or dying once instead of being diffused and scattered creatures drawn blindly from a grab bag and assembled"—a world in which men were, "integer for integer," more simple and complete.

If it be objected that Faulkner's view is unrealistic, that had the old order satisfied human needs it would have survived, and that it is sentimental to hold that it was killed from the outside, the answer is clear in the work: the old order did not satisfy human needs—the Southern old order or any other—for it, not being founded on justice, was "accursed" and held the seeds of its own ruin in itself. But even in terms of the curse the old order, as opposed to the new order (in so far as the new is to be equated with Snopesism), allowed the traditional man to define himself as human by setting up codes, concepts of virtue, obligations, and by accepting the risks of his humanity. Within the traditional order was a notion of truth, even if man in the flow of things did not succeed in realizing that truth. Take, for instance, the passage from "The Bear":

"All right," he said. "Listen," and read again, but only one stanza this time and closed the book and laid it on the table. "She cannot fade, though thou hast not thy bliss," McCaslin said: "Forever wilt thou love, she be fair."

"He's talking about a girl," he said.

"He had to talk about something," McCaslin said. Then he

said, "He was talking about truth. Truth is one. It doesn't change. It covers all things which touch the heart — honor and pride and pity and justice and courage and love. Do you see now?"

The human effort is what is important, the capacity to make the effort to rise above the mechanical process of life, the pride to endure, for in endurance there is a kind of self-conquest.

When it is said, as it is often said, that Faulkner's work is "backward-looking," the answer is that the constant ethical center is to be found in the glorification of the human effort and of human endurance, which are not in time, even though in modernity they seem to persist most surely among the despised and rejected. It is true that Faulkner's work contains a savage attack on modernity, but it is to be remembered that Elizabethan tragedy, for instance, contained just such an attack on its own special "modernity." (Ambition is the most constant tragic crime, and ambition is the attitude special to an opening society; all villains are rationalists and appeal to "nature" beyond traditional morality for justification, and rationalism is, in the sense implied here, the attitude special to the rise of a secular and scientific order before a new morality can be formulated.)

It is not ultimately important whether the traditional order (Southern or other) as depicted by Faulkner fits exactly the picture which critical historical method provides. Let it be granted, for the sake of discussion, that Faulkner does oversimplify the matter. What is ultimately important, both ethically and artistically, is the symbolic function of that order in relation to the world which is set in opposition to it. The opposition between the old order and the new does not, however, exhaust the picture. What of the order to come? "We will have to wait," old Ike McCaslin says to the mulatto girl who is in love with a white man. A curse may work itself out in time; and in such glimpses, which occur now and then, we get the notion of a grudging meliorism, a practical supplement to the idealism, like Ike McCaslin's, which finds compensation in the human effort and the contemplation of "truth."

The discussion, even at a larger scope and with more satisfactory analysis, of the central theme of Faulkner would not exhaust the interest of his work. In fact, the discussion of this question always runs the risk of making his work appear too schematic, too dry and too complacent when in actual fact it is full of rich detail, of shadings and complexities of attitude, of ironies and ambivalences. Cowley's introduction cautions the reader on this point and suggests various fruitful topics for investigation and thought. But I shall make bold—and in the general barrenness of criticism on Faulkner it does not require excessive boldness—to list and comment on certain topics which seem to me to demand further critical study.

Nature. The vividness of the natural background is one of the impressive features of Faulkner's work. It is accurately observed, but observation only provides the stuff from which the characteristic effects are gained. It is the atmosphere which counts, the poetry, the infusion of feeling, the symbolic weight. Nature provides a backdrop—of lyric beauty (the meadow in the cow episode of *The Hamlet*), of homely charm (the trial scene of the "Spotted Horses" story from the same book), of sinister, brooding force (the river in "Old Man" from *The Wild Palms*), of massive dignity (the forest in "The Bear")—for the human action and passion. The indestructible beauty is there: "God created man," Ike McCaslin says in "Delta Autumn," "and He created the world for him to live in and I reckon He created the kind of world He would have wanted to live in if He had been a man."

Ideally, if man were like God, as Ike McCaslin puts it, man's attitude toward nature would be one of pure contemplation, pure participation in its great forms and appearances; the appropriate attitude is love, for with Ike McCaslin the moment of love is equated with godhood. But since man "wasn't quite God himself," since he lives in the world of flesh, he must be a hunter, user, and violator. To return to McCaslin: God "put them both here: man and the game he would follow and kill, foreknowing it. I believe He said, 'So be it.' I reckon He even foreknew the end. But He said, 'I will give him his chance. I will give him warning and foreknowledge too, along with the desire to follow and the power to slay. The woods and the fields he ravages and the game he devastates will be the consequence and signature of his crime and guilt, and his punishment.' "

There is, then, a contamination implicit in the human condition—a kind of Original Sin, as it were—but it is possible, even in the contaminating act, the violation, for man to achieve some measure of redemption, a redemption through love. For instance, in "The Bear," the great legendary beast which is pursued for years to the death is also an object of love and veneration, and the symbol of virtue, and the deer hunt of "Delta Autumn" is for Ike McCaslin a ritual of renewal. Those who have learned the right relationship to nature—"the pride and humility" which young Ike McCaslin learns from the half-Negro, half-Indian Sam Fathers—are set over against those who have not. In "The Bear," General Compson speaks up to Cass McCaslin to defend the wish of the boy Ike McCaslin to stay an extra week in the woods: "You got one foot straddled into a farm and the other foot straddled into a bank; you ain't even got a good hand-hold where this boy was already an old man long before you damned Sartorises and Edmondses invented farms and banks to keep yourselves from having to find out what this boy was born knowing and fearing too maybe, but without being afraid, that could go ten miles on a compass because he wanted to look at a bear none of us had ever got near enough to put a bullet in and looked at the bear and came the ten miles back on the compass in the dark; maybe by God that's the why and the wherefore of farms and banks."

Those who have the wrong attitude toward nature are the pure exploiters, the apostles of abstractionism, the truly evil men. For instance, the very opening of *Sanctuary* presents a distinction on this ground between Benbow and Popeye. While the threat of Popeye keeps Benbow crouching by the spring, he hears a Carolina wren sing, and even under these circumstances tries to recall the local name for it. And he says to Popeye: "And of course you don't know the name of it. I don't suppose you'd know a bird at all, without it was singing in a cage in a hotel lounge, or cost four dollars on a plate." Popeye, as we may remember, spits in the spring (he hates nature and must foul it), is afraid to go through the woods ("Through all them trees?" he demands when Benbow points out the short cut), and when an owl whisks past them in the twilight, claws at Benbow's coat with almost hysterical fear ("It's just an owl," Benbow says. "It's nothing but an owl.").

The pure exploiters, though they may gain ownership and use of a thing, never really have it; like Popeye, they are impotent. For instance, Flem Snopes, the central character and villain of *The Hamlet,* who brings the exploiter's mentality to Frenchman's Bend, finally marries Eula Varner, a kind of fertility goddess or earth goddess; but his ownership is meaningless, for she always refers to him as "that man" (she does not even have a name for him), and he has only got her after she has given herself willingly to one of the bold, hot-blooded boys of the neighborhood. In fact, nature can't, in one sense, be "owned." Ike McCaslin, in "The Bear," says of the land which has come down to him: "It was never Father's and Uncle Buddy's to bequeath me to repudiate, because it was never Grandfather's to bequeath them to bequeath me to repudiate, because it was never old Ikkemotubbe's to sell to Grandfather for bequeathment and repudiation. Because it was never Ikkemotubbe's fathers' father's to bequeath Ikkemotubbe to sell to Grandfather or any man because on the instant when Ikkemotubbe discovered, realized, that he could sell it for money, on that instant it ceased ever to have been his forever, father to father, to father, and the man who bought it bought nothing."

The right attitude toward nature is, as a matter of fact, associated with the right attitude toward man, and the mere lust for power over nature is associated with the lust for power over other men, for God gave the earth to man, we read in "The Bear," not "to hold for himself and his descendants inviolable title forever, generation after generation, to the oblongs and squares of the earth, but to hold the earth mutual and intact in the communal anonymity of brotherhood, and all the fee He asked was pity and humility and sufferance and endurance and the sweat of his face for bread." It is the failure of this pity which curses the earth (the land in Faulkner's particular country is "accursed" by chattel slavery, but slavery is simply one of the possible forms of the failure). But the rape of nature and the crime against man are always avenged. The rape of nature, the mere exploitation of it without love, is always avenged because the attitude which commits that crime also commits the crime against men which in turn exacts vengeance, so that man finally punishes himself. It is only by this line of reasoning that one can, I think, read the last page of "Delta Autumn":

This land which man has deswamped and denuded and derivered in two generations so that white men can own plantations and commute every night to Memphis and black men own plantations and ride in Jim Crow cars to Chicago to live in millionaires' mansions on Lake Shore Drive; where white men rent farms and live like niggers and niggers crop on shares and live like animals; where cotton is planted and grows man-tall in the very cracks of the sidewalks, and usury and mortgage and bankruptcy and measureless wealth, Chinese and African and Aryan and Jew, all breed and spawn together until no man has time to say which one is which nor cares. . . . No wonder the ruined woods I used to know don't cry for retribution! he thought: The people who have destroyed it will accomplish its revenge.

The attitude toward nature in Faulkner's work, however, does not involve a sinking into nature. In Faulkner's mythology man has "suzerainty over the earth," he is not of the earth, and it is the human virtues which count—"pity and humility and sufferance and endurance." If we take even the extreme case of the idiot Snopes and his fixation on the cow in *The Hamlet* (a scene whose function in the total order of the book is to show that even the idiot pervert is superior to Flem), a scene which shows the human being as close as possible to the "natural" level, we find that the scene is the most lyrical in Faulkner's work: even the idiot is human and not animal, for only human desires, not animal, clothe themselves in poetry. I think that George Marion O'Donnell is right in pointing to the humanism-naturalism opposition in

Faulkner's work, and over and over again we find that the point of some novel or story has to do with the human effort to find or create values in the mechanical round of experience—"not just to eat and evacuate and sleep warm," as Charlotte Rittenmeyer says in *The Wild Palms,* "so we can get up and eat and evacuate in order to sleep warm again," or not just to raise cotton to buy niggers to raise cotton to buy niggers, as it is put in another place. Even when a character seems to be caught in the iron ring of some compulsion, of some mechanical process (the hunted Negro of "Red Leaves," the tall convict of *The Wild Palms,* Christmas of *Light in August*), the effort may be discernible. And in Quentin's attempt, in *The Sound and the Fury,* to persuade his sister Caddy, who is pregnant by one of the boys of Jefferson, to confess that she has committed incest with him, we find among other things the idea that "the horror" and "the clean flame" would be preferable to the meaninglessness of the "loud world."

Humor. One of the most important remarks in Cowley's introduction is that concerning humor. There is, especially in the later books, "a sort of homely and sober-sided frontier humor that is seldom achieved in contemporary writing." Cowley continues: "In a curious way, Faulkner combines two of the principal traditions in American letters: the tradition of psychological horror, often close to symbolism, that begins with Charles Brockden Brown, our first professional novelist, and extends through Poe, Melville, Henry James (in his later stories), Stephen Crane and Hemingway; and the other tradition of frontier humor and realism, beginning with Augustus Longstreet's *Georgia Scenes* and having Mark Twain as its best example." The observation is an acute one, for the distortions of humor and the distortions of horror in Faulkner's work are closely akin and frequently, in a given instance, can scarcely be disentangled.

It is true that the most important strain of humor in Faulkner's work is derived from the tradition of frontier humor (though it is probable that he got it from the porches of country stores and the courthouse yards of county-seat towns and not from any book), and it is true that the most spectacular displays of Faulkner's humor are of this order—for example, the "Spotted Horses" episode from *The Hamlet* or the story "Was." But there are other strains which might be distinguished and investigated. For example, there is a kind of Dickensian humor; the scene in the Memphis brothel from *Sanctuary*, which is reprinted here under the title "Uncle Bud and the Three Madams," is certainly more Dickensian than frontier. There is a subdued humor, sometimes shading into pathos, in the treatment of some of the Negro characters and in their dialogue. And there is an irony ranging from that in the scene in *Sanctuary* where Miss Reba, the madam, in offended decency keeps telling Temple, "Lie down and cover up your nekkidness," while the girl talks with Benbow, to that in the magnificently sustained monologue of Jason at the end of *The Sound and the Fury*.

In any case, humor in Faulkner's work is never exploited for its own sake. It is regularly used as an index, as a lead, to other effects. The humor in itself may be striking, but Faulkner is not a humorist in the sense, say, that Mark Twain is. His humor is but one perspective on the material and it is never a final perspective, as we can see from such an example as the episode of "Spotted Horses." Nothing could be more wide of the point than the remark in Maxwell Geismar's essay on Faulkner to the effect that Faulkner in *The Hamlet* "seems now to accept the antics of his provincial morons, to enjoy the chronicle of their low-grade behavior; he submerges himself in their clownish degradation." All the critic seems to find in Mink Snopes' victim with his life-long devotion to the memory of his dead wife, and in Ratliff with his good heart and ironical mind and quiet wisdom, is comic "descendants of the gangling and giggling Wash Jones."

The Poor White. The above remark leads us to the not un-common misconception about the role of the poor white in Faulkner's work. It is true that the Snopeses are poor whites, descendants of bushwhackers (and therefore outside society, as the bushwhacker was outside society, had no "side" in the Civil War but tried to make a good thing of it), and it is true that Snopes-ism represents a special kind of villainy and degradation, the form that the pure doctrine of exploitation and degradation takes in the society of which Faulkner writes, but any careful reader realizes that a Snopes is not to be equated with a poor white. For instance, the book most fully about the poor white, *As I Lay Dying*, is full of sympathy and poetry. There are a hundred touches like that in Cash's soliloquy about the phonograph: "I reckon it's a good thing we aint got ere a one of them. I reckon I wouldn't never get no work done a-tall for listening to it. I dont know if a little music aint about the nicest thing a fellow can have. Seems like when he comes in tired of a night, it aint nothing could rest him like having a little music played and him resting." Or like the long section toward the middle of the book devoted to Addie Bundren, a section which is full of eloquence like that of this paragraph: "And then he died. He did not know he was dead. I would lie by him in the dark, hearing the dark land talking of God's love and His beauty and His sin; hearing the dark voicelessness in which the words are the deeds, and the other words that are not deeds, that are just the gaps in peoples' lacks, coming down like the cries of geese out of the wild darkness in the old terrible nights, fumbling at the deeds like orphans to whom are pointed out in a crowd two faces and told, That is your father, your mother." Do these passages indicate a relish in the "antics of his provincial morons"?

The whole of *As I Lay Dying* is based on the heroic effort of the Bundren family to fulfill the promise to the dead mother, to take her body to Jefferson; and the fact that Anse Bundren, after the heroic effort has been completed, immediately gets him a new wife, the "duck-shaped woman" with the "hard-looking popeyes," does not negate the heroism of the effort nor the poetry and feeling which give flesh to the book. We are told by one critic that "what should have been the drama of the Bundrens thus becomes in the end a sort of brutal farce," and that we are "unable to feel the tragedy because the author has refused to accept the Bundrens, as he did accept the Compsons, as tragic." Rather, I should say, the Bundrens may come off a little better than the latter-day Compsons, the whining mother, the promiscuous Caddy, the ineffectual Quentin, and the rest. The Bundrens, at least, are capable of the heroic effort, and the promise is fulfilled. What the conclusion indicates is that even such a fellow as Anse Bundren (who is not typical of his family, by the way), in the grip of an idea, in terms of promise or code, is capable of rising out of his ordinary level; Anse falls back at the end, but only after the prop of the idea and obligation have been removed. And we may recall that even the "gangling and giggling Wash Jones" has always been capable of some kind of obscure dream and aspiration (his very attachment to Sutpen indicates that), and that in the end he achieves dignity and manhood.

The final and incontrovertible evidence that Snopes is not to be equated with poor white comes in *The Hamlet* (though actually most of the characters in the book, though they may be poor, are not, strictly speaking, "poor whites" at all, but rather what uninstructed reviewers choose to call by that label). The point of the book is the assault made on a solid community of plain, hard-working small farmers by Snopeses and Snopesism. Ratliff is not rich, but he is not Flem Snopes. And if the corruption of Snopesism does penetrate into the community, there is no one here who can be compared in degradation and vileness to Jason of *The Sound and the Fury,* the Compson who has embraced Snopesism. In fact, Popeye and Flem, Faulkner's best advertised villains, cannot, for vileness and ultimate meanness, touch Jason.

The Negro. In one of Faulkner's books it is said that every white child is born crucified on a black cross. Remarks like this have led to a gross misconception of the place of the Negro in Faulkner's work, to the notion that Faulkner "hates" Negroes. For instance, we find Maxwell Geismar exclaiming what a "strange inversion" it is to take the Negro, who is the "tragic consequence," and to exhibit him as the "evil cause" of the failure of the old order in the South.

This is a misreading of the text. It is slavery, not the Negro, which is defined, quite flatly, as the curse, over and over again, and the Negro is the black cross in so far as he is the embodiment of the curse, the reminder of the guilt, the incarnation of the problem. That is the basic point. But now and then, as a kind of tangential irony, we have the notion, not of the burden of the white on the black, but of the burden of the black on the white, the weight of obligation, inefficiency, and so on, as well as the weight of guilt (the notion we find in the old story of the plantation mistress who, after the Civil War, said: "Mr. Lincoln thought he was emancipating those slaves, but he was really emancipating me").

For instance, we get hints of this notion in "Red Leaves": one of the Indians, sweating in the chase of the runaway Negro who is to be killed for the Man's funeral, says, "Damn that Negro," and the other Indian replies, "Yao. When have they ever been anything but a trial and a care to us?" But the black cross is, fundamentally, the weight of the white man's guilt, the white man who now sells salves and potions to "bleach the pigment and straighten the hair of Negroes that they might resemble the very race which for two hundred years had held them in bondage and from which for another hundred years not even a bloody civil war would have set them completely free." The curse is still operative, as the crime is still compounded.

The actual role of the Negro in Faulkner's fiction is consistently one of pathos or heroism. It is not merely, as has been suggested more than once, that Faulkner condescends to the good and faithful servant, the "white folks' nigger." There are figures like Dilsey, but they are not as impressive as the Negro in "Red Leaves" or Sam Fathers, who, with the bear, is the hero of "The Bear." The fugitive, who gains in the course of the former story a shadowy symbolic significance, is told in the end by one of the Indians who overtake him, "You ran well. Do not be ashamed," and when he walks among the Indians, he is "the tallest there, his high, close, mud-caked head looming above them all." And Sam Fathers is the fountainhead of the wisdom which Ike McCaslin finally gains, and the repository of the virtues which are central for Faulkner—"an old man, son of a Negro slave and an Indian king, inheritor on the one hand of the long chronicle of a people who had learned humility through suffering and learned pride through the endurance which survived suffering, and on the other side the chronicle of a people even longer in the land than the first, yet who now existed there only in the solitary brotherhood of an old and childless Negro's alien blood and the wild and invincible spirit of an old bear."

Even Christmas, in *Light in August,* though he is sometimes spoken of as a villain, is a mixture of heroism and pathos. He is the lost, suffering, enduring creature (the figure like Sam Fathers, the tall convict of *The Wild Palms,* or Dilsey in *The Sound and the Fury*), and even the murder he commits at the end is a fumbling attempt to define his manhood, is an attempt to break out of the iron ring of mechanism, to lift himself out of "nature," for the woman whom he kills has become a figure of the horror of the human which has surrendered the human attributes. (We may compare Christmas to Mink Snopes in *The Hamlet* in this respect: Mink, mean and vicious as he is, kills out of a kind of warped and confused pride, and by this affirmation is set off against his kinsman Flem, whose only values are those of pure Snopesism.)

Even such a brief comment on the Negro in Faulkner's work cannot close without this passage from "The Bear":

"Because they will endure. They are better than we are. Stronger than we are. Their vices are vices aped from white men or that white men and bondage have taught them: improvidence and intemperance and evasion—not laziness: evasion: of what white men had set them to, not for their aggrandizement or even comfort but his own—" and McCaslin

"All right. Go on: Promiscuity. Violence. Instability and lack of control. Inability to distinguish between mine and thine—" and he

"How distinguish when for two hundred years mine did not even exist for them?" and McCaslin

"All right. Go on. And their virtues—" and he

"Yes. Their own. Endurance—" and McCaslin

"So have mules:" and he

"—and pity and tolerance and forbearance and fidelity and love of children—" and McCaslin

140

ROBERT PENN WARREN

"So have dogs:" and he

"—whether their own or not or black or not. And more: what they got not only from white people but not even despite white people because they had it already from the old free fathers a longer time free than us because we have never been free—"

And there is the single comment under Dilsey's name in the annotated genealogy of the Compsons which Faulkner has prepared for the present volume: "They endured."

Technique. There are excellent comments on this subject by Cowley, Conrad Aiken, Warren Beck, Joseph Warren Beach, and Alfred Kazin, but the subject has not been fully explored. One difficulty is that Faulkner is an incorrigible and restless experimenter, is peculiarly sensitive to the expressive possibilities of shifts in technique and has not developed (like Hemingway or Katherine Anne Porter—lyric rather than dramatic writers, artists with a great deal of self-certainty) in a straight line.

Provisionally, we may distinguish in Faulkner's work three basic methods of handling a narrative. One is best typified in *Sanctuary,* where there is a tightly organized plot, a crisp, laconic style, an objective presentation of character—an impersonal method. Another is best typified by *As I Lay Dying* or *The Sound and the Fury,* where each character unfolds in his own language or flow of being before us—a dramatic method in that the author does not obtrude, but a method which makes the subjective reference of character the medium of presentation. Another is best typified by "Was," "The Bear," or the story of the tall convict in *The Wild Palms,* where the organization of the narrative is episodic and the sense of a voice, a narrator's presence (though not necessarily a narrator in the formal sense), is almost constantly felt—a method in which the medium is ultimately a "voice" as index to sensibility. The assumptions underlying these methods, and the relations among them, would provide a study.

Cowley's emphasis on the unity of Faulkner's work, the fact that all the novels and stories are to be taken as aspects of a single, large design, is very important. It is important, for one thing, in regard to the handling of character. A character, Sutpen, for instance, may appear in various perspectives, so that from book to book we move toward a final definition much as in actual life we move toward the definition of a person. The same principle applies to event, as Conrad Aiken has pointed out, the principle of the spiral method which takes the reader over and over the same event from a different altitude, as it were, and a different angle. In relation to both character and event this method, once it is understood by the reader, makes for a kind of realism and a kind of suspense (in the formal not the factual sense) not common in fiction.

The emphasis on the unity. of Faulkner's work may, however, lead to an underrating of the degree of organization within individual works. Cowley is right in pointing out the structural defect in *Light in August,* but he may be putting too much emphasis on the over-all unity and not enough on the organization of the individual work when he says that *The Hamlet* tends to resolve into a "series of episodes resembling beads on a string." I think that in that novel we have a type of organization in which the thematic rather than the narrative emphasis is the basic. principle, and once we grasp that fact the unity of the individual work may come clear. In fact, the whole subject of the principle of thematic organization in the novels and long stories, "The Bear," for instance, needs investigation. In pieces which seem disjointed, or which seem to have the mere tale-teller's improvisations, we may sometimes discover the true unity if we think of the line of meaning, the symbolic ordering, and surrender ourselves to the tale-teller's "voice." And it may be useful at times to recall the distinction between the formal, forensic realism of Ibsen as opposed to the fluid, suggestive realism of Chekhov.

Symbol and Image. Cowley and O'Donnell have given acute readings of the main symbolic outline of Faulkner's fiction, but no one has yet devoted himself to the study of symbolic motifs which, though not major, are nevertheless extremely instructive. For instance, the images of the hunt, the flight, the pursuit, such as we have in "Red Leaves," *The Wild Palms,* the episode of "Peter Grimm" in *Light in August,* "The Bear," "Delta Autumn,"

"Was," and (especially in the hordes of moving Negroes) in *The Unvanquished*. Or there is the important symbolic relationship between man and earth. Or there is the contrast between images of compulsion and images of will or freedom. Or there is the device of what we might call the frozen moment, the arrested action which becomes symbolic, as in the moment when, in "An Odor of Verbena" (from *The Unvanquished*), Drusilla offers the pistols to the hero.

Polarity. To what extent does Faulkner work in terms of polarities, oppositions, paradoxes, inversions of roles? How much does he employ a line of concealed (or open) dialectic progression as a principle for his fiction? The study of these questions may lead to the discovery of principles of organization in his work not yet defined by criticism.

The study of Faulkner is the most challenging single task in contemporary American literature for criticism to undertake. Here is a novelist who, in mass of work, in scope of material, in range of effect, in reportorial accuracy and symbolic subtlety, in philosophical weight, can be put beside the masters of our own past literature. Yet this accomplishment has been effected in what almost amounts to critical isolation and silence, and when the silence has been broken it has usually been broken by someone (sometimes one of our better critics) whose reading has been hasty, whose analysis unscholarly and whose judgments superficial. The picture of Faulkner presented to the public by such criticism is a combination of Thomas Nelson Page, a fascist and a psychopath, gnawing his nails. Of course, this picture is usually accompanied by a grudging remark about genius.

Cowley's book, for its intelligence, sensitivity, and sobriety in the introduction, and for the ingenuity and judgment exhibited in the selections, would be valuable at any time. But it is especially valuable at this time. Perhaps it can mark a turning point in Faulkner's reputation. That will be of slight service to Faulkner, who, as much as any writer of our place and time, can rest in confidence. He can afford to wait. But can we?

143

Manners, Morals, and the Novel

THE invitation that was made to me to address you this evening
was couched in somewhat uncertain terms. Time, place, and
cordiality were perfectly clear, but when it came to the subject
our hosts were not able to specify just what they wanted me to
talk about. They wanted me to deal with literature in its relation to manners—by which, as they relied on me to understand,
they did not really mean *manners*. They did not mean, that is, the
rules of personal intercourse in our culture; and yet such rules
were by no means irrelevant to what they did mean. Nor did
they quite mean manners in the sense of *mores*, customs, although—again—these did bear upon the subject they had in
mind.

I understood them perfectly, as I would not have understood
them had they been more definite. For they were talking about
a nearly indefinable subject.

Somewhere below all the explicit statements that a people
makes through its art, religion, architecture, legislation, there is
a dim mental region of intention of which it is very difficult to
become aware. We now and then get a strong sense of its existence

NOTE. This paper was originally prepared for delivery at the second Kenyon College Conference on the Heritage of the English Speaking Peoples and Their Responsibility, September 1947. In its present revised form it appeared in the
Kenyon Review, 1948 (copyright 1947). It is reprinted by permission of the
Conference Office, the editors of the *Kenyon Review*, and the author.

when we deal with the past, not by reason of its presence in the past but by reason of its absence. As we read the great formulated monuments of the past, we notice that we are reading them without the accompaniment of something that always goes along with the great formulated monuments of the present. The voice of multifarious intention and activity is stilled, all the buzz of implication which always surrounds us in the present, coming to us from what never gets fully stated, coming in the tone of greetings and the tone of quarrels, in slang and humor and popular songs, in the way children play, in the gesture the waiter makes when he puts down the plate, in the nature of the very food we prefer.

Some of the charm of the past consists of the quiet—the great distracting buzz of implication has stopped and we are left only with what has been fully phrased and precisely stated. And part of the melancholy of the past comes from our knowledge that the huge, unrecorded hum of implication was once there and left no trace—we feel that because it is evanescent it is especially human. And we feel, too, that the truth of the great preserved monuments of the past does not fully appear without it. From letters and diaries, from the remote, unconscious corners of the great works themselves, we try to guess what the sound of the multifarious implication was and what it meant.

Or when we read the conclusions that are drawn about our own culture by some gifted foreign critic—or by some stupid native one—who is equipped only with a knowledge of our books, when we try in vain to say what is wrong, when in despair we say that he has read the books "out of context," then we are aware of the matter I have been asked to speak about tonight.

What I understand by manners, then, is a culture's hum and buzz of implication. I mean the whole evanescent context of its explicit statements. It is that part of a culture which is made up of half-uttered or unuttered or unutterable expressions of value. They are hinted at by small actions, sometimes by the arts of dress or decoration, sometimes by tone, gesture, emphasis, or rhythm, sometimes by the words that are used with a special

145

frequency or a special meaning. They are the things that for good or bad draw the people of a culture together and that separate them from the people of another culture. It is the part of a culture which is not art, nor religion, nor morals, nor politics, and yet it relates to all these highly formulated departments of culture. It is modified by them; it modifies them; it is generated by them; it generates them. In this part of culture assumption rules, which is often so much stronger than reason.

The right way to begin to deal with such a subject is to gather together as much of its detail as we possibly can. Only by doing so will we become fully aware of what the gifted foreign critic or the stupid native one was not aware of, that in any complex culture there is not a single system of manners but a conflicting variety of manners, and that what we mean by a culture is the adjustment of this conflict.

But the nature of our present occasion does not permit this accumulation of detail and so I shall try to drive toward a generalization and a hypothesis which, however wrong they may be, will at least permit us to circumscribe the subject. I propose to generalize the subject of American manners by talking about the attitude of Americans toward the subject of manners itself. And since in a complex culture there are, as I say, many different systems of manners and since I cannot talk about them all, I shall select the manners and the attitude toward manners of the literate, reading, responsible middle class of people who are ourselves. I specify that they be reading people because I shall draw my conclusions from the novels they read. The hypothesis I propose is that our attitude toward manners is the expression of a particular conception of reality.

All literature tends to be concerned with the question of reality — I mean quite simply the old opposition between reality and appearance, between what really is and what merely seems.

"Don't you *see*?" is the question we want to shout at Oedipus as he stands before us and before fate in the pride of his rationalism. And at the end of *Oedipus Rex* he demonstrates in a particularly direct way that he now sees what he did not see before.

"Don't you *see?*" we want to shout again at Lear and Gloucester, the two deceived, self-deceiving fathers: blindness again, resistance to the clear claims of reality, the seduction by mere appearance. The same with Othello — reality is right under your stupid nose, how *dare* you be such a gull? So with Molière's Orgon — my good man, my honest citizen, merely *look* at Tartuffe and you will know what's what. So with Milton's Eve — "Woman, watch out! Don't you see — anyone can see — that's a *snake!*"

The problem of reality is central, and in a special way, to the great forefather of the novel, the great book of Cervantes, whose four-hundredth birthday we celebrate this year. There are two movements of thought in *Don Quixote,* two different and opposed notions of reality. One is the movement which leads toward saying that the world of ordinary practicality *is* reality in its fullness. It is the reality of the present moment in all its powerful immediacy of hunger, cold, and pain, making the past and the future, and all ideas, of no account. When the conceptual, the ideal, and the fanciful come into conflict with this, bringing their notions of the past and the future, then disaster results. For one thing, the ordinary proper ways of life are upset — the chained prisoners are understood to be good men and are released, the whore is taken for a lady. There is general confusion. As for the ideal, the conceptual, the fanciful, or romantic — whatever you want to call it — it fares even worse: it is shown to be ridiculous.

Thus one movement of the novel. But Cervantes changed horses in mid-stream and found that he was riding Rosinante. Perhaps at first not quite consciously — although the new view is latent in the old from the very beginning — Cervantes begins to show that the world of tangible reality is not the real reality after all. The real reality is rather the wildly conceiving, the madly fantasying mind of the Don: people change, practical reality changes, when they come into its presence.

In any genre it may happen that the first great example contains the whole potentiality of the genre. It has been said that all philosophy is a footnote to Plato. It can be said that all prose fiction is a variation on the theme of *Don Quixote*. Cervantes sets for the novel the problem of appearance and reality: the shifting and conflict of social classes becomes the field of the problem which at that very moment of history is vexing the philosophers and scientists. And the poverty of the Don suggests that the novel is born with the appearance of money as a social element—money, the great solvent of the solid fabric of the old society, the great generator of illusion. Or, which is to say much the same thing, the novel is born in response to snobbery.

Snobbery is not the same thing as pride of class. Pride of class may not please us but we must at least grant that it reflects a social function. A man who exhibited class pride—in the day when it was possible to do so—may have been puffed up about what he *was*, but this ultimately depended on what he *did*. Thus, aristocratic pride was based ultimately on the ability to fight and administer. No pride is without fault, but pride of class may be thought of as today we think of pride of profession, toward which we are likely to be lenient.

Snobbery is pride in status without pride in function. And it is an uneasy pride of status. It always asks, "Do I belong—do I really belong? And does he belong? And if I am observed talking to him, will it make me seem to belong or not to belong?" It is the peculiar vice, not of aristocratic societies, which have their own appropriate vices, but of bourgeois democratic societies. For us the legendary strongholds of snobbery are the Hollywood studios, where two thousand dollars a week dare not talk to three hundred dollars a week for fear they be taken for nothing more than fifteen hundred dollars a week. The dominant emotions of snobbery are uneasiness, self-consciousness, self-defensiveness, the sense that one is not quite real but can, in some way, acquire reality.

Money is the medium that, for good or bad, makes for a fluent society. It does not make for an equal society but for one in which there is a constant shifting of classes, a frequent change in the personnel of the dominant class. In a shifting society great emphasis is put on appearance—I am using the word now in the common meaning, as when people say that "a good appearance is very important in getting a job." To appear to be established is one of the ways of being established. The old notion of the solid merchant who owns far more than he shows increasingly gives way to the ideal of signalizing status by appearance, by showing more than you have: status in a democratic society is presumed to come not with power but with the tokens of power. Hence the development of what Tocqueville saw as a mark of democratic culture, what he called the "hypocrisy of luxury"—instead of the well-made peasant article and the well-made middle-class article, we have the effort of all articles to appear as the articles of the very wealthy.

And a shifting society is bound to generate an interest in appearance in the philosophical sense. When Shakespeare lightly touched on the matter that so largely preoccupies the novelist—that is, the movement from one class to another—and created Malvolio, he immediately involved the question of social standing with the problem of appearance and reality. Malvolio's daydreams of bettering his position present themselves to him as reality and in revenge his enemies conspire to convince him that he is literally mad and that the world is not as he sees it. The predicaments of the characters in *A Midsummer Night's Dream* and of Christopher Sly seem to suggest that the intermingling of social extremes always suggested to Shakespeare's mind some doubting of the senses.

The characteristic work of the novel is to record the illusion that snobbery generates and to try to penetrate to the truth which, it assumes, lies hidden beneath all the false appearances. Money, snobbery, the ideal of status, these become in themselves the objects of fantasy, the support of the fantasies of love, freedom, charm, power, as in *Madame Bovary,* whose heroine is the sister at a three-centuries' remove of Don Quixote. The greatness of *Great Expectations* begins in its title: modern society bases itself on great expectations which, if ever they are realized, are found to exist by reason of a sordid, hidden reality. The real thing is not the gentility of Pip's life but the hulks and the murder and the rats and decay in the cellarage of the novel.

An English writer, recognizing the central concern of the novel with snobbery, recently cried out half ironically against it. "Who cares whether Pamela finally exasperates Mr. B. into marriage, whether Mr. Elton is more or less than moderately genteel, whether it is sinful for Pendennis nearly to kiss the porter's daughter, whether young men from Boston can ever be as truly refined as middle-aged women in Paris, whether the District Officer's fiancée ought to see so much of Dr. Aziz, whether Lady Chatterley ought to be made love to by the game-keeper, even if he was an officer during the war. Who cares?"

The novel, of course, tells us much more about life than this. It tells us about the look and feel of things, how things are done and what things are worth and what they cost and what the odds are. If the English novel in its special concern with class does not, as the same writer says, explore the deeper layers of personality, then the French novel in exploring these layers must start and end in class; and the Russian novel exploring the ultimate possibilities of spirit, does the same—every situation in Dostoevski, no matter how spiritual, starts with a point of social pride and a certain number of rubles. The great novelists knew that manners indicate the largest intentions of men's souls as well as the smallest and they are perpetually concerned to catch the meaning of every dim implicit hint.

The novel, then, is a perpetual quest for reality, the field of its research being always the social world, the material of its analysis being always manners as the indication of the direction of man's soul. One can understand the pride of profession that moved D. H. Lawrence to say, "Being a novelist, I consider myself superior to the saint, the scientist, the philosopher and the poet. The novel is the one bright book of life."

Now the novel as I have described it has never really established itself in America. Not that we have not had very great novels but that the novel in America diverges from its classic intention, which, as I have said, is the investigation of the problem of reality beginning in the social field. The fact is that American writers of genius have not turned their minds to society. Poe and Melville were quite apart from it; the reality they sought was only tangential to society. Hawthorne was acute when he insisted that he did not write novels but romances — he thus expressed his awareness of the lack of social texture in his work. Howells never fulfilled himself because, although he saw the social subject clearly, he would never take it with full seriousness. In the nineteenth century, Henry James was alone in knowing that to scale the moral and esthetic heights in the novel one had to use the ladder of social observation.

There is a famous passage in James' life of Hawthorne in which James enumerates the things which are lacking to give the American novel the thick social texture of the English novel — no State; barely a specific national name; no sovereign; no court; no aristocracy; no church; no clergy; no army; no diplomatic service; no country gentlemen; no palaces; no castles; no manors; no old country houses; no parsonages; no thatched cottages; no ivied ruins; no cathedrals; no great universities; no public schools; no political society; no sporting class — no Epsom, no Ascot! That is, no sufficiency of means for the display of a variety of manners, no opportunity for the novelist to do his job of searching out reality, not enough complication of appearance to make the job interesting. Another great American novelist of very different temperament had said much the same thing some decades before: James Fenimore Cooper had said that American manners were too simple and dull to nourish the novelist.

This is cogent but it does not explain the condition of the American novel at the present moment. For life in America has increasingly thickened since the nineteenth century. It has not, to be sure, thickened so much as to permit my students to understand the characters of Balzac — to understand, that is, life in a crowded country where the competitive pressures are great, forcing intense passions to express themselves fiercely and yet within the limitations set by a strong and complicated tradition of manners. Still, life here has become more complex and more pressing. And even so we do not have the novel that touches significantly on society, on manners. Whatever the virtues of Dreiser may be, he could not report the social fact with the kind of accuracy it needs. Sinclair Lewis is shrewd, but no one, however charmed with him as a social satirist, can believe that he does more than a limited job of social understanding. John Dos Passos sees much, sees it often in the great way of Flaubert, but can never use social fact as more than either backdrop or "condition." Of our novelists today perhaps only William Faulkner deals with society as the field of tragic reality and he has the disadvantage of being limited to a provincial scene.

It would seem that Americans have a kind of resistance to looking closely at society. They appear to believe that to touch accurately on the matter of class, to take full note of snobbery, is somehow demeaning. It is as if we felt that one cannot touch pitch without being defiled—which, of course, may possibly be the case. Americans will not deny that we have classes and snobbery, but they seem to hold it to be indelicate to take precise cognizance of these phenomena. Consider that Henry James is, among a large part of our reading public, held to be to blame for noticing society as much as he did. Consider the conversation that has, for some interesting reason, become a part of our literary folklore. Scott Fitzgerald said to Ernest Hemingway: "The very rich are different from us." Hemingway replied, "Yes, they have more money." I have seen the exchange quoted many times and always with the intention of suggesting that Fitzgerald was infatuated by wealth and had received a salutary rebuke from his democratic friend. But the truth is that after a certain point quantity of money does indeed change into a quality of personality: in an important sense the very rich *are* different from us. So are the very powerful, the very gifted, the very poor. Fitzgerald was right, and almost for that remark alone he has been received in Balzac's bosom in the heaven of novelists.

And if I may bring my own experience into evidence, I can adduce the response to a review of mine in which I praised John O'Hara's gift of acute observation of snobbery. Friends took me seriously to task, acquaintances greeted me coolly. It was clear to everyone that I had said that snobbery was a good thing.

LIONEL TRILLING

It is of course by no means true that the American reading class has no interest in society. Its interest fails only before society as it used to be represented by the novel. And if we look at the successful serious novels of the last decade, we see that almost all of them have been written from an intense social awareness— it might be said that our definition of a serious book is one which holds before us some image of society to consider and condemn. What is the situation of the dispossessed Oklahoma farmer and whose fault it is, what situation the Jew finds himself in, what it means to be a Negro, how one gets a bell for Adano, what is the advertising business really like, what it means to be insane and how society takes care of you or fails to do so—these are the matters which are believed to be most fertile for the novelist and certainly they are the subjects most favored by our reading class.

The public is probably not deceived about the quality of most of these books. If the question of quality is brought up, the answer is likely to be: no, they are not great, they are not "literature." But there is an unexpressed addendum: and perhaps they are all the better for that—they are not literature, they are reality, and *in a time like this* what we need is reality in large doses.

When, generations from now, the historian of our times undertakes to describe the assumptions of our culture, he will surely discover that the word *reality* is of central importance in his understanding of us. He will observe that for some of our philosophers the meaning of the word was a good deal in doubt, but that for our political writers, many of our literary critics, and most of our reading public, the word did not open discussion but, rather, closed it. Reality, as conceived by us, is whatever is external and hard, gross, unpleasant. Involved in its meaning is the idea of power conceived in a particular way. Some time ago I had occasion to remark how, in the critical estimates of Theodore Dreiser, it is always being said that Dreiser has many faults but that it cannot be denied that he has great power. No one ever says "a kind of power." Power is assumed to be always "brute" power, crude, ugly, and undiscriminating, the way an elephant appears to be. It is seldom understood to be the way an elephant is, precise and discriminating; or the way electricity is, swift and absolute and scarcely embodied.

The word *reality* is an honorific word and the future historian will naturally try to discover our notion of its pejorative opposite, appearance, mere appearance. He will find it in our feeling about the internal: whenever we detect evidences of style and thought we suspect that reality is being a little betrayed, that "mere subjectivity" is creeping in. There follows from this our feeling about complication, modulation, personal idiosyncrasy, and about social forms, both the great and the small.

Having gone so far, our historian is then likely to discover a puzzling contradiction. For we claim that the great advantage of reality is its hard, bedrock, concrete quality, yet everything we say about it tends toward the abstract and it almost seems that what we want to find in reality is abstraction itself. Thus we believe that one of the unpleasant bedrock facts is social class, but we become extremely impatient if ever we are told that social class is indeed so real that it produces actual differences of personality. The very people who talk most about class and its evils think that Fitzgerald was bedazzled and Hemingway right. Or again, it might be observed that in the degree that we speak in praise of the "individual" we have contrived that our literature should have no individuals in it—no people, that is, who are shaped by our liking for the interesting and memorable and special and precious.

Here, then, is our generalization: that in proportion as we have committed ourselves to our particular idea of reality we have lost our interest in manners. For the novel this is a definitive condition because it is inescapably true that in the novel manners make men. It does not matter in what sense the word *manners* is taken —it is equally true of the sense which so much interested Proust or of the sense which interested Dickens or, indeed, of the sense which interested Homer. The Princesse de Guermantes, unable to delay departure for the Duchesse's party to receive properly from her friend Swann the news that he is dying, but able to delay to change the red slippers her husband objects to; Mr. Pickwick and Sam Weller; Priam and Achilles—they exist by reason of their observed manners.

So true is this, indeed, so creative is the novelist's awareness of manners, that we may say that it is a function of his love. It is some sort of love that Fielding has for Squire Western that allows him to note the great, gross details that bring that insensitive, sentient being into existence for us. If that is true, we are forced to certain conclusions about our literature and about the particular definition of reality that has shaped it. The reality we admire tells us that the observation of manners is trivial and even malicious, that there are things much more important for the novel to consider. As a consequence our social sympathies have indeed broadened, but in proportion as they have done so we have lost something of our power of love, for our novels can never create characters who truly exist. We make public demands for love, for we know that broad social feelings should be infused with warmth, and we receive a kind of public product which we try to believe is not cold potatoes. The reviewers of Helen Howe's novel thought that its satiric first part, an excellent satire on the manners of a small but significant segment of society, was ill-natured and unsatisfactory, but they approved the second part, which is the record of the heroine's self-accusing effort to come into communication with the great soul of America. Yet it should have been clear that the satire had its source in a kind of affection, in a real community of feeling, and told the truth, while the second part, said to be so "real," was mere abstraction, one more example of our public idea of ourselves and our national life. The novelist John Steinbeck satisfies our desire for reality the more by being an amateur scientist, and it is believed that his representations of reality are infused with warm-heartedness. In his latest novel the lower-class characters receive a doctrinaire affection in proportion to the suffering and sexuality which define their existence, while the ill-observed middle-class characters are made to submit not only to moral judgment but to the withdrawal of all fellow feeling, being mocked for their very misfortunes and almost for their susceptibility to death. Only a little thought or even less feeling is required to perceive that the basis of his creation is the coldest response to abstract ideas.

Two novelists of the older sort had a prevision of our present situation. In Henry James' *The Princess Casamassima* there is a scene in which the heroine is told about the existence of a conspiratorial group of revolutionaries pledged to the destruction of all existing society. She has for some time been drawn by a desire for social responsibility; she has wanted to help "the people," she has longed to discover just such a group as she now hears about, and she exclaims in joy, "Then it's real, it's solid!" We are intended to hear the Princess' glad cry with the knowledge that she is a woman who despises herself, "that in the darkest hour of her life she sold herself for a title and a fortune. She regards her doing so as such a terrible piece of frivolity that she can never for the rest of her days be serious enough to make up for it." She seeks out poverty, suffering, sacrifice, and death because she believes that these things alone are real; she increasingly believes that art is contemptible; she more and more withdraws her awareness and love from the one person of her acquaintance who most deserves her awareness and love and she increasingly scorns all that suggests variety and modulation and is dissatisfied with the humanity of the present in her longing for the more perfect humanity of the future. It is one of the great points the novel makes that with each step that she takes toward the real, the solid, she in fact moves farther away from it.

In E. M. Forster's *The Longest Journey* there is a young man named Stephen Wonham who, although a gentleman born, has been carelessly brought up and has no real notion of the responsibilities of his class. He has a friend, a country laborer, a shepherd, and on two occasions he outrages the feelings of certain intelligent, liberal, democratic people in the book by his treatment of this friend. Once, when the shepherd reneges on a bargain, Stephen quarrels with him and knocks him down; and in the matter of the loan of a few shillings he insists that the money be paid back to the last farthing. The intelligent, liberal, democratic people know that this is not the way to act to the poor. But Stephen cannot think of the shepherd as the poor, nor, although he is a country laborer, as an object of research by J. L. and Barbara Hammond; he is rather a reciprocating subject in a relationship of affection—as we say, a friend—and therefore liable to anger and required to pay his debts. But this view is held to be deficient in intelligence, liberalism, and democracy.

In these two incidents we have the premonition of our present cultural and social situation, the passionate self-reproachful addiction to a "strong" reality which must limit its purview to maintain its strength, the replacement with abstraction of natural, direct human feeling.

It is worth noting, by the way, how clear is the line by which the two novels descend from *Don Quixote*—how their young heroes come into life with large preconceived ideas and are knocked about in consequence; how both are concerned with the problem of appearance and reality, *The Longest Journey* quite explicitly, *The Princess Casamassima* by indirection; how both evoke the question of the nature of reality by contriving a meeting and conflict of diverse social classes and take great note of the differences of manners. Both have as their leading characters people who are specifically and passionately concerned with social injustice and both agree in saying that to act against social injustice is right and noble but that to choose to act so does not settle all moral problems but, on the contrary, generates new ones of an especially difficult sort.

I have elsewhere given the name of moral realism to the perception of the dangers of the moral life itself. Perhaps at no other time has the enterprise of moral realism ever been so much needed, for at no other time have so many people committed themselves to moral righteousness. We have the books that point out the bad conditions, that praise us for taking progressive attitudes. We have no books that raise questions in our minds not only about conditions but about ourselves, that lead us to refine our motives and ask what might lie behind our good impulses.

There is nothing so very terrible in discovering that something does lie behind. Nor does it need a Freud to make the discovery. Here is a publicity release sent out by one of our oldest and most respectable publishing houses. It bears the heading: "What Makes Books Sell?" "Blank & Company reports that the current interest in horror stories has attracted a great number of readers to John Dash's novel . . . because of its depiction of Nazi brutality. Critics and readers alike have commented on the stark realism of Dash's handling of the torture scenes in the book. The publishers originally envisaged a woman's market because of the love story, now find men reading the book because of the other angle." This does not suggest a more than usual depravity in the male reader, for "the other angle" has always had a fascination, no doubt a bad one, even for those who would not themselves commit or actually witness an act of torture. I cite the extreme example only to suggest that something may indeed lie behind our sober intelligent interest in moral politics. In this instance the pleasure in the cruelty is protected and licensed by moral indignation. In other instances moral indignation, which has been said to be the favorite emotion of the middle class, may be in itself an exquisite pleasure. To understand this does not invalidate moral indignation but only sets up the conditions on which it ought to be entertained, only says when it is legitimate and when not.

But, the answer comes, however important it may be for moral realism to raise questions in our minds about our motives, is it not at best a matter of secondary importance? Is it not of the first importance that we be given a direct and immediate report on the reality that is daily being brought to dreadful birth? The novels that have done this have effected much practical good, bringing to consciousness the latent feelings of many people, making it harder for them to be unaware or indifferent, creating an atmosphere in which injustice finds it harder to thrive. To speak of moral realism is all very well. But it is an elaborate, even fancy, phrase and it is to be suspected of having the intention of sophisticating the simple reality that is easily to be conceived. Life presses us so hard, time is so short, the suffering of the world is so huge, simple, unendurable—anything that complicates our moral fervor in dealing with reality as we immediately see it and wish to drive headlong upon it, must be regarded with some impatience.

True enough: and therefore any defense of what I have called moral realism must be made not in the name of some highflown fineness of feeling but in the name of simple social practicality. There is a simple social fact to which moral realism has a simple practical relevance, but it is a fact very difficult for us to perceive. It is that the moral passions are even more willful and imperious and impatient than the self-seeking passions. All history is at one in telling us that their tendency is to be not only liberating but restrictive.

It is probable that at this time we are about to make great changes in our social system. The world is ripe for such changes, and if they are not made in the direction of greater social liberality, the direction forward, they will, almost of necessity, be made in the direction backward, of a terrible social niggardliness. We all know which of these two directions we want. But it is not enough to want it, not even enough to work for it—we must want it and work for it with intelligence. Which means that we must be aware of the dangers which lie in our most generous wishes. Some paradox of our natures leads us, when once we have made our fellow men the objects of our enlightened interest, to go on to make them the objects of our pity, then of our superior wisdom, ultimately of our coercion. It is to prevent this corruption, the most ironic and tragic that man knows, that we stand in need of the moral realism which is the product of the free play of the moral imagination.

For our time the most effective agent of the moral imagination has been the novel of the last two hundred years. It was never, either esthetically or morally, a perfect form and its faults and failures can be quickly enumerated. But its greatness and its practical usefulness lay in its unremitting work of involving the reader himself in the moral life, inviting him to put his own motives under examination, suggesting that reality is not as he sees it. It taught us, as no other genre ever did, the extent of human variety and the value of variety. It was the literary form to which the emotions of understanding and forgiveness were indigenous, as if by the definition of the form itself. At the moment its impulse does not seem strong, for there never was a time when the virtues of its greatness were so likely to be thought of as weaknesses. Yet there never was a time when its particular activity was so much needed, was of so much practical, political, and social use — so much so that if its impulse does not respond to the need, we can be sad not only over a waning form of art but also over a waning freedom.

ᴥᶑ E. K. BROWN

The Revival of E. M. Forster

THOSE of us who have long admired Mr. Forster and hoped that his work would have the permanent life of distinguished minor fiction—the kind of life that Fromentin's *Dominique* has had in France and *The Country of the Pointed Firs* in America—have found 1943 a white milestone. For years Mr. Forster had been scarcely a name to the general reader, and critical comment upon him except as a theorist about the novel had been scanty and commonplace. Within the year came reprints of four novels, *A Room with a View* and *The Longest Journey* from New Directions, *Where Angels Fear To Tread* and *Howards End* from Alfred Knopf. The fifth of his novels, *A Passage to India*, preserved its place, with a temporary eclipse because of the shortage of paper, in the inexpensive Modern Library series. A penetrating and essentially sympathetic estimate, the first book on Mr. Forster to come from America, was brought out by the eminent Arnoldian, Professor Lionel Trilling. From some critics of the extreme Left there was faint praise, there were even a very few rude outcries; but otherwise the reception of the reprints and the estimate was no less delightful to the faithful reader of Mr. Forster than their appearance. Today he stands in this country as the greatest living English master of the novel.

NOTE. Reprinted from the *Yale Review*, 1944, by permission of the editors and the author.

The spurt in Mr. Forster's reputation is the more notable, and the more surprising, coming when interest in his admired, and admiring, friend Mrs. Woolf has receded. Through the later thirties it was apparent that her fiction was not wearing well. *The Years* was a disappointment, appearing, as it did, to surrender her peculiar virtues and to abandon her peculiar methods, and to win in compensation little beyond the range of a dozen novelists of the time. Some of us thought that nemesis was at work as Mrs. Woolf, who had been so supercilious toward the formula of Galsworthy, tried in this book something he had often performed —and was, at best, but moderately successful. *Between the Acts* was far from a sufficient offset for either the flatness of *The Years* or the imperfections now felt so acutely in Mrs. Woolf's earlier and more characteristic fiction. The almost fretful delicacy of touch, the arch and even coy quality in her humor, her style, and even in her manipulation of incident, narrative, and character, told against her; the implied scheme of moral and social values was no longer found to be stimulating to the conscience or liberating to the imagination.

The present decline of interest in Mrs. Woolf—a trend which time may, of course, reverse—has had no full parallel in the reputation of the master experimenter of the twenties. Still, *Finnegans Wake,* the labor of fifteen years, has had no impact comparable with that of *Ulysses*; viewed as a whole it has been less formative, perhaps even less impressive, than some of the parts published much earlier, "Haveth Childers Everywhere" and "Anna Livia Plurabelle." Since its publication the comments on Joyce's work as a whole have struck notes of firmer and sadder reservation than modern-minded critics had sounded before. It is far too early to say that the Joyce chapter in English or American fiction has closed; but it is safe to say that the culminating pages of the chapter have been turned.

The deaths of Mrs. Woolf and Mr. Joyce in the early months of the war seemed to symbolize the end of a movement and a period in English fiction. Yet now the third great experimenter of the group—the third distinguished novelist of the life within, of peculiar states of being of peculiar people — stands higher than ever, in this country at least. This, then, is the moment for some thought about the qualities of fiction so unexpectedly and so vigorously revived, and about its chances for permanent life either in a somewhat small circle or among readers generally.

In a preface to a novel that no one reads any longer, even in France, Paul Bourget speaks interestingly of the novel of ideas, and links it with the name of Balzac. Balzac, he says, was addicted to the novel of ideas, the novel occupied with what goes on within the mind. By the novel of ideas Balzac, I think, understood something much more definite: for him it was a novel illustrating a theory about what goes on within the mind, and indeed about life in general. Such an approach to fiction, rare among our less speculative English novelists, has its peculiar dangers — dangers clearly seen and strongly felt by George Eliot, our first, and I should argue, our greatest novelist of ideas. In a letter to Frederic Harrison she spoke of "the severe effort of trying to make certain ideas incarnate, as if they had revealed themselves to me first in the flesh"; and of "the sort of agonizing labor to an English-fed imagination to make out a sufficiently real background for the desired picture — to get breathing individual forms, and to group them in the needful relations, so that the presentation will lay hold on the emotions as human experience — will, as you say, flash conviction on the world by means of aroused sympathy." I know of no other presentation of the plight of the novelist of ideas which can compare with this for clearness and suggestive power. Everyone is familiar with the weight George Eliot carried, as she sought again and again to lend the breath of life to her master altruists, to make the noble ideals of her version of Comtism flash conviction on the Victorian world; and the figures she intended to be so moving and winning remained stiff and absurd, while the irrelevant Mrs. Poysers, the deplored Casaubons, the muddled Lydgates breathed with overflowing life.

Since the time of George Eliot the novel of ideas has had honor in England: she was almost what Lord David Cecil calls her — the point of junction between the old novel and the new. Of the old in her dependence on typed characters and clean and complicated plots, she was of the new, as he says, because she explored depths in her main personages which would have gone unsounded by Fielding or Thackeray, and also, I should add, because she put forward a detailed redemptive theory about life. At the center of a George Eliot novel there is a stretch which might be compared with Paul's experience on the road to Damascus, if in addition to his regeneration he had been provided with the Athanasian creed. In her works the way to salvation is always neatly codified. And so it has been with Meredith, with Hardy, with Samuel Butler, with Wells, and with Forster.

In our time, perhaps the subtlest effort to write the novel of ideas in England has been Forster's. He would writhe to hear it, but he is the lawful issue of George Eliot. He has been more clearly conscious of the danger to vitality in characters that the novel of ideas offers, and far more cunning in his means of parrying the danger. For instance, in *The Longest Journey*, he has his redemptive character safely in his grave before the book begins. How much better it would have been if all we had been allowed to see of Will Ladislaw was an exquisite miniature such as we are shown of some of his female relatives! Or a lock of that wonderful curly blond hair! If we could have been spared Will's taking his careless elegant ease on the fur rug by Rosamond Vincy's fireside, or trying to say profound things to Dorothea Brooke! The great man in *The Longest Journey*, Anthony Failing, used to live in Wiltshire; and as we approach the house on the downs, we see his widow sitting in her arbor and beginning to write a memoir of her husband. The horrible, heartless old woman begins: "The subject of this memoir first saw the light at Wolverhampton on May the 14th, 1842." She scores out the dead words and begins again: "The subject of this memoir first saw the light in the middle of the night. It was twenty to eleven. His pa was a parson, but he was not his pa's son, and never went to heaven." Mr. Forster is determined that right from the beginning he will make the reader feel the lash of the world's whip, and the force of the world's snigger against his ideal characters; they are not to be plaster saints, they are to have qualities which will seem disagreeable or laughable; and so, he hopes, as Balzac did, we may find them believable, breathing beings.

He used the same means in another early novel, *A Room with a View*. The redemptive character, old Mr. Emerson, lives in an English pension at Florence. Two culture-seeking English ladies arrive and are upset to find that, instead of the rooms with a view over the Arno they had been promised, they have been installed in rooms on the wrong side of the house. Mr. Emerson's rooms are on the Arno side, and he offers them. Everything in his way of offering them from his appearance, through the tone of his voice, to the state of mind he expresses is wrong in their conventional eyes. They do take his rooms, however; all that one of them can do is bar the shutters and search the room for a dangerous hidden entrance; but the other, over whose unformed being so many forces are to play during the novel, "opened the window, and breathed the clean night air, thinking of the kind old man who had enabled her to see the lights dancing in the Arno, and the cypresses of San Miniato, and the foothills of the Apennines, black against the rising moon." Mr. Emerson may not be so impressive as George Eliot's Dinah Morris, that admirable unbreathing statue, but like her, he gets his way, and unlike her, for a moment he inspires belief. His absurdities make him life size.

But we do not continue to believe he breathes. He becomes only an eloquent voice encased in a body which appears to have no integral relation to it. I can fancy Mr. Forster taking stock of Mr. Failing and Mr. Emerson and deciding that they would not do. I can imagine him saying that there was something rootless in their spirits, something a little too suggestive of the kindly prosing idealism of the scientific socialist of the late nineteenth century, something too close to the Labor intellectual. At any moment, we fear, they might begin to talk with the bombinating eloquence of Mr. Ramsay MacDonald. Those books, I can imagine him saying, must be re-done, and one must go a great deal deeper in the new versions. It seems to me that *Howards End* is the re-doing of *The Longest Journey*, with a far deeper redemptive character, and the world of business substituted for the smaller world of public school masters and their wives. "*A Passage to India* I take to be a re-doing of *A Room with a View,* with the deepest of all Mr. Forster's redemptive characters, and the English in their life-and-death relation with the major peninsula of India replacing the English in their superficial relation with the minor peninsula of Italy.

Before we look at these later novels, on which I believe Mr. Forster's claims will more and more depend, there is another type of character, not quite redemptive, which we must understand and value. This is the Panic being, first entering his fiction in the earliest of his novels, *Where Angels Fear To Tread,* in the person of Gino Carella. Gino is not a wholly satisfactory portrait; but he is a much more living type of the natural man than the gamekeeper in *Lady Chatterley's Lover* or indeed any of Lawrence's glorifications of huge limbs, curt speech, and unquenchable sexuality. Gino can be charming, but he can also be stupid, cleverly cruel, and abysmally self-centered. He is a sort of Pan, fighting civilization with the weapons of "those childlike ruffians, his ancestors, who flung each other from the towers" of their hill towns. Gino is just a sketch for the portrait of the natural man in Stephen Wonham in *The Longest Journey.*

Stephen Wonham is a pure expression of the novel of ideas: he is nature—an illegitimate child, a farmer and wanderer over the downs, with that antique harshness and egoism which mark the male nature symbols in the poems of Robinson Jeffers. He has just that disgust and fear for the symbols of civilization that Jeffers' men have: the spire of Salisbury Cathedral frightens him just as the bridges over California rivers frighten the wild men in Jeffers. And yet for Mr. Forster, a supremely civilized being, a devotee of tradition, Stephen Wonham is in some degree exemplary. "Look how much better, how much wiser, how much surer than my conventionalists, my intellectuals, this animal is!" Mr. Forster is always telling us. This is because Stephen, within his narrow range, is better in relations with others than the civilized and the conventional can be. But do we believe in Stephen? Does he breathe? He is much more flesh and blood than the Emersons and the Failings. Still the idea obtrudes very often in Stephen, just as the idea obtruded in Hawthorne's faun. Not from Stephen can we take conviction that Mr. Forster can set in the framework of a novel of ideas a movingly real breathing being. For this conviction we must look to two women characters, who will have something of Stephen in them, and something of Mr. Emerson and Mr. Failing, and something else too, something more precious and more vivid. We must look to Mrs. Wilcox in *Howards End* and Mrs. Moore in *A Passage to India*.

Mrs. Wilcox we shall meet at the beginning of *Howards End*. The page in which she comes before us, by which she is realized for us forever, is so admirable that I wish to give it in full. I think it can be put beside that high moment in *The Ambassadors* when Strether, in Gloriani's garden, the finest people in Europe walking and talking in the alleys and the bells of a seminary sounding from beyond the wall, appreciates the thinness of life in Woollett, Massachusetts.

The novel has a running start, and some background is needed if the beauty of the page is to be seen in its splendor and power. One of the Schlegel girls has come to stay with the Wilcoxes, and has speedily become engaged to the younger Wilcox son; she has wired the great news to her sister, and their aunt, dear meddlesome old Mrs. Munt, has hurried down to the Wilcoxes' country place to survey the ground; at the station Mrs. Munt was met by the elder Wilcox son; and supposing he was to be her nephew-in-law she has congratulated him, thus giving him the first news of what was afoot. Driving from the station she and the boy have fought a stiff battle, and the moment he comes within speaking range he shouts out to his brother:

"Paul, Paul, Paul, is there any truth in this?"
"I didn't — I don't —"
"Yes or no, man; plain question, plain answer. Did or didn't Miss Schlegel —"
"Charles dear," said a voice from the garden. "Charles, dear Charles, one doesn't ask plain questions. There aren't such things."

They were all silent. It was Mrs. Wilcox.

She approached just as Helen's letter had described her, trailing noiselessly over the lawn, and there was actually a wisp of hay in her hands. She seemed to belong not to the young people and their motor, but to the house, and to the tree that overshadowed it. One knew that she worshipped the past, and that the instinctive wisdom the past can alone bestow had descended upon her—that wisdom to which we give the clumsy name of aristocracy. High-born she might not be [she came of yeoman stock]. But assuredly she cared about her ancestors, and let them help her. When she saw Charles angry, Paul frightened, and Mrs. Munt in tears, she heard her ancestors say, "Separate those human beings who will hurt each other most. The rest can wait." So she did not ask questions. Still less did she pretend that nothing had happened, as a competent society hostess would have done. She said, "Miss Schlegel, would you take your aunt up to your room or my room, whichever you think best. Paul, do find Evie, and tell her lunch for six, but I'm not sure whether we shall all be downstairs for it [they were not]." And when they had obeyed her, she turned to her elder son, who still stood in the throbbing, stinking car, and smiled at him, with tenderness, and without saying a word, turned away from him towards her flowers.

"Mother," he called, "are you aware that Paul has been playing the fool again?"

"It's all right, dear. They have broken off the engagement."

"Engagement—!"

"They do not love any longer, if you prefer it put that way," said Mrs. Wilcox, stooping down to smell a rose.

In no space at all character has been shaped and colored; we have been taken to a plane far above the normal level of human relations. Mrs. Wilcox is not always on that rare plane. She can be a quite simple and even dreary creature, complaining of the service on the railway, and worrying about Christmas cards. The great point is that when she ceases to be dreary and soars, she takes us with her: we believe in her. Mr. Somerset Maugham, after expressing warm admiration for the art of Mr. Forster, finds it necessary to make a heavy reservation. He says: "He can create characters that are freshly seen and vividly alive: then he makes them do things that you know very well, so roundly and soundly has he set them before you, they couldn't possibly do.

168

. . . You don't believe." What Mr. Maugham objects to, I am sure, is the soaring, such as Mrs. Wilcox has done in the page quoted. Probably he has been too devoted a reader of Anatole France to accept the plane to which Mrs. Wilcox soars as a part of life.

It is certain — this may be said in support of Mr. Maugham's doubts — that words were not framed to express what goes on when a character reaches this plane. Mrs. Wilcox shies away from words: her failures to communicate her deepest insights have taught her that words are not her instruments. In trying to help the character who is most nearly sympathetic to her she flounders sadly and abounds in such phrases of desperation as "I almost think" and "I only meant." Her gentle charm becomes a veil over depths, and so it is best to leave her and turn to her more sharply featured sister character, Mrs. Moore in *A Passage to India*.

Mrs. Moore is by much the most wonderful of all Mr. Forster's wonderful old women, not so softly appealing as Mrs. Wilcox but more solid a being, more startling to the imagination, and more richly satisfying to the lover of reality. On her I should most surely base the claim that he has involved in a novel of ideas a character who is at once a complex and effective symbol and a genuine human being. There is just as rare stuff in her as in Mrs. Wilcox — it is not quite the same stuff — and she undergoes a rare type of experience beyond the gamut of Mrs. Wilcox; and yet she remains a visible being, with a jolly red face and a mass of fine white hair, and a piece of sure humanity.

She will come before us best if we see her at the moment when she is called upon to rise from her seat among the other English personages and begin her great experience. With her son's fiancée she has come to a tea party given by an unconventional education officer so that the two women can touch India. India is represented by a Mohammedan doctor, superficially Europeanized, and an old Brahman, Professor Godbole. One of the pleasures Mrs. Moore had been promised was that Godbole would sing. The party has taken a rather unsatisfying course: no revelation of India has appeared. At the very close, just as the English women are about to leave, Godbole sings. The song was a maze of noise, now and then it took on rhythm, or the shadow of melody; but there was no continuity of either, and one might either suppose that it was something primitive and insignificant, or be devastated by an impression that it was shot through with meaning so deep that a Western personality could not seize it. Mrs. Moore took the second interpretation; from the moment she hears the song, she is struck with unphraseable intuitions, jaded, muddled, eager to escape from the network of personal and social relationships, ready to die.

All through the next great scene of the novel — its central scene for plot — Mrs. Moore reveals, one by one, the phases of feeling I have mentioned. And as she reveals them she does not cease to be a real personage. We do not cease to believe in her. She is veiled from us, we grope for her, but we do not give up the conviction that she is a human being. This, it seems to me, is Mr. Forster's triumph. And round about Mrs. Moore, just as if he were bearing in mind George Eliot's formula, he has grouped other characters, Indian and English, who are breathing individuals (as well as palpable symbols) and set them in fruitful relationships, and drawn about them a fiercely vivid setting, also symbolic. Throughout the scene — it is, of course, the cave scene — symbol and reality interfuse.

In these two scenes he has exhausted his power. All that Mrs. Moore can do henceforth is to depart and die. She will remain throughout the rest of the book as an inescapable presence, as Mrs. Wilcox did. It was hard to believe in the shade that Mrs. Wilcox cast after her death: some of the characters pleaded with us to believe in it, the plot emphatically demanded belief; but the shade was not impressive to the imagination. Mrs. Moore's shade is also invoked by some of the characters; it almost dominates plot; and, what is much more, there are beautiful moments which irresistibly compel belief. There is the moment when the Mohammedan doctor, meeting a younger son of Mrs. Moore for the first time, years after her death, appreciates that she was the greatest experience of his life; and there is the moment when the education officer, married to her daughter, confesses that all his labors toward liberality of mind and spirit have left him on the poorer side of a chasm which separates him from his wife and his wife's mother; and there is the moment, equally long after Mrs. Moore's death, the rarest moment of all, when Godbole in the ecstasy of adoration finds that this old English woman, met only once, is the surest link between him and the One. In the felicity of his invention here, and in the vitality with which he endows the scenes in which it flowers forth, Mr. Forster appears to show his gift as a novelist of ideas at its purest. Here he comes within reach of the author of "La Recherche de l'Absolu."

What of the conventionalists who abound in these novels, as foils for the characters who have been considered? Do they come to life? There can, I think, be no doubt that the atmosphere of conventional groups carries conviction. That pension in Florence, the house at the public school in *The Longest Journey*, the club at Chandrapore in *A Passage to India*, are richly human in the manner of the Maison Vauquer. The individuals do not live so fully. So great is Mr. Forster's impatience with conventionalist women he seldom makes them credible: Agnes Pembroke, in *The Longest Journey*, the two Herriton females, in *Where Angels Fear To Tread*, Evie Wilcox, are just a few lines dashed down in hasty anger. The best of the conventionalists are men. In Mrs. Wilcox's husband and in Mrs. Moore's elder son, there is a sturdy vitality such as George Eliot could impart to her worldly clergy or gentry and Thackeray to the best of his club men.

This is a severe limitation, and there are other limitations in Mr. Forster's handling of character. If I were seeking to express by a single image the effect that his novels make upon a responsive reader, I should compare them to narrow dark paths across a world of light, paths irradiated for a moment now and then by splinters shooting through the darkness. In one of his short stories —a parable as most of them are— he likens life to a road, lined on one side by a hedge through which an occasional plodder finds his way into a superior level of being. Before one reaches the middle of any of his novels, one has a distinct sense of two levels on which one cannot focus at once. This notion of inability to focus is a favorite of his. Contrasting George Eliot and Dostoevski he says that for her God is on the same plane as chairs and tables, but for him the focus changes as one leaves the tables and chairs, and comes to God. In a comment on Mrs. Wilcox, made by a sympathetic character, the image comes again—and the two passages are separated by fifteen years: "She and daily life were out of focus; one or the other must show blurred. And at lunch she seemed more out of focus than usual and nearer the line that divides daily life from a life that may be of greater importance." The collection of short stories to which he gave the title *The Celestial Omnibus* is a set of illustrations of this image. They are beautiful parables, but like all parables they rest on an enormous and incredible simplification of material. *Life is not in the least like that!* we say as we read these stories, just as we say this in reading *Mosses from an Old Manse*.

We do not keep on saying so as we read the novels, but we do say so at important crises in each of them. Notice the queer way in which Mr. Forster approaches the fact of death. At the end of an early chapter in *The Longest Journey* — Mr. Trilling has seized on this before me—an athlete, Gerald, has boasted of his strength. The next chapter opens: "Gerald died that afternoon. He was broken up in the football match." Surely this is all too close to the tone of Mr. Failing's widow. Again and again, death is touched with this light unfeeling hand. When Mrs. Moore dies aboard the homeward-bound *P. and O.*, it is just as quietly and coldly done. In *To the Lighthouse* Mrs. Woolf, whom Mr. Forster so warmly admires, kills her main personage in a single clause in the middle of a long sentence which is set off from the main course by brackets. Here are striking instances of the way in which the novel of ideas can fail: it fails because a theory which the novelist is illustrating is inconsistent with reality as we know and appraise it. We do not feel about death as the authors of these sentences feel: our feeling may not approach the frenzy of Dickens, but we cannot go along with Mrs. Woolf and Mr. Forster. Their failure here is the same as Hardy's when he sinks hagridden by his theory of an actively malevolent fate.

Whatever a novel may or may not do, it must be realistic. It is as true today as it was when Brunetière said it, that the end of fiction is the realistic representation of life. When the great datum of a novel is inconsistent with such a representation, however lifelike some of its scenes and persons may be, the novel is ruined. A novel is not saved by a great theme. No theme greater than Mr. Forster's opposition between two levels of being can be conceived. The weakness is in failing to find adequate vesture for the theme, in letting the bones obtrude. Mr. Trilling has remarked on the inadequacy of Mr. Forster's secondary characters to the ideas they incarnate. Speaking of *A Passage to India* he says: "To represent the official English as so unremittingly bad, and the Indians as so unremittingly feeble is to prevent the story from being sufficiently worked out in terms of the characters." I should like to put in a good word for McBryde among the English, and for Aziz among the Indians. (Godbole I assume Mr. Trilling did not have in mind at all in making the criticism.) Still, as a general objection to *A Passage to India,* and to the other novels, Mr. Trilling's remark holds. What is criticized here is the same inability, of which other instances have been given, to animate character, to create realistic form, credible form, moving form.

The answer to the central question, Can Mr. Forster give us a realistic representation of life? is not a simple one. Often his fiction falls into unrealism: Mr. Maugham is right in some of his moments of discomfort. Still, the creation of Mrs. Moore, and in only less degree of Mrs. Wilcox, is a very notable achievement in fiction. To some readers it may seem that Mrs. Moore and Mrs. Wilcox are like genii which now and again swell out of the slender vases in which they are contained, and take on forms so huge and vague that the eye cannot focus on them as wholes. Perhaps genii which perform in this fashion are not the best material for fiction; but the reader who can focus on them as wholes will return to the scenes in which they reach their full grandeur in quest of a pleasure that is to be found in no other novels.

For the strange silence which has followed *A Passage to India,* a silence broken by essays, pageants, and a suggestive biography, I find a ready explanation. I believe that Mr. Forster appreciated that his ideas were not only agonizingly difficult to incarnate, but inappropriate to the novel, and that he elected to retain the ideas —it is stupid, perhaps, to speak of electing, for doubtless the decision was inevitable—and to abandon the novel. Lest it be thought that I am becoming too speculative, I shall now cite the best of witnesses. After he had read an article of mine upon his ideas, written some ten years ago, he said, with his usual generosity: "It is a great novelty to be written about like that. I have been praised for my character drawing, sense of social distinctions, etc., but seldom for the things which really interest me, and which I have tried to express through the medium of fiction." That sentence mirrors a state of mind in which the ideas are more important than the characters, the plots, or the settings. It is very near to the state of mind reflected in the letter from George Eliot to Frederic Harrison. Such are the struggles of the novelist of ideas. I do not think it is hard to understand why such a person should cease to be a novelist.

The present revival will doubtless fail to make of Mr. Forster a major figure in fiction, a figure comparable with Conrad; but the art he uses is so delicate at many points, and the ideas he expresses so wholly admirable, that we may delight in any movement to make the works more widely read and the man more deeply honored.

✒ CARLOS LYNES, JR.

André Gide and the
Problem of Form in the Novel

FEW writers of any age have been more consciously and acutely
aware of the problem of form in the novel and few have provided
us with more complete records of their wrestling with the difficulties of transforming the reality of experience into the autonomous reality of fiction than has the author of *Les Faux-
Monnayeurs*. If Gide has failed in this work to achieve a real
masterpiece of the novel, he has nevertheless given us an extraordinarily interesting and enlightening book — a critical novel or a
critique of the novel which, together with the *Journal des Faux-
Monnayeurs* in which the author notes the problems, the doubts,
and the tentative solutions which he formulated during the period
of gestation of his fiction, deserves our closest scrutiny.

It is possible now, a generation after the appearance of *Les
Faux-Monnayeurs,* to consider the novel itself and Gide's theory
with detachment, an attitude which most critics — French as well
as foreign — have been loath to accord a work that seemed to
outrage moral and critical conventions alike. Because of the moral
implications of all his writings, Gide has been the constant prey
of the moralistic critics, and after Ramon Fernandez' excellent
study of some years ago it was only in 1938 that Jean Hytier
produced his brilliant analysis of Gide's art by heeding the au-

NOTE. Reprinted from the *Southern Review,* 1941, by permission of the author.

FORMS OF MODERN FICTION

thor's own advice: "Le point de vue esthétique est le seul où il faille se placer pour parler de mon oeuvre sainement."*

It is this point of view that must be adopted, of course, if we wish to learn anything from Gide about the problem of form in the novel. One fact only must be noted about Gide the man, which is that his whole life has been an effort to realize and to harmonize all the rich and conflicting possibilities which he felt within himself—to reconcile these possibilities not by suppressing some of them in accordance with a convention imposed from without or an ideal set up from within but by including them all in a synthesis, a "perilous balance," which would be authentic and sincere, vital and mobile, the perfect realization of a man within the limits set by his own physical and spiritual nature. To what extent Gide the man has approached this goal need not concern us directly here, though human limitations being what they are and Gide's problem being more difficult than most because of the anomaly which he has revealed to us so frankly in *Si le grain ne meurt* . . . it seems obvious that achievement of this goal in his life could be but partial. In fact Gide soon understood that complete realization was no doubt impossible in life, but he believed that it could be attained, virtually at least, in the work of art.

This conception of the work of art as the reconciling of opposites and the resolving of discords in a form that recognizes and respects the variety and complexity of experience was not new, of course, but it was something which too many writers and literary schools had in practice forgotten. Gide was unable even to approach this goal at first, all the more so because he began his literary activity under the aegis of symbolism—not what Mr. Edmund Wilson has called the "conversational-ironic" type of symbolism represented by Laforgue and Corbière but rather the "serious-esthetic" kind of symbolism turned inward represented by Verlaine. This turning inward gave Gide one kind of reality—a kind which the naturalists had too long neglected—but it was only one element in the complexity of experience.

* André Gide, *Journal, 1889-1939*. Paris: *Nouvelle Revue Française*, "Bibliothèque de la Pléiade," 1939. Entry under date April 25, 1918.

CARLOS LYNES, JR.

Aside from their intrinsic esthetic value, Gide's writings during the long interval between his youthful symbolistic writings (which began to appear in 1891) and *Les Faux-Monnayeurs* (1926) reveal the author's groping toward the kind of artistic synthesis which he early recognized as his goal. Before attempting such a synthesis in a comprehensive literary form, Gide preferred to prepare himself by treating the elements separately, first in the little compositions that he calls "traités" and later in the short fictions that he designates as "récits" or "soties" rather than as novels. Or doubtless it was not really a matter of preference but simply the fact that until late middle age he hesitated even to attempt the difficult problem of harmonizing in a single work themes as varied as the ones stated separately in *L'Immoraliste, La Porte étroite, Isabelle,* and *Les Caves du Vatican.* When he published *Isabelle* (1911) he planned a preface to explain that this book, as well as *L'Immoraliste* and *La Porte étroite,* is termed a "récit" because it does not correspond to his conception of the novel. Similarly, in the dedication of *Les Caves du Vatican* he asserts that he does not wish people to take his fictions as novels and then accuse him of violating the rules of the genre and "de manquer par exemple de désordre et de confusion."* He feels that his short fictions, which he insists are "ironical" or "critical," represent conflicting tendencies or possibilities of his own nature — tendencies coexisting and held in check in Gide the man but here isolated as a pathologist might isolate bacilli for study and placed under a light so clear and direct that each element stands out in sharp relief. The criticism and irony are only implicit in the individual fictions, partly because Gide understands that the work of art itself is the only proper solution to the "problems" that it raises, but above all because the real criticism of *L'Immoraliste* lies in *La Porte étroite* just as the criticism of *La Porte étroite* is found in *L'Immoraliste.* Gide understands, moreover, the close relationship among these works as well as his own inability, at the time of their composition, to harmonize their

* André Gide, *Oeuvres complètes.* Paris: *Nouvelle Revue Française,* 1932–39. Vol. VII, p. 408.

diverse themes in the complex unity of a real novel. Thus he considers the idea of writing a preface for *Les Caves du Vatican* in which he would make it clear that: "Tous ces sujets se sont développés parallèlement, concurremment—et si j'ai écrit tel livre avant tel autre c'est que le sujet m'en paraissait plus 'at hand' comme dit l'Anglais. Si j'avais pu, c'est *ensemble* que je les aurais écrits" (*Journal,* July 12, 1914).

Realization of such a synthesis, granted that the artist's experience is sufficiently rich and his attitude sufficiently comprehensive and profound, is essentially a problem of form, since form —in all the arts—is what has been called "the artistically expressive organization . . . of the medium in which it has its being." The novelist, to borrow the words of the late Professor Rogers, "is attempting to convey a summation of the way life is grouped, at a particular moment or period, a summation, of course, which may give way to others in the future." To convey this summation he must, as Mr. Tate has said that the poet must do, apprehend and concentrate our experience in the mysterious limitations of form. Mr. Ransom has defined poetry as "a structure with a texture." This definition, freely interpreted, may be applied to any type of imaginative literature. And both the structure and the texture have to do with the problem of form, since artistic form comes into being only when the two elements are successfully fused in the specific objectivity of the poem or the play or the novel.

All this implies no shallow "art for art's sake" doctrine or exclusively formalist esthetic, however, nor any belief in a priori patterns of composition, especially in the novel, which has always enjoyed more freedom than any other literary type. Gide would certainly subscribe to Percy Lubbock's assertion that "The best form is that which makes the most of its subject—there is no other definition of the meaning of form in fiction." Yet in France during the late nineteenth and early twentieth centuries there had developed a type of "well-made" novel which, fortified by the academic prejudice that the French alone know how to "compose" and that such formal "composition" is essential to litera-

ture, tended to crystallize in a strict conventional mold into which
the individual novelist was expected to stuff whatever material
came to hand instead of actively shaping his experience into the
unique form required by the subject. Against this kind of unin-
telligent, inartistic doctrine Gide rebels—Gide the master of
style and composition himself and the exponent of the vital kind
of "classicism" which he defines as the integration of the totality
of the moral, intellectual, and emotional preoccupations of one's
age in a synthesis allowing all the elements to assume their proper
reciprocal relationships (*Oeuvres,* XI, 42–43). He is unwilling to
accept any such ready-made frame for his own composition because he understands that the true novelist is a poet or "maker"
whose task and privilege it is to shape his material into the specific form which *is* the novel just as surely as the form *is* the
statue. As he insists in a preface written for a special edition of
Baudelaire's *Fleurs du mal*: "La forme est le secret de l'oeuvre"
(*Oeuvres,* VII, 500).

Les Faux-Monnayeurs is all the more interesting for the study
of Gide's esthetic of the novel because it is, in a much truer sense
than any of Zola's fiction, an "experimental" novel—a work in
which the real subject is largely the novelist's effort to transform
the reality of experience into the ideal reality of the work of art
or, as Gide says, "la lutte entre ce que lui offre la réalité et ce
que, lui, prétend en faire." Though published separately, the
novel itself and the *Journal des Faux-Monnayeurs* were so closely
linked in the author's consciousness that he thought more than
once of pouring the *Journal* into his imaginative creation and
attempting to fuse the two in a still more complex synthesis. Yet
the novel was already sufficiently complex, for by a curious
"doubling" of his subject (a type of composition already used,
though less elaborately, in several earlier writings) Gide places
within *Les Faux-Monnayeurs* a novelist who is writing a novel
with the same title as Gide's and who, in turn, plans to place a
novelist in *his* story.

This doubling of the subject is one of the elements in the solution which Gide gives to the problem of the point of view in his

fiction. As Henry James and Percy Lubbock have shown us, the "post of observation," or the point of view from which the story is presented, largely determines the form which a novel assumes. Gide recognizes this fact in several passages of the *Journal des Faux-Monnayeurs* and he has his novelist Édouard, too, note its importance in his effort to narrate little Georges Molinier's abortive theft of a book from one of the stalls along the Seine. Fifteen years previously Gide had written that the true novel, as contrasted with the "récit," "comporte une diversité de points de vue, soumise à la diversité des personnages qu'il met en scène" (*Oeuvres*, VI, 361–62).

Gide's specific solution to the problem of the point of view depends ultimately, perhaps, upon what Professor Rogers would have called his "basic organization," that is, upon the general pattern which he gives to life and experience. More immediately, however, it depends upon the subject of the particular novel as he envisages it, with appropriate modifications as the work develops. The two extremes in the method of presenting the subject matter of a novel are direct narration—a sort of "pictorial summary," as Percy Lubbock phrases it—from the point of view of the author, and the type of rigorously dramatic presentation that gives not an account or a report of what has happened but a direct sight of the matter itself while it is passing. Modern fiction generally lies between these extremes, where there is room for the greatest variety and freedom, the only requirement for the novelist being that the presentation he adopts should be the one which makes the most of the subject.

For the subjects of works like *L'Immoraliste, La Porte étroite,* and *La Symphonie pastorale,* Gide found the first-person narrative by a character in the story admirably suited, but when he wishes to harmonize a number of varied and conflicting themes within the structure of a single complex novel the problem of the point of view again presents itself. At first he considers having Lafcadio, the hero of *Les Caves du Vatican,* serve as narrator for *Les Faux-Monnayeurs,* but he soon doubts that everything can be presented from the highly individual point of view of this youth. Then he thinks of using Lafcadio's diary for certain chapters, Édouard's *Journal* for others, and perhaps the files of a lawyer for still other chapters. Finally he decides that he cannot entirely avoid the use of impersonal narration, since his novel is to consist of so many strands of action, but he modifies and supplements this traditional method so abundantly that his novel acquires a highly original structure with a texture of unusual richness. Because he knows himself to be much better at making others speak than in speaking directly himself, he presents much of the story by means of dramatic dialogues and even allows the characters to take over the narration of events which he prefers not to tell in impersonal narrative or in dramatic scenes. Moreover, the same happenings are sometimes presented from different angles by different characters and Gide welcomes the slight distortion which results because it calls for the active collaboration of the reader to correct the image. Sometimes letters assist in telling the story and here again Gide is glad to relinquish direct narration from the author's point of view for what he considers a more objective method.

An especially large part of the story is presented indirectly by means of the *Journal* of Édouard. Gide's use of the *Journal* for this purpose has been criticized by Jean Hytier, who points out that it introduces a confusion in the structure of the novel without any important compensation. Édouard's "reality" is the story told by Gide and what one expects to find in his *Journal* is, on the one hand, reflections on the problems encountered in writing his novel and, on the other hand, chapters of his novel which by contrast with the "real" events of Gide's story would show how the reality furnished by experience is transformed by the artist into something which is his own unique creation. But Gide disappoints us in this expectation, under the pretext that Édouard is an "amateur," a "raté" who will never be able to write his novel at all because he lacks the faculty of being able to give himself up wholeheartedly to reality outside himself. As a result, Édouard's *Journal* is used partly as a means for Gide to consider the esthetic of the novel without having to commit himself fully

on any point and partly as a medium for the indirect presentation of incidents in Gide's own story from a rather detached point
of view similar to but not identical with the author's point of
view.

But even this diversity in the method and point of view finally
seems insufficient to Gide. After re-reading *Tom Jones* he decides
that, in spite of Flaubert's example and the advice of Martin du
Gard, he will intervene directly in his novel to comment on the
characters and action. This he does in numerous instances, notably in the final chapter of Part Two, which is entirely given over
to the author's review of his characters. Gide handles this method
rather more subtly and critically than did the eighteenth- and
nineteenth-century novelists who had used a similar technique,
and it becomes a factor in the deliberate rejection of "realism"
that he wishes his novel to be. To make this break with realism
even sharper, he tries to introduce epic elements in *Les Faux-
Monnayeurs* and, though most of these attempts, especially with
respect to the fantastic or the marvelous, fall rather flat, he occasionally strikes a minor epic note in such a passage as the following, where he intervenes with poetic omniscience to survey the
story from on high:

C'est l'heure où, dans une triste chambre d'hôtel, Laura, sa
maîtresse [celle de Vincent] d'hier, après avoir longtemps pleuré,
longtemps gémi, va s'endormir. Sur le pont du navire qui le
ramène en France, Édouard, à la première clarté de l'aube, relit
la lettre qu'il a reçue d'elle, lettre plaintive et où elle appelle au
secours. Déjà, la douce rive de son pays natal est en vue, mais,
à travers la brume, il faut un oeil exercé pour la voir. Pas un nuage
au ciel, où le regard de Dieu va sourire. La paupière de l'horizon
rougissant déjà se soulève. Comme il va faire chaud dans Paris!
Il est temps de retrouver Bernard. Voici que dans le lit d'Olivier
il s'éveille [*Oeuvres*, XII, 87].

Of fundamental importance to his conception of form in the
novel is Gide's rejection of any a priori plan, any set mold into
which the material has to be stuffed according to fixed patterns
or rules. Thus Édouard, speaking for Gide, writes in his *Journal*:

"X. [almost certainly Martin du Gard] soutient que le bon roman-

CARLOS LYNES, JR.

cier doit, avant de commencer son livre, savoir comment ce livre finira. Pour moi, qui laisse aller le mien à l'aventure, je considère que la vie ne nous propose jamais rien qui, tout autant qu'un aboutissement, ne puisse être considéré comme un nouveau point de départ. 'Pourrait être continué . . .' c'est sur ces mots que je voudrais terminer mes Faux-Monnayeurs" [*Oeuvres,* XII, 471–72].

This rejection of the traditional framework and the conventional "plot" does not mean, of course, that the novel for Gide is to be a formless, undisciplined growth, but only that "form" and "content" are to be wrought into a unique organic whole outside of which neither element has any relevant meaning. Composition is of first importance in a book, Gide believes, but he adds that the best procedure is to "laisser l'oeuvre se composer et s'ordonner elle-même, et surtout ne pas la *forcer*" (*Journal,* p. 716. 1921). He recognizes that because of the variety and complexity of the themes which he seeks to harmonize in *Les Faux-Monnayeurs* it is necessary in some way to "établir une relation contue entre les éléments épars." To do this he wishes, in Édouard's words, to make of his novel something like Bach's *Art of Fugue* (*Oeuvres,* XII, 275).

In this attempt, I think, he is not completely successful. As Gide himself recognizes, there are two centers to *Les Faux-Monnayeurs*—the objective story and Édouard's effort to convert this "reality" into a novel. Moreover, since we are given no glimpse of Édouard's accomplishment (except in his tentative narration of Georges Molinier's attempt to steal the book), the two centers never really coincide. And the relationship among the different strands of the narrative is tenuous and sometimes arbitrary, so that one cannot help believing that Gide—who is admirably gifted for the "récit"—lacks the specific ability required to integrate these separate themes in a contrapuntal texture from which they could not easily be detached. Gide himself was acutely aware of these difficulties and in the early stages of the composition of his novel he revealed his misgivings about the new task before him when he wrote, with reference to his short fictions, that "ces petits récits épurés . . . ont plus d'espoir de durer que le complexe roman que je souhaite d'écrire aujourd'hui" (*Journal,* pp. 686–87. November 23, 1921). He was in any case unwilling to adopt the facile, ready-made solution that a conventional "plot" would have provided. Nor could he bring himself now to break his conception up and treat the various stories in separate "récits" (though he admits that without the influence of Martin du Gard he might have had recourse to this). We may be grateful that Gide did stick to his determination to make his novel a complex synthesis of his experience, for even if *Les Faux-Monnayeurs* is not the great masterpiece of the novel that we might wish, it is still the most complete expression of a great artist.

The question of the "roman pur" which comes up in *Les Faux-Monnayeurs* and in the *Journal des Faux-Monnayeurs* need not detain us long, for like the debate over "la poésie pure" which has caused so much French critical ink to be expended, it leads only to a sterile impasse if it is pushed very far. As a reaction against the material clutter of the naturalists and their twentieth-century survivors and disciples, Gide wished—in Édouard's phrase—to "Dépouiller le roman de tous les éléments qui n'appartiennent pas spécifiquement au roman." This rather vague phrase he goes on to explain as follows:

De même que la photographie naguère, débarrassa la peinture du souci de certaines exactitudes, le phonographe nettoiera sans doute demain le roman de ses dialogues rapportés, dont le réaliste souvent se fait gloire. Les événements extérieurs, les accidents, les traumatismes, appartiennent au cinéma; il sied que le roman les lui laisse. Même la description des personnages ne me paraît point appartenir proprement au genre. Oui vraiment, il ne me paraît pas que le roman *pur* . . . ait à s'en occuper. Non plus que ne fait le drame . . . —Le romancier, d'ordinaire, ne fait point suffisamment crédit à l'imagination du lecteur [*Oeuvres,* XII, 113–14].

The answer to this, I think, is obvious. If Gide chooses to eliminate from his own fictions everything except the inner life of his characters there is no reason why he should not attempt to do so, but neither is there any reason why his taste in this matter should be set up as a general rule for the novel. Gide seems to realize this, for after discussing the problem of the "roman pur" in the *Journal des Faux-Monnayeurs* he decides to place these ideas in Édouard's *Journal* because in this way he can avoid committing himself definitely on all the points raised, however judicious some of them may seem to him at the moment.

The final point that I wish to discuss is the reason for the disconcerting, even slightly irritating, impression made upon the reader of novels by the form of *Les Faux-Monnayeurs*. The characters in the book are admirably introduced and awakened to a life of their own and the individual chapters of the story have a vitality which reveals Gide's exceptional narrative and dramatic gifts. Yet from chapter to chapter, and accordingly in the work as a whole, there is a sense of discontinuity, of failure on the author's part to "follow through" once he sets his characters on their feet and his themes in motion. The effect on the reader is a vague dissatisfaction that prevents the novel from firing his imagination and possessing him utterly in the way that the greatest masterpieces of fiction tend to do. This effect is not due to carelessness or ineptitude in Gide but rather to a deliberate principle of his esthetic of the novel. Gide was certainly not taking the easy or the popular way, for the rule that he set himself in *Les Faux-Monnayeurs*—"ne jamais profiter de l'élan acquis"—made it almost as difficult for him to launch each chapter as it was to get the book itself under way.

This peculiar method of composition, which tends to take away the reader's spontaneous pleasure in the narrative in proportion as it is applied more rigorously, undoubtedly corresponds to a basic element in Gide's attitude toward life—to his desire to be always sincere, "authentique," "disponible," and not to commit himself by his present choice in such a way that the spontaneity of his future actions may be in any way impaired. The fullest expression of this attitude occurs in the early *Nourritures terrestres* (1897), but to a marked degree the tendency has remained characteristic of Gide the artist and the man throughout the years. A knowledge of this attitude helps us to understand Gide's observation in the *Journal des Faux-Monnayeurs*: "Ne pas établir la suite de mon roman dans le prolongement des lignes déjà tracées; voilà la difficulté. Un surgissement perpétuel; chaque nouveau chapitre doit poser un nouveau problème, être une ouverture, une direction, une impulsion, une jetée en avant—de l'esprit du lecteur" (*Oeuvres*, XII, 53).

The result of this attitude and of this method of composition is that though Gide suggests infinitely rich possibilities in the characters and action of *Les Faux-Monnayeurs*, he does not go very far in developing them. Here too one must recognize something intentional (unless Gide attempts to rationalize a lack that he feels within himself), for in the *Journal des Faux-Monnayeurs* we read: "La vie nous présente de toutes parts quantité d'amorces de drames, mais il est rare que ceux-ci se poursuivent et se dessinent comme a coutume de les filer un romancier. Et c'est là précisément l'impression que je voudrais donner dans ce livre . . ." (*Oeuvres*, XIII, 57–58). Even the conclusion to *Les Faux-Monnayeurs* is meant to intensify this effect, for Gide says that the novel "s'achèvera brusquement, non point par épuisement du sujet, qui doit donner l'impression de l'inépuisable, mais au contraire, par son élargissement et par une sorte d'évasion de son contour. Il ne doit pas se boucher, mais s'éparpiller, se défaire . . ." (*Oeuvres*, XIII, 60).

One may concede that this theory (though it is in no sense a doctrine of universal application) might under ideal circumstances produce a great masterpiece of the novel. It obviously requires the most active collaboration of the reader, but this is something that the novelist, no less than the poet, has the right as a serious artist to demand. But in the specific case of *Les Faux-Monnayeurs*, I think, Gide's application of his theory, sincere as it is, gives the impression of a somewhat too conscious technique, almost a tour de force, and the pleasure which the reader derives from collaborating with the novelist to follow through his leads verges on the pleasure that is derived from sheer mental gymnastics. One cannot help echoing the comment made by Bernard, the thorough-going realist in the novel, after hearing Édouard attempt to explain the esthetic of his projected book: "Un bon roman s'écrit plus naïvement que cela" (*Oeuvres*, XII, 294). It is possible that Gide is too much of an artist to take his place among the greatest novelists, though I do not wish by this remark to suggest that artistry and craftsmanship are less desirable in the novel than in other literary types. But as Gide himself realized, even though he has expressed confidence that his novel will eventually win praise for the very things which critics still question, the type of composition that he adopted in *Les Faux-Monnayeurs* was a risk (*Journal,* p. 1050. June 12, 1931). It was, in fact, a sort of wager, and unfortunately Gide did not emerge so clearly the winner that his work may be termed an unqualified success as the great novel, the rich synthesis of the author's experience in the complex unity of a solid masterpiece, which he strove so hard to achieve.

In view of this incomplete success, we may ask in conclusion, what is the lesson to be learned from Gide—from his theory and his practice—with respect to the problem of form in the novel? On the one hand, it seems to me, Gide has proved that for any novelist who is a sincere and serious artist the old, conventional, stereotyped "form" which the Paul Bourgets and the Henry Bordeaux' accepted without question is gone forever. The novelist may not care to discard "plot" or he may develop his fiction in such a way that this element loses its traditional identity; the important thing is that the novelist, no less than the poet, is an imaginative artist whose task and privilege it is to create for each subject a form that will fuse so inseparably with the matter that a work of art in all its specific objectivity comes into being. This valuable lesson, which each new generation of writers and critics needs to have brought before it in concrete examples, was especially appropriate for the generations that have looked to Gide as a courageous master.

But on the other hand, Gide's attempt to achieve a great novel in *Les Faux-Monnayeurs* shows clearly that it is not enough for the novelist to be an intelligent, skillful, sensitive artist and to reject the old forms for a new design showing rare inventiveness and superb craftsmanship. What is necessary is something at the same time simpler and much more difficult, for the novelist's success depends upon his making the reader accept his creation as living and true—not, of course, true only in the narrow realistic sense, but true in that the artist so captures our imagination that we cease to regard mere reason as the sole criterion of truth and attend to his creation with all our faculties at once. In *Les Faux-Monnayeurs,* Gide fails to an appreciable degree in this essential matter, it seems to me, and this in spite of his admirable effort to synthesize his experience in the complex structure of a single work and in spite of the exceptional artistic and intellectual gifts which he brings to the task. This failure, moreover, strikes me as a failure to achieve a perfect solution to the problem of form, since it comes largely from the author's conscious artistic procedure of refusing to "follow through" either his characters or his story. This refusal, I have noted, is a manifestation of one of the basic traits of Gide's make-up—his unwillingness to compromise the spontaneity of his future responses by his present choice. In a novelist, no less than in a man of action, such a trait is a handicap if it becomes dominant, and the result in this instance is that while *Les Faux-Monnayeurs* is the work most fully representative of its author and one of the most interesting pieces of fiction in an age that has produced the writings of Thomas Mann, Marcel Proust, and James Joyce, it fails to sustain that mysterious quality of life which would place it among the real masterpieces of the novel.

◄ξ FREDERICK J. HOFFMAN

Aldous Huxley and the Novel of Ideas

IN HIS *Point Counter Point,* Aldous Huxley has Philip Quarles occasionally jot down in his notebook random observations on the craft of fiction. These may be considered a kind of handbook for a study of the "novel of ideas"— not the novel which incidentally *illustrates* ideas but the novel which uses them in default of characterization and other qualities of the traditional narrative. These passages from the notebook are, of course, immensely valuable for those who wish to investigate Huxley as artist and thinker, but their principal advantage is the way in which they illuminate an art form almost peculiar to twentieth-century literary history. This note, for example, is a "statement of principle" for such a novel:

Novel of ideas. The character of each personage must be implied, as far as possible, in the ideas of which he is the mouthpiece. In so far as theories are rationalizations of sentiments, instincts, dispositions of soul, this is feasible. The chief defect of the novel of ideas is that you must write about people who have ideas to express— which excludes all but about .01 per cent. of the human race. Hence the real, the congenital novelists don't write such books. But then, I never pretended to be a congenital novelist.

At first glance, the notion that ideas might take precedence

NOTE. Reprinted from *College English,* 1946, by permission of the editors and the author.

over characters in a novel seems no less than monstrous; and of this reaction Quarles is himself aware: "People who can reel off neatly formulated notions aren't quite real; they're slightly monstrous. Living with monsters becomes rather tiresome in the long run." But Huxley has often demonstrated in his novels the fact that ideas may possess qualities which are comparable with those which animate persons—and this particularly in a period of time when ideas are not fixed, calculated, or limited by canons of strict acceptance or rejection. Ideas, as they are used in Huxley, possess, in other words, *dramatic* qualities. Dominating as they very often do the full sweep of his novels, they appropriate the fortunes and careers which ordinarily belong to persons.

I should like to draw further upon the ideas of Philip Quarles as they relate to this unusual and interesting adaptation of a respectable art form. To begin with, Philip is in a very special sense a "modern intellectual." He finds a much greater charm in ideas than in persons. For the ordinary, passive, "idea-less" men of the streets and tearooms—who, of course, exist on all levels of society—he cannot bring himself to command any respect or affection. In fact, in the world of human relationships he is "curiously like a foreigner, uneasily not at home among his fellows, finding it difficult or impossible to enter into communication with any but those who could speak his native intellectual language of ideas."

He meets each personal word, each expression of feeling or intimacy, with a generalization—one which includes his own circumstances and indicates understanding but is safely removed from the danger of immediate participation. His reaction to the personal circumstances which ordinarily demand intimate contact for their proper treatment is an understanding, bulwarked by such generalizations as make that understanding universally applicable. All of which distresses his wife Elinor, who is often hurt by his kind indifference and puzzled rather than made happy by his "occasional and laborious essays at emotional intimacy," but who is also attracted by his intelligence, "that quick, comprehensive, ubiquitous intelligence that could understand everything, including the emotions it could not feel and the instincts it took care not to be moved by."

Philip's unwillingness to be involved in the affairs of ordinary mortals has no small relevance for his attitude toward his art. For him, *persons* are either specimens, or statistics, or demonstrations—anything which can conveniently be lifted from the personal to the abstract. Thus, too, his humor, which takes the form of wit, of exaggeration, of caricature. To the unregenerate intellectual, persons are seldom if ever three-dimensional or actual; or, if they accidentally become so (as they do occasionally for Philip), the experience is a bit disagreeable, even shocking and disturbing. In consequence, his *idea* of personality is substituted for actual *evidence* of personality; ideas are acted out by characters, or demonstrated by them; and finally, a character often assumes the monstrous appearance of such a demonstration. He becomes a caricature which incorporates the furthest possible human demonstration of an attitude with certain grotesque inadequacies of person to which his whimsical creator condemns him. As if in compensation for not having given a character some personal symmetry and identity, he extends beyond credibility the one or few attributes which he does confer upon him.

Philip is a man of great sensitivity to philosophies and points of view. He is capable of accommodating each in its turn. This generosity toward influences is in essence a kind of ever-shifting eclecticism, as a result of which each form of thought may at one time attract him and then be deserted for some other.

The essential character of the self consisted precisely in that liquid and undeformable ubiquity; in that capacity to espouse all contours and yet remain unfixed in any form; to take, and with an equal facility efface, impressions. To such moulds as his spirit might from time to time occupy, to such hard and burning obstacles as it might flow round, submerge, and, itself cold, penetrate to the fiery heart of, no permanent loyalty was owing. The moulds were emptied as easily as they had been filled, the obstacles were passed by. But the essential liquidness that flowed where it would, the cool indifferent flux of intellectual curiosity— that persisted and to that his loyalty was due.

Such a point of view is ideal — indeed, it is almost necessary — for the novelist of ideas. And at one time in Huxley's career, this it is which both Philip Quarles and his creator upheld. The true way of looking at things is "multiplicity," says Philip to his wife on one occasion. Each point of view differs from every other; and all are valid. A large and ample demonstration of the several approaches to morality and fact serves to bring one as close to truth as one may get. "Multiplicity of eyes and multiplicity of aspects seen," explains Philip. "For instance, one person interprets events in terms of bishops; another in terms of the price of flannel camisoles; another, like that young lady from Gulmberg," he nodded after the retreating group, "thinks of it in terms of good times. And then there's the biologist, the chemist, the physicist, the historian. Each sees, professionally, a different aspect of the event, a different layer of reality. What I want to do is to look with all those eyes at once."

II

This generous point of view is explained at some length in several of the essays published in the volume *Do What You Will*. They constitute the platform for the novelist of ideas. An idea, or large generalization about human behavior, when it is joined to a character in such a novel, is modified to become an attitude or mood. In the interests of narrative and dramatic movement, this attitude or mood leads to action — but it is always *typical* or *characteristic* action, the adventure not so much of a person as of an idea in its contemporary world. The formal essay proves; the novel of ideas demonstrates. Each is strongly dominated by the intellectual character of its author.

As explanation of this point of view, Huxley discusses, in *Do What You Will*, the psychological nature of truth. Truth, he says, is internal. A "psychological fact" is valid for the person who holds it, if for no other. This makes for a diversity of truths, for an infinite variety of interpretations, and for an emphasis upon *attitude* as the determinant of the quality of truth. Opposed to this point of view is the tendency toward unity — purely intellectual knowledge which secures a unity from diversity of experience and holds tenaciously to that unity. The weaknesses of Philip Quarles' kind of intellectual are admitted by Huxley in these essays. One must accept life in all its manifestations, he says in one place, condemning Swift for having failed in this regard; and, speaking of Wordsworth's "Handy Manual for Nature Lovers," he suggests that "it is fear of the labyrinthine flux and complexity of phenomena that has driven men to philosophy, to science, to theology — fear of the complex reality driving them to invent a simpler, more manageable, and therefore consoling fiction."

Each of us searches for his own way of accommodating himself to the universe. But we are frequently afraid of the reality we see and experience, and we hasten to impose upon it some form of order, original or borrowed. We are seldom hospitable toward mere diversity in itself; we are too often afraid of it. Huxley would have us accept the immediate first record of our senses, to be not affrighted but thrilled by their gift of disorder to our minds.

The principal defect in this philosophy of knowing is its marginless and limitless generosity to flux itself — so that one actually escapes the responsibility of *any* interpretation of life by accepting and entertaining momentarily *each* of them. Its value is great, however, for us who wish to apply it to our investigation of the twentieth-century novel of ideas. For it allows for a generous accommodation of all the currents of thought which have been influential in our times.

III

The novel of ideas is a narrative form peculiar to an "unstable" age — one in which standards are not fixed beyond removal or alteration. It assumes a diversity of mood and intention, but it is careful not merely to label its characters. They are not allegorical figures, for there is no single thing which the drama of their interaction is designed to illustrate. The novel which Philip Quarles wants to write is a novel of diversity in points of view, in each of which the intellectual nature is modified by the local circumstances governing it. Such a novel has a development which consists mainly of the demonstration in terms of human events of the effects of a point of view upon the person who holds it. The drama implicit in an idea becomes explicit when it is shown as a point of view which a *person* holds and upon which he acts. The comedy implicit in an idea is revealed in a concrete demonstration of its inherent untenability. But one cannot repeat too often that there is no "moral" to be drawn from the career and fate of ideas in such a novel. There is never any fixed contest between right and wrong, or between the true and the false, from which we are supposed to get what comfort or instruction we can.

One of the chief objectives of the novelist of ideas is to include men of varying temperaments and attitudes within the scope of one narrative and thus to dramatize the clash of these attitudes in his novel. Each character thus has given him (if little else!) a point of view drawn from the prevailing intellectual interests of his creator. On this point of view the character stands, wavers, or falls. Thus, implicit in this type of novel is the drama of ideas rather than of persons, or, rather, the drama of individualized ideas. The structural requirements of such a novel are perhaps simpler than they at first appear. One requirement is to get these people, or as many of them as is possible, together in one place where circumstances are favorable to a varied expression of intellectual diversity. The drawing room, the party, the dinner— these are all favorite points of structural focus. To supplement them, there are the notebooks (as in *Point Counter Point*), correspondence (which serves as a substitute for conversation and varies the narrative procedure), the casual or accidental meeting of two or three persons, who continue their discussions in one form or another, and the prolonged exposition, in essay form, of any given or chance suggestion which the narrative may allow.

The best examples of the novel of ideas are Huxley's novels of the 1920's. To be sure, he did not always use this form; nor is any of his novels purely a novel of ideas. In his shorter pieces, most notably in "Uncle Spencer," "Two or Three Graces," and "Young Archimedes," Huxley writes charmingly and sympathetically of persons and reveals a remarkable talent for a complete delineation of characters who are interesting almost exclusively as persons. But the works which mark the development of Huxley as a novelist—*Chrome Yellow, Antic Hay, Those Barren Leaves,* and *Point Counter Point*—are, each in its own way, novels of ideas. Rarely does a Huxley character give himself away directly; rarely if ever does Huxley fail to give him away. The position, the point of view, of the Huxley character is usually revealed in the course of Huxley's discussion of his tastes, his intellectual preferences, his manner of behaving himself in the society of his fellows. Thus the *idea* which each is to demonstrate becomes in the novel the point of view he adopts—or, actually, *is.* There are varying shades of characterization, ranging from gross caricature to sympathetic exposition. There are degrees of the grotesque in the points of view described in Huxley's novels. Thus Lypiatt of *Antic Hay* is at times grotesque, at times pathetic, but almost always absurd. Gumbril Jr. is a pleasant enough grotesque, though his weaknesses at times make of him a pathetic figure. Other characters, like Mercaptan, are consistently and superbly themselves on all or almost all occasions.

These persons in *Antic Hay* have ample opportunity to express their individualities in an early gathering in a restaurant—a favorite setting, one in which points of view are given an opportunity for "free-lance" expression. Lypiatt's hostility to Mercaptan is one theme of the novel; it is an opposition of points of view much more than of wills. Lypiatt, the frustrated, would-be genius, is never a match for the genteelly cynical Mercaptan. The inequality reduces the conflict to an absurdity. Typically revealing examples of their conversation illustrate well their points of view and may help to show how the Huxley novel of ideas works:

Lypiatt went on torrentially. "You're afraid of ideals, that's what it is. You daren't admit to having dreams. . . . Ideals— they're not sufficiently genteel for you civilised young men.

You've quite outgrown that sort of thing. No dream, no religion, no morality." . . .

"*What* there is to be ashamed of in being civilised, I *really* don't know," [Mercaptan] said, in a voice that was now the bull's, now the piping robin's. "No, if I glory in anything, it's in my little rococo boudoir, and the conversations across the polished mahogany, and the delicate, lascivious, *witty* little flirtations on ample sofas inhabited by the soul of Crébillon Fils. We needn't *all* be Russians, I hope. These revolting Dostoievskys."

This clash between the vigorous but pathetically awkward and mistaken artist and the mild but venomously precious esthete and critic rises and subsides throughout the novel, until it issues in physical violence. In the novel we also find the scientist, the incorrigibly self-sacrificing laboratory scientist, devoted to a ceaseless experimenting with endless demonstrations of a fragment of hypothesis. His point of view, consistent to the last lost shred of dignity, is portrayed by Huxley as one of the more pathetic of the grotesques in his fiction.

Perhaps because *Point Counter Point* is more deliberately planned, that novel seems at least to have given each of its points of view some discoverable beginning, middle, and end. By interweaving these points of view, giving them a thematic structure, Huxley has placed a large premium upon his view of supplementary ideas. The interesting fact about this novel is that the several points of view are acted out, tested as it were, in the modern world, and the limitations of each are demonstrated in the individual fates of the persons who hold them. Spandrell, in himself not concerned with large social issues, lends courage to Illidge, scientist-Communist, so that Webley, Fascist, comes to a violent end. Lord Edward's devotion to science is free, because he chooses it to be, of the embarrassing complications which Illidge suffers through involvement in political action. He has instead what his assistant calls "a shameful and adulterous passion for idealistic metaphysics." In each case, the point of view, which becomes quite clear very early in the novel, is so given as to form a core of responsibility for the action consequent upon differences of opinion and opposing and clashing ideas.

IV

"Put a novelist into the novel" (that is, as one of the characters), Philip Quarles advises himself in his notebook. "He justifies aesthetic generalizations, which may be interesting — at least
to me. He also justifies experiment. Specimens of his work may
illustrate other possible or impossible ways of telling a story. And
if you have him telling parts of the same story as you are, you
can make a variation on the theme." Philip is, of course, talking
here of a novelist as one of the characters, not of *the* novelist,
not of himself. He does not consider it wise to set up the novelist
in a place of authority, so that the other characters may consult
him on occasion about what they are to do next, or how they
are to feel about what they have just done.

But the author of a novel of ideas is a *person* of much greater
stature in his own novel — and his presence is much more obvious,
too. And, at least in the case of Huxley, there is a close interaction
of the essayist with the novelist. They parallel each other for a
time; they frequently supplement each other. The essayist is a
sort of "supply station," to which the novelist has recourse. He is
the "port of call" at which the novelist stops, to take on necessary and staple goods. The reputation of Huxley is chiefly that
of the novelist. In another sense, however, he is the essayist-
commentator upon twentieth-century morals and ideas. Just as
his characters are often subordinate as persons to the ideas or
points of view they express, so his novels as a whole are often
mere carriers for the cargo of ideas which their author must
retail.

The essayist's attempt to give animation to his ideas leads to
the novel of ideas. In the course of Huxley's development as
novelist, the characters of his creation stumble, swagger, or are
carried through his novels, supported almost always by the essayist. Feelings, such as those mixed feelings with which Walter
Bidlake contemplates both his mistresses, are freighted with ratioc-
ination. The great difference between this kind of exposition
and the *exempla* of medieval sermons is that in the former there
is no fixed point of view to bring home to the reader. Rather,

there are many points of view; and the reader is asked not so much to appraise as to enjoy them. To illustrate, Walter Bidlake's conquest of Lucy Tantamount proceeds by stages of speculation and comment, the essayist explaining and analyzing to the last detail of sentiment and caprice. Walter, says Huxley, "treated Lucy, not as the hard, ruthless amusement-hunter he had so clearly recognized her as being before he became her lover, but as an ideally gracious and sensitive being, to be adored as well as desired, a sort of combined child, mother, and mistress, whom one should maternally protect and be maternally protected by, as well as virilely and — yes! — faunishly make love to."

This much one wants, needs, by way of establishing the mood of the occasion. There follows an elaborate essay on sensuality and sentiment, based upon the relationship between Walter and Lucy, but a separate thing as well, an essay on the subject, broken occasionally to allow for a further demonstration of the points it is making. The commentator says: "This is a situation worthy of lengthy comment, because it illustrates what I have long thought to be true of modern moralities. Let me speak my mind, and in a short while I shall have these two characters back. In what they do you will see that I am right in my analysis." The essay begins: "Sensuality and sentiment, desire and tenderness are as often friends as they are enemies." A comment generalized from experience not real but imagined, projected upon the essayist's screen, to which he points in support of it. Some sentences further, the essayist permits Walter to assume his role as specific example, but the comment is itself a generalization: "Walter's desire to justify his longings by love was only, on final analysis, the articulately moral expression of his natural tendency to associate the act of sexual enjoyment with a feeling of tenderness, at once chivalrously protective and childishly self-abased."

Lucy and Walter — sensuality and sentiment, touching each other, embracing, and then separate, isolated points of view, their inherent conflict restored after a brief moment of self-indulgent union. "Living modernly's living quickly," says Lucy to Walter, as if to underline finally the fact that, in these times at any rate, sensuality and sentiment do not mix well. "You can't cart a wagonload of ideals and romanticisms about with you these days. When you travel by airplane, you must leave your heavy baggage behind. The good old-fashioned soul was all right when people lived slowly. But it's too ponderous nowadays. There's no room for it in the airplane."

In the novels of the 1920's, the essayist in Huxley strode along with the novelist. The essays he wrote for the *Athanaeum* and for *Vanity Fair* are matched by the conversation and contemplation recorded in the novels; and there is a supporting theory of composition to be found in certain of the essays. Beginning, perhaps, with *Eyeless in Gaza,* the essayist far exceeds the novelist. What has happened? The novel of ideas requires a poise, a balance, and most of all an eclectic faith in the democracy of ideas. Once the novelist deserts this position, his novels have only one of two ways to go: they may become novels not of ideas but of persons; this seldom occurs, because the conversion of a novelist of ideas is scarcely ever an esthetic conversion. Or they may become essays almost purely, and the narrative itself a setting for the *exposition* rather than the *dramatization* of ideas. This latter is what occurred in Huxley's later novels. He is alternately a caricaturist and an essayist; he is no longer a novelist of ideas, but a philosopher who knows not how gracefully to leave the house in which he has lived so graciously all his life. There are occasional delightful exceptions in *Eyeless in Gaza, After Many a Summer,* and *Time Must Have a Stop.* But in each case one feels that the essayist is impatient for the artist to finish building the platform, so that he may mount it for his "lesson." Anthony Beavis and Miller *of Eyeless in Gaza,* Propter of *After Many a Summer,* Bruno Rontini and his disciple, Sebastian Barnack, of *Time Must Have a Stop*—to these persons Huxley gives the responsibility for showing the development of the point of view which he himself presents at length in *Ends and Means.*

Huxley is no longer a novelist. His recent novels are lengthy essays, to which are added entertainments. But his novels of the 1920's *are* novels of ideas—ideas clothed, ideas given flesh and bone and sent out into a world in which they may test themselves. What is grotesque or pathetic or noble in each of them is revealed in various ways as the dramatic equivalent of its intellectual status. Compare the dialogue in any of Jane Austen's novels with that, let us say, in *Point Counter Point*. In the one, the larger morality of the day is taken for granted, and only the peculiarities of persons residing in a relatively fixed world receive treatment. In the other, nothing is taken for granted; everything is accepted, but only as it meets and clashes with everything else.

Huxley's novels of ideas are an expression of the tremendous vitality which ideas had in the 1920's; they are also a testimony of the intellectual confusion of that period. To record that confusion requires a tolerance of it and, above all, a willingness to grant for the moment at least that ideas may have a vitality and attraction quite apart from their more sober values, those values they possess when they remain confined within the limits of systematic philosophy or science. Most important of all, these novels are a brilliant portrait of the age, or at least of its intellectual interests and habits. Whatever defects of manner the novels of Huxley suffer, his vital interest in the intellectual concerns of his time has resulted in several dramatic portraits of contemporary life and thought.

⊌§ C. W. M. JOHNSON

Tone in *A la recherche du temps perdu*

A l'ombre des jeunes filles en fleurs brings Marcel to his first meeting with Bergotte, at the home of Madame Swann, and there the action is suspended to allow for a lengthy analysis of the qualities of that author's conversation. Several points are discussed, most of them suggesting comparison with characteristics of his literary style. The qualities of Bergotte's voice were altered, we are told, by the thought behind what he was saying, by "un frisonnement d'idées précises" which his imitators could not reproduce in their works. At times

Bergotte avait l'air de parler presque à contre-sens, psalmodiant certains mots et, s'il poursuivait au-dessous d'eux une seule image, les filant sans intervalle comme un même son, avec une fatigante monotonie.

These images possessed a family resemblance, but

chacune de ces beautés . . . restait cependent particulière, comme la découverte qui l'avait mise à jour.

He had applied his mind "avec précision à la réalité qui lui plaisait." He ignored familiar aspects of a question, and sometimes became difficult to follow, simply because he had successfully eliminated "[le] poncif auquel nous étions habitués et qui nous semblait la réalité même." He wearied his listeners by seeming always to be talking in metaphors. One feature of his literary

201

style was the illumination which arises from the necessity for reading printed phrases with a certain vocal inflection, an inflection that Bergotte had successfully captured in his prose. Essentially, Bergotte was

un homme qui au fond n'aimait vraiment que certaines images et . . . que les composer et les peindre sous les mots. . . . Et s'il avait eu à se défendre devant un tribunal, malgré lui il aurait choisi ses paroles non selon l'effet qu'elles pouvaient produire sur le juge mais en vue d'images que le juge n'aurait certainement pas aperçues.

It is plain that in this analysis Proust is thinking as much of his own characteristics as of those of any actual author who may have served as a model for Bergotte, in the sense of suggesting the "nez rouge en forme de coquille de colimaçon" so incongruent with Marcel's idealized preconception of his favorite writer. It should also be apparent that the points so far summarized do not present separate issues, but are all concerned in some way with problems of imagery and tone and their relation to one type of literary excellence. Two further observations suggested by qualities of Bergotte's conversation should be noted, although they carry us somewhat into the realm of psychology. One is that no "déterminisme" can ever predict the variety, the unexpected turns, present in the work of a man who is not bound by the cliché:

La vraie variété est dans cette plénitude d'éléments réels et inattendus, dans le rameau chargé de fleurs bleues qui s'élance contre toute attente, de la haie printanière qui semblait déjà comble . . .

The other is an illustration of Bergotte's subtle use of imagery as he takes part in a mild dispute. When the conversation gets under way, Marcel and Bergotte discuss Berma's Phèdre. Marcel had admired a scene in which a green light had been played upon Phèdre, and Bergotte had not, for

"la petite Phèdre là-dedans fait trop branche de corail au fond d'un aquarium. . . . Ce que Racine a raconté ce ne sont pas les amours des oursins."

With these figures Bergotte has given Marcel's mind something pleasant to play with, so that the fact of the disagreement is softened. Marcel is impressed by Bergotte's technique of conciliatory argumentation and contrasts it favorably with the flat contradictions of M. de Norpois, that enemy of Art for Art's sake, whose method of disputation quickly put a stop to all talk. Bergotte's method was better because

Une idée forte communique un peu de sa force au contradicteur. Participant à la valeur universelle des esprits, elle s'insère, se greffe en l'esprit de celui qu'elle réfute, au milieu d'idées adjacents, à l'aide desquelles, reprenant quelque avantage, il la complète, la rectifie; si bien que la sentence finale est en quelque sort l'oeuvre des deux personnes qui discutaient.

Marcel's meeting with Bergotte is notable for several reasons; it affords an early instance of the failure of Marcel's preconceptions to coincide with reality; and it suggests formative influences in Bergotte's past and significant disparities between the moral tone of his works and certain details of his private life. But my purpose in selecting these passages has been to lay a foundation for an analysis of a quality of Proust's writing which, while it is apparent enough, is somewhat difficult to isolate and discuss.

The reader of *A la recherche du temps perdu* becomes increasingly aware of the importance of tone as he progresses through the work, and on rereading it he feels that the successful realization in tone is without doubt its most pervasive achievement. Tone is an impressionistic term, but it stands for something perceptible enough in literature. At one end it shades off into considerations of style (but those elements of tone dependent upon the spoken word survive even less well than stylistic features in translation), and at the other it can be confused with emotions arising out of the conflict. It is influenced by qualities of character and of setting. But it is nevertheless separable from these considerations; passages may be conspicuous for tone in which nothing in particular is happening except for an adjustment of intimacy between narrator and reader—digressions from the main stream of the narrative, or introductory and cadential sections. Such parts of a work could be effective in tone for purely stylistic reasons, but they could hardly be notable if entirely free of imagery. For tone is very dependent upon imagery, and especially, in a work of fiction, upon images that have a meaning for someone in the story.

Some of these statements will take on more meaning if, keeping them in mind, we turn to the last words in the passage devoted to the death of Bergotte. Proust has carried Bergotte through his final agonies, but he feels the need for some kind of peroration to round out the episode. He gets under way by raising the question of the survival of the soul:

Ce qu'on peut dire, c'est que tout se passe dans notre vie comme si nous y entrions avec le faix d'obligations contractées dans une vie antérieure; il n'y a aucune raison dans nos conditions de vie sur cette terre pour que nous nous croyions obligés à faire le bien, à être délicats, même à être polis, ni pour l'artiste cultivé à ce qu'il se croie obligé de recommencer vingt fois un morceau dont l'admiration qu'il excitera importera peu à son corps mangé par les vers, comme le pan de mur jaune que peignit avec tant de science et de raffinement un artiste à jamais inconnu, à peine identifié sous le nom de Ver Meer. Toutes ces obligations qui n'ont pas leur sanction dans la vie présente semblent appartenir à un monde différent, fondé sur la bonté, le scrupule, le sacrifice, un monde entièrement différent de celui-ci, et dont nous sortons pour naître à cette terre, avant peut-être d'y retourner revivre sous l'empire de ces lois inconnues auxquelles nous avons obéi parce que nous en portions l'enseignement en nous, sans savoir qui les y avait tracées,—ces lois dont tout travail profond de l'intelligence nous rapproche et qui sont invisibles seulement—et encore!—pour les sots. De sorte que l'idée que Bergotte n'était pas mort à jamais est sans invraisemblance.

On l'enterra, mais toute la nuit funèbre, aux vitrines éclairées, ses livres disposés trois par trois veillaient comme des anges aux ailes éployées et semblaient, pour celui qui n'était plus, le symbole de sa résurrection.

These sentences hardly differ in stylistic structure from those discussing the word *pissotière* three pages later. But there is something in them, some quality of tone, only superficially dependent upon the vocal inflection with which one might read the words,

C. W. M. JOHNSON

or upon the somewhat conventional and, I believe, insincere Platonism which keeps the sentences going. There is the image of the yellow wall, now full of meaning because in the episode just closed it has undergone a development. Appearing originally as another instance of Bergotte's love of images, and one that is to be the death of him, it becomes a symbol of artistic perfection when Bergotte says to himself at the gallery, "C'est ainsi que j'aurais dû écrire. . . . Mes derniers livres sont trop secs. . . ." The image is in Bergotte's mind as he dies (a source of consolation of a nonreligious sort, perhaps). And now it is evoked once more, with a fresh perspective, for we are reminded that the artist who created this bit of perfection is unknown, and that the good artist can never be certain even of the meager reward of being remembered. Images of the moment also impart an emotional coloring to the passage: "son corps mangé par les vers" (a cliché, but rhetorically effective here), Bergotte's books in lighted windows (suggesting the homes of all his readers), "disposés trois par trois" (a number with associations of piety), "comme des anges aux ailes éployées" (Proust pictures them opened for reading). The Platonism is a vehicle for these sober reflections, and for establishing between the narrator and Bergotte a spiritual kinship in their scrupulous devotion to the laws of literature, "ces lois inconnues auxquelles nous avons obéi." We know that Proust reworked this passage during his last illness, but even if we did not, we could hardly fail to read these words in the light of Marcel's sympathy for his "doux Chantre aux cheveux blancs."

Hence the importance in *A la recherche du temps perdu* of a first-person narrator, in spite of the liberties Proust takes with the form and the troubles it gets him into when he is forced to maintain it,* for almost as important as the images themselves is the fact that they are being realized in the mind of a character whose whole background and temperament have been revealed to the reader. The images take on a context from the fact of their presence in Marcel's mind. Proust has said that genius consists "dans

* Literal-minded critics are unable to see the Charlus-Jupien episode as a problem in point of view, and denounce Marcel, or Proust himself, as an eavesdropper.

le pouvoir réfléchissant et non dans la qualité intrinsèque du spectacle reflété," and by placing the author in the story he has focused on that reflective power as well as on the imagery and established the kind of intimacy between author and reader in which things take on the most overtones.

It takes time to develop that intimacy. At first it is established between Marcel and Swann, as a means of blurring the confusion in technique arising from a simultaneous use in this part of the story of the omniscient and the limited point of view. Scenes come to us filtered through the consciousness of Swann and again through the mind of a first-person narrator whose own nature is being established for the reader at the same time, primarily in terms of its similarity to Swann's. Gradually the reader begins to accept Marcel, outrageous neurotic though he is, and, seduced by the incantation of Proust's style and charmed by the range of his perceptions, to identify himself with the narrator. And the second time through the work his resistance is down from the start. He now has the advantage of the narrator's own orientation in the story, can look both ways in time, can see each clue as it is planted and respond because the context of its fullest development is already in his mind.

This intimacy aids, in a broad sense, in setting the tone of the work, but to account for the great range of tone in Proust we must consider certain technical devices at work, devices concerned above all with a judicious and disciplined control of imagery. All authors use imagery in the sense that descriptive passages demand some kind of specification. But

la littérature qui se contente de "[décrire] les choses", d'en donner seulement un misérable relevé de lignes et de surfaces, est celle qui tout en s'appelant réaliste est la plus éloignée de la réalité, celle qui nous appauvrit et nous attriste le plus, car elle coupe brusquement toute communication de notre moi présent avec le passé dont les choses gardaient l'essence et l'avenir, où elles nous incitent à le goûter de nouveau. C'est elle que l'art digne de ce nom doit exprimer . . .

Now Proust's artistic intentions were, even for a literary man, remarkably conscious and clear; and he brought to the task of their realization a knowledge of how the mind works and of the difficulties in his way. The subjective is the realm of tone, and to communicate on that level he needed something beyond the technique of the surface realist. Figurative language was a help, for figures can take on a function other than mere ornamentation when they become a means of getting at the quality of an event through the suggestion of unexpected similarities in otherwise divergent types of experience. The work abounds in similes employed for that purpose. It would, however, be most appropriate here to cite the instance when, at Mme Swann's party, Marcel suddenly learns that Bergotte is present:

Ce nom de Bergotte me fit tressauter comme le bruit d'un revolver, qu'on aurait déchargé sur moi, mais instinctivement pour faire bonne contenance je saluai; devant moi, comme ces prestidigitateurs qu'on aperçoit intacts et en redingote dans la poussiere d'un coup de feu d'où s'envole une colombe, mon salut m'était rendu par un homme jeune, rude, petit, râblé et myope, à nez rouge en forme de coquille de colimaçon et à barbiche noire J'étais mortellement triste . . .

There are many cases where figures are invoked because the emotion to be grasped is of a less communicable nature, but as an example of the use of appropriate imagery to intensify the tone of a ludicrous situation one could hardly wish a better passage. Marcel's start, embarrassing to him because it is one of several gauche responses on the occasion of his first appearance in society, suggests the response to a pistol shot, and that image in combination with the astonishment he feels on seeing Bergotte for the first time suggests a magician's act with something absurd and unexpected materializing out of the smoke of the pistol; finally, there is a hint that Bergotte, with his red nose and tufted chin, looks like a magician. In a sense he is one, but his appearance, at least, has far less dignity than that of the frail, white-haired man Marcel had constructed in his imagination.

It is almost a pity that the reader has so little time to explore the implications of some of this figurative language. However, the most effective device Proust found for penetrating the subjective was one directed toward the associative powers of the mind as they operate in a moment of vivid recollection. There is no need to establish the fact that Proust understood and valued these associative powers; they are the foundation of the main issue in the work—the philosophical treatment of time. But the associations of value to Proust should be differentiated from what usually passes for memory in our looser thinking on the subject:

Peu à peu conservée par la mémoire, c'est la chaîne de toutes les impressions inexactes, où ne reste rien de ce que nous avons réellement éprouvé, qui constitue pour nous notre pensée, notre vie, la réalité, et c'est ce mensonge-la que ne ferait que reproduire un art soi-disant "vécu", simple comme la vie, sans beauté, double emploi si ennuyeux et si vain de ce que nos yeux voient et de ce que notre intelligence constate qu'on se demande où celui qui s'y livre, trouve l'étincelle joyeuse et motrice, capable de le mettre en train et de le faire avancer dans sa besogne.

It is our failure to keep in mind this distinction between what we might call contextual recall and the shoddy abstraction and distortion we take for memory that obscures for us the point of Proust's main argument. Proust has tackled the old problem of "emotion recollected in tranquility," has seen this type of vivid recall as a source of poetry, and has set a form for his work that recreates for the reader the conditions necessary for experiencing such recall. The reader has only to respond to imagery as in life he would, in favorable circumstances, respond to evocative sense impressions.

A la recherche du temps perdu is a matrix of images related to each other in subtle ways. These images thread through the story, undergo development, and in general behave like the main characters, at times just present in a scene, at other times taking the center of the stage and delivering long monologues, and often demanding a reorientation of our thinking because of the metamorphoses they undergo. The figure is extravagant; but it points to an unrecognized source of unity in the work.

To exploit imagery in this fashion takes time and a prodigious amount of space. The reader must be occupied with other matters and allowed to forget, before conditions are right for recall and further development; but after the image has undergone several such variations it becomes so charged with associations that the slightest allusion to it is evocative. One thinks at once of the perhaps too-often cited "petite phrase de la sonate de Vinteuil," which gets its development rather early and rapidly becomes a symbol of the power of all beauty to cause suffering. But the list could be extended indefinitely: * the madeleine, the pink hawthorns, the three bell towers, the reflection of the sea in the bookcases of Marcel's hotel room at Balbec, all the little clues Marcel is able to gather about Albertine's life apart from him, which at first appease his jealousy and later cause him so much anguish.

The big themes in the work — the relativity of our subjective impressions and the self-deception implied in the concept of objectivity, the dependence of love upon incomplete possession, the conception of art as a discipline rewarding its followers with a grasp of reality and with selfhood — these themes all originate from concrete images, which still hover in the air when the large ideas to which they gave rise are being explored, and impart an undercurrent of emotion, a quality of poetry, to passages where it would otherwise be lacking. And just as in a philosophical discussion one is able to bring in a multitude of related facts, to refer indeed to a whole system, merely by mentioning a philosopher's name, so the images in Proust's story carry with them the weight of the themes to which they give rise, and evoke them by virtue of their power as referents. The depth of communication thus established is favorable to the realization of tone, the kind of tone sometimes noticeable in the works of a philosopher with a good sense of style.

* Raoul Celly's *Répertoire des thèmes de Marcel Proust* (Paris: Gallimard, 1935) is helpful in tracing some of these images as they undergo development, but less helpful than it might have been. Only the most conspicuous are indexed, for *thème* is taken to mean any pronouncement on a large issue (*Amour*, for example) and passages are cited only when the key word is specified. Thus *Relativisme* has only one entry, yet the entire work is in a sense a treatise on the subject. Passages containing an implied relativism can be located by consulting *Temps (deuxième sens)*.

The reader finally accepts Marcel and begins to think in his terms; and while it is impossible to name a point in the story where this is likely to occur, it must be at a time when he feels the impact of thought in what the narrator is saying. The mind of the narrator engages us because, long before he dramatizes the separation by shutting himself off to write, we see that mind apart from the world of the story, detached and amused. Two of the quotations above show Proust working out a definition of reality — a definition in which the term has a meaning for him almost synonymous with value. In his search for value Proust found it, not in events themselves, but in imagery, and in the memory which links events together.

ॐ ROBERT BECHTOLD HEILMAN

The Turn of the Screw as Poem

THERE is probably no other short work of fiction which has been the center, during the first fifty years of its life, of such regular attention and speculation as have been called forth by Henry James' *The Turn of the Screw*. The more obvious reasons for this phenomenon—those summarized, for instance, in Heywood Broun's rather uncomplex description of *The Turn* as "the thriller of thrillers, the last word in creeping horror stories"—actually explain almost nothing. For thrillers that exert a "hideous thrall-dom" are incontinently begotten and die, like movies, each year; and the continuing devotion to *The Turn* has hardly been that of the multitudes in search of hashish. That devotion is significant, indeed, because it has been critical; *The Turn* has elicited special comment from such writers as Edmund Wilson, Philip Rahv, F. O. Matthiessen, Katherine Anne Porter, Mark Van Doren, Allen Tate.

Since the book first appeared, there has been a series of interpretations; as these come forth periodically, and as the alterations in them show the different decades endeavoring to adjust James' materials to new interpretative methods, what is unmistakable is that James has hit upon some fundamental truth of

NOTE. This article appears in the Summer 1948 issue of the *University of Kansas City Review*.

experience that no generation can ignore and that each generation wishes to restate in its own terms. For half a century sensitive readers have felt the story exert a pull that far transcends any effects springing from the cool manipulations of mystery-mongers. Mr. Matthiessen's remark that the story exhibits James' "extraordinary command of . . . the darkness of moral evil" suggests the nature of the almost unique reality with which the story is infused. For critical readers the problem has been the definition of evil, and the identification of the methods by which the awareness of evil is brought to disturbing intensity.

It is probably safe to say that the Freudian interpretation of the story, of which the best known exponent is Edmund Wilson, no longer enjoys wide critical acceptance.* If, then, we cannot account for the evil by treating the governess as pathological, we must seek elsewhere an explanation of the story's hold. I am convinced that, at the level of action, the story means exactly what it says: that at Bly there are apparitions which the governess sees, which Mrs. Grose does not see but comes to believe in because they are consistent with her own independent experience, and of which the children have a knowledge which they endeavor to conceal. These dramatic circumstances have a symbolic import which seems not too difficult to get hold of: the ghosts are evil, evil which comes subtly, conquering before it is wholly seen; the governess, Cassandra-like in the intuitions which are inaccessible to others, is the guardian whose function it is to detect and attempt to ward off evil; Mrs. Grose—whose name, like the narrator's title, has virtually allegorical significance—is the commonplace mortal, well-intentioned, but perceiving only the obvious; the children are the victims of evil, victims who, ironically,

---

* Philip Rahv calls attempts to explain away the ghosts "a fallacy of rationalism," and asserts, I think correctly, that the Freudian view narrows and conventionalizes the story in a way that contradicts both James' intentions and artistic habits, and, I might add, our own sense that large matters are at stake. In their symposium in *Invitation to Learning*, Katherine Anne Porter, Mark Van Doren, and Allen Tate have all specifically denied the validity of the Freudian reading of the story. I have attempted, in some detail, to show how Wilson's account of *The Turn* runs afoul of both the story and James' preface (*Modern Language Notes*, 1946, pp. 433–45).

practice concealment—who doubtless must conceal—when not to conceal is essential to salvation. If this reading of the symbolism be tenable, we can understand in part the imaginative power of the story, for, beneath the strange and startling action-surface, we have the oldest of themes—the struggle of evil to possess the human soul. And if this struggle appears to resolve itself into a Christian form, that impulse, as it were, of the materials need not be surprising.

But the compelling theme and the extraordinarily vivid plot-form are not the entirety of *The Turn of the Screw*; there are other methods by which James extends and intensifies his meaning and strikes more deeply into the reader's consciousness. Chief of these is a highly suggestive and even symbolic language which permeates the entire story. After I had become aware of and begun to investigate this phenomenon, I found Mr. Matthiessen, in quite fortuitous corroboration of my own critical method, commenting on the same technical aspect of James' later works—his ability to "bind together his imaginative effects by subtly recurrent images of a thematic kind" and to "extend a metaphor into a symbol," and the fact that later in his career "realistic details had become merely the covering for a content that was far from realistic." In *The Turn* there is a great deal of recurrent imagery which powerfully influences the tone and the meaning of the story; the story becomes, indeed, a dramatic poem, and to read it properly one must assess the role of the language precisely as one would if public form of the work were poetic. For by his iterative imagery and by the very unobtrusive management of symbols, which in the organic work cofunction with the language, James has severely qualified the bare narrative; and, if he has not defined the evil which, as he specified, was to remain at the level of suggestion, he has at least set forth the mode and the terms of its operation with unrecognized fullness.

For a mature reader it is hardly necessary to insist that the center of horror is not the apparitions themselves, though their appearances are worked out with fine uniqueness, but is the children, and our sense of what is happening to them. What is happening to them is Quint and Jessel; the governess' awareness of the apparitions is her awareness of a change within the children; the shock of ghostly appearances is the shock of evil perceived unexpectedly, suddenly, after it has secretly made inroads. Matthiessen and R. P. Blackmur both refer, as a matter of course, to the corruption of the children; E. M. W. Tillyard, in a volume on Shakespeare, remarks incidentally that James "owes so much of the power with which evil is conveyed to showing it in the minds of children; where it should least be found." Perhaps two modern phenomena, the sentimentalizing of children and the disinclination to concede to evil any status more profound than the melodramatic, account for a frequent unwillingness to accept what the story says. James is not disposed to make things easier; he emphasizes that it is the incorruptible who have taken on corruption. He introduces no mere pathos of childhood catastrophe; his are not ordinary children. He is at pains to give them a special quality — by repetition which in so careful an artist can hardly have been a clumsy accident. As the repeated words achieve a cumulative tonal force, we can see the working of the poetic imagination.

Flora has "extraordinary charm," is "most beautiful." Miles is "incredibly beautiful." Both have "the bloom of health and happiness." Miles is "too fine and fair" for the world; he is a "beautiful little boy." The governess is "dazzled by their loveliness." They are "most loveable" in their "helplessness." Touching their "fragrant faces" one could believe only "their incapacity and their beauty." Miles is a "prodigy of delightful, loveable goodness." In midstory Flora still emerges from concealment "rosily," and one is caught by "the golden glow of her curls," by her "loveliest, eagerest simplicity," by "the excess of something beautiful that shone out of the blue" of her eyes, by "the lovely little lighted face." In both, "beauty and amiability, happiness and cleverness" are still paramount. Miles has still the "wonderful smile" and the "beautiful eye" of "a little fairy prince." Both write letters "too beautiful to be posted." On the final Sunday the governess sees still Miles' "beautiful face" and talks of him as "beautiful and perfect"; he smiles at her "with the same loveliness" and spars verbally with "serenity" and "unimpeachable gaiety." Even after Flora is gone, Miles is "the beautiful little presence" as yet with "neither stain nor shadow"; his expression is "the most beautiful" the governess has ever known.

James devotes an almost prodigal care to creating an impression of special beauty in the children, an impression upon which depends the extraordinary effectiveness of the change which takes place in them. In such children the appearance of any imperfection is a shock. The shock is emphasized when the governess wonders whether she must "pronounce their loveliness a trick of premature cunning" and reflects upon the possibility that "the immediate charm . . . was studied"; when Miles' "sweet face" must be described as a "sweet ironic face"; when his "happy laugh" goes off into "incoherent, extravagant song"; and when, above all, the governess must declare with conviction that their "more than earthly beauty, their absolutely unnatural goodness is a game . . . a policy and a fraud." Is James, then, laboriously overusing the principle of contrast, clothing the children with an astonishing fascination merely to accentuate the shock of their being stripped bare? Obviously not. Beneath the superficial clash we can already sense a deeper paradox. When James speaks of Miles' "beautiful fevered face" and says that he "lives in a setting of beauty and misery," he puts into words what the reader has already come to feel—that his real subject is the dual nature of man, who is a little lower than the angels, and who yet can become a slave in the realm of evil. The children's beauty, we have come to feel, is a symbol of the spiritual perfection of which man is capable. Thus the battle between the governess and the demons becomes the old struggle of the morality play in a new dress.

But that statement of the struggle is much more general and abstract than the formulation of it made by the story itself. When James speaks of "any clouding of their innocence," he reminds us again of a special quality in their beauty which he has quietly stressed with almost thematic fullness. The *clouding* suggests a *change* in a characteristic brightness of theirs, a brightness of which we are made aware by a recurrent imagery of light. Flora, at the start, "brightly" faces the new governess; hers is a "radiant" image; the children "dazzle" the governess; Flora has "a lovely little lighted face," and she considers "luminously"; in his "brightness" Miles "fairly glittered"; he speaks "radiantly"; at his "revolution" he speaks with "extraordinary brightness." This light-giving quality of theirs is not a mere amplification of a charm shockingly to be destroyed; it is difficult not to read it as a symbol of their being, as it were, at the dawn of existence. For they are children, and their radiance suggests the primal and the universal. This provisional interpretation is supported by another verbal pattern which James uses to describe the children. Miles has a "great glow of freshness," a "positive fragrance of purity," a "sweetness of innocence"; the governess comments again on the "rose-flush of his innocence"; in him she finds something "extraordinarily happy, that . . . struck me as beginning anew each day"; he could draw upon "reserves of goodness." Then, as things change, the governess remarks, on one occasion, that "He couldn't play any longer at innocence," and mentions, on another, his pathetic struggles to "play . . . a part of innocence."

To the emphasis upon beauty, then, is added this emphasis upon brightness and freshness and innocence. What must come across to us, from such a context, is echoes of the Garden of Eden; we have the morality play story, as we have said, but altered, complemented, and given unique poignance by being told of mankind at its first radical crisis, in consequence of which all other morality stories are; Miles and Flora become the childhood of the race. They are symbolic children as the ghosts are symbolic ghosts. Even the names themselves have a representative quality as those of James' characters often do: Miles—the soldier, the archetypal male; Flora—the flower, the essential female. Man and woman are caught even before the first hint of maturity, dissected, and shown to have within them all the seeds—possible of full growth even now—of their own destruction.

James' management of the setting and of other ingredients in the drama deepens one's sense of a story at once primeval and eternal, lurking beneath the surface of the action. Bly itself is almost an Eden with its "lawn and bright flowers"; the governess comments, "The scene had a greatness . . ." Three times James writes of the "golden" sky, and one unconsciously recalls that Flora was a "rosy sprite" with "hair of gold." Miss Jessel first appears "in the garden," where "the old trees, the thick shrubbery, made a great and pleasant shade." Here, for a time, the three "lived in a cloud of music and love"; the children are "extraordinarily at one" in "their quality of sweetness." Now it is significant that James uses even the seasons to heighten his drama: the pastoral idyl begins in June, when spring is at the full, and then is gradually altered until we reach the dark ending of a November whose coldness and deadness are unobtrusively but unmistakably stressed. ". . . the autumn had dropped . . . and blown out half our lights" (a variation of the light pattern); the governess now notices "grey sky and withered garlands," "bared spaces and scattered leaves." What might elsewhere be Gothic trimming is here disciplined by the pattern. When, on the final Sunday night, the governess tries hard to "reach" Miles, there is "a great wind"; she hears "the lash of rain and the batter of the gusts"; at the climax there is "an extraordinary blast and chill," and then darkness. The next afternoon is "damp and grey." After Flora's final escapade at the pond, James stresses the governess' feelings at the end of the day; the evening is "portentous" without precedent; she blows out the candles and feels a "mortal coldness." On the final day with Miles she notices "the stupid shrubs," "the dull things of November," "the dim day." So it is not merely the end of a year but the end of a cycle: the spring of gay, bright human innocence has given way to the dark autumn — or, as we might pun, to the dark *fall*.

And in the darkness of the latter end of things we might note the special development of the light which, to the sensitive governess, the children seem actually to give off. It is, I think, more than a coincidence that, when the governess mentions Miss

Jessel, Flora's face shows a "quick, smitten glare," and that, in the final scene, Miles is twice said to be "glaring"—the same verb which has been used to describe Quint's look. All three characters, of course, look with malevolence; yet *glare* must suggest, also, a hard, powerful, ugly light—an especially effective transformation of the apparently benign luminousness of the spring.

The same movement of human experience James portrays in still another symbolic form. As the light changes and the season changes and the children's beauty becomes ambiguous, another alteration takes place in them. Their youth, of course, is the prime datum of the story, and of it we are ever conscious; and at the same time we are aware of a strange maturity in them—in, for instance, their poise, their controlled utilization of their unusual talents to give pleasure. Our sense of something that transcends their youth is first defined overtly late in the story when the governess speaks of her feeling that Miles is "accessible as an older person." Though she does not speak of change, there is subtly called forth in us a conviction that years have been added to Miles. So we are not surprised when the governess assures Mrs. Grose, and goes out of her way, a little later, to remind her of the assurance, that, at meetings with Miss Jessel, Flora is "not a child" but "an old, old woman"—an insight that receives a measure of authentication, perhaps, by its reminiscence of the Duessa motif.

The suggestion that Flora has become older is skillfully conveyed, in the pond scene, by her silence (and silence itself has an almost symbolic value throughout the story), by her quick recovery of her poised gaiety, and especially by the picture of her peeping at the governess over the shoulder of Mrs. Grose, who is embracing her—the first intimation of a cold adult calculatingness which appears in all her remaining actions. The governess says, "her incomparable childish beauty had suddenly failed, had quite vanished . . . she was literally . . . hideously, hard; she had turned common and almost ugly." Mrs. Grose sums up, "It has made her, every inch of her, quite old." More effective, however, than any of this direct presentation of vital change is a delicate symbol which may pass almost unnoticed: when she is discovered at the pond, Flora picks up, and drops a moment later, "a big, ugly spray of withered fern"—a quiet commentary on the passage of symbolic spring, on the spiritual withering that is the story's center. When, at the end of the scene, the governess looks "at the grey pool and its blank, haunted edge," we automatically recall "The sedge has withered from the lake"—the imagery used by Keats in his account of an ailing knight-at-arms in another bitter autumn.

Besides the drying of foliage and the coming of storms and darkness there is one other set of elements, loosely working together and heavy with implications, which suggest that this is a story of the decay of Eden. At Quint's first appearance Bly "had been stricken with death." After Miles' nocturnal exploit the governess utters a cliché that, under the influence of the context, becomes vigorously meaningful: "you . . . caught your death in the night air!" There are, further, some arresting details in the description of Quint: "His eyes are sharp, strange—awfully . . . rather small and very fixed. His mouth's wide, and his lips are thin . . ." These are unmistakably the characteristics of a snake. James is too fine an artist to allegorize the point, but, as he has shaped the story, the coming of Quint is the coming of the serpent into the little Eden that is Bly (both Miss Porter and Mr. Tate have noted other physical characteristics of Quint which traditionally belong to the devil). Quint's handsomeness and his borrowed finery, by which he apes the gentleman, suggest, perhaps, the specious plausibleness of the visitor in the Garden. As for the "fixed eyes": later we learn that Miss Jessel "only fixed the child" and that the apparition of Quint "fixed me exactly as it had fixed me from the tower and from the garden."

Of Quint's position at Bly Mrs. Grose says, "The master believed in him and placed him here because he was supposed not to be well and the country air so good for him." The master, in other words, has nourished a viper in his bosom. The secret influence upon Miles the governess describes as "poison," and at the very end she says that the demonic presence "filled the room like the taste of poison." In the first passage the governess equates "poison" with "secret precocity"; toward the end she emphasizes Miles' freedom and sorrowfully gives up "the fiction that I had anything more to teach him." Why is it a fiction? Because he already knew too much, because he had eaten of the fruit of the tree of knowledge? We have already been told of the "dark prodigy" by which "the imagination of all evil *had* been opened up to him," and his being "under some influence operating in his small intellectual life as a tremendous incitement."

We should not press such analogies too hard, or construct inflexible parables. Our business is rather to trace all the imaginative emanations that enrich the narrative, the associations and intimations by which it transcends the mere horror story and achieves its own kind of greatness. But by now it must be clear from the antipodal emphases of the story that James has an almost religious sense of the duality of man, and, as if to manifest an intention, he makes that sense explicit in terms broadly religious and even Christian. The image of Flora's "angelic beauty" is "beatific"; she has "the deep, sweet serenity . . . of one of Raphael's holy infants"; she has "placid heavenly eyes." In Miles there is "something divine that I have never found to the same degree in any child." In a mildly humorous context the children are called "cherubs." Seeing no signs of suffering from his school experience, the governess regards Miles as an "angel." Mrs. Grose imputes to Flora a "blessed innocence," and the governess surrenders to the children's "extraordinary childish grace"—a noun which in this patterned structure can hardly help being ambivalent. In midstory Flora has still a "divine smile"; both children remain "adorable." This verbal pattern, which is too consistent to be coincidental, irresistibly makes us think of the divine in man, of his capability of salvation. Now what is tragic and terrifying in man is that to be capable of salvation is to be capable also of damnation—an equivocal potentiality suggested early by the alternation of moods in the newly arrived governess, who senses immediately a kind of wavering, a waiting for determination, at Bly. And James, to present the spiritual decline of the children, finds terms which exactly balance those that connote their spiritual capabilities.

We are never permitted to see the apparitions except as moral realities. Miss Jessel is a figure of "unmistakable horror and evil . . . in black, pale and dreadful." She is a "horror of horrors," with "awful eyes," "with a kind of fury of intention," and yet "with extraordinary beauty." Again she is described as "Dark as midnight in her black dress, her haggard beauty, and her unutterable woe . . ." It is brilliant to give her beauty, which not only identifies her with Flora and thus underscores the dual possibilities that lie ahead of Flora, but also enriches the theme with its reminder of Milton's fallen angels who retain something of their original splendor—"the excess / Of glory obscured." So, with the repeated stress upon her woe, we almost expect the passage which tells us that she "suffers the torments . . . of the damned": she is both damned and an agent of damnation—another reminiscence of the Miltonic myth. She is called later a "pale and ravenous demon," not "an inch of whose evil . . . fell short"—which reminds us of James' prefatory insistence that the apparitions were to be thought of as demons. Again, she is "our infernal witness"; she and Quint are "those fiends"; "they were not angels," and they could be bringing "some yet more infernal message." "And to ply them with that evil still, to keep up the work of demons, is what brings the others back." They are "tempters," who work subtly by holding out fascinating "suggestions of danger." In the last scene Quint presents—the phrase is used twice—"his white face of damnation."

By this series of words, dispersed throughout the story yet combining in a general statement, James defines as diabolic the forces attacking the children of whose angelic part we are often reminded. Now these attacking forces, as often in Elizabethan drama, are seen in two aspects. Dr. Faustus has to meet an enemy which has an inner and an outer reality—his own thoughts, and Mephistopheles; James presents evil both as agent (the demons) and as effect (the transformation in the once fresh and beautiful and innocent children). The dualistic concept of reality appears most explicitly when Mrs. Grose asks, "And if he was so bad there as that comes to, how is he such an angel now?" and the governess replies, "Yes, indeed—and if he was a fiend at school!" by the *angel-fiend* antithesis James underscores what he sees as a central human contradiction, which he emphasizes throughout the book by his chosen verbal pattern. The governess speaks of the children's "love of evil" gained from Quint and Miss Jessel, of Miles' "wickedness" at school.

In such a context the use of the word *revolution* to describe Miles' final taking matters up with the governess—a move by which, we should remember, he becomes completely "free"—cannot help calling to mind the Paradise and Eden revolutions of Judaeo-Christian mythology. The revolutionary change in character is nicely set forth by the verbal counterpoint in one passage. "He found the most divine little way," the governess says, "to keep me quiet while she went off." " 'Divine'?" Mrs. Grose asks, and the governess replies, "Infernal then!" The divine has paradoxically passed into the infernal. Then we see rapidly the completed transition in Flora: she turns upon the governess an expression of "hard, fixed gravity" and ignores the "hideous plain presence" of Miss Jessel—"a stroke that somehow converted the little girl herself into the very presence that could make me quail." In Miles, by contrast, we see a protracted struggle, poignantly conveyed by a recurrent metaphor of illness. Early in the story Miles is in "the bloom of health and happiness," but near the end he seems like a "wistful patient in a children's hospital," "like a convalescent slightly fatigued." At the end he shows "bravery" while "flushing with pain"; he gives "a sick little headshake"; his is a "beautiful fevered face." But the beauty goes, the fever gains; Miles gives "a frantic little shake for air and light"; he is in a "white rage." The climax of his disease, the binding together of all the strands we have been tracing, is his malevolent cry to the governess—"you devil!" It is his final transvaluation of values: she who would be his savior has become for him a demon. His face gives a "convulsive supplication"—that is, actually, a prayer, for and to Quint, the demon who has become his total deity. But the god isn't there, and Miles despairs and dies. We need not labor the dependence of this brilliant climax upon the host of associations and evocations by which, as this outline endeavors to show, James prepares us for the ultimate resolution of the children's being.

There are glimmerings of other imaginative kinships, such as that already mentioned, the Faustian. Miles' "You devil" is in one way almost identical with Faustus's savage attack, in Marlowe's play, upon the Old Man who has been trying to save him; indeed James' story, in its central combat, is not unlike the Faustus story as it might be told by the Good Angel. But whereas Dr. Faustus is a late intellectualist version of Everyman, James, as we have said, weaves in persuasive hints, one after another, of mankind undergoing, in his Golden Age, an elemental conflict; thus we have the morality play, but in a complicated, enriched, and intensified version. When the governess first sees Quint, she is aware of "some challenge between us"; the next time it seems "as if I had been looking at him for years and had known him always"; near the end she says, "I *was* . . . face to face with the elements," and, of the final scene, "It was like fighting with a demon for a human soul."

What, then, does the story say about the role of the governess, and how does this contribute to the complex of the impressions built up in part by James' language? From the start the words used by the governess suggest that James is attaching to her the quality of savior, not only in a general sense, but with certain Christian associations. She uses words like "atonement"; she speaks of herself as an "expiatory victim," of her "pure suffering," and at various times—twice in the final scene—of her "torment." Very early she plans to "shelter my pupils," to "absolutely save" them; she speaks variously of her "service," "to protect and defend the little creatures . . . bereaved . . . loveable." When she fears that she cannot "save or shield them" and that "they're lost," she is a "poor protectress." At another time she is a "sister of charity" attempting to "cure" Miles. But by now what we cannot mistake is the relation of pastor and flock, a relationship which becomes overt when the governess tells Miles, "I just want you to help me to save you." It is in this sense that the governess "loves" Miles—a loving which must not be confused, as it is confused by some critics, with "making love to" or "being in love with" him. Without such pastoral love no guardian would consider his flock worth the sacrifice.

The governess' priestly function is made still more explicit by the fact that she comes ultimately to act as confessor and to use every possible means to bring Miles to confession; the long final scene really takes place in the confessional, with the governess as priest endeavoring, by both word and gesture, to protect her charge against the evil force whose invasion has, with consummate irony, carried even there. In one sense the governess must elicit confession because, in her need for objective reassurance, she will not take the lead as accuser; but securing the confession is, more importantly, a mitigation of Miles' own pride, his self-will; it could soften him, make him accessible to grace. The experience has a clear sacramental quality: the governess says that Miles senses "the need of confession . . . he'll confess. If he confesses, he's saved." It is when he begins to break and confess that "the white face of damnation" becomes baffled and at a vital moment retreats; but it returns "as if to blight his confession," and it is in part through the ineptitude of the governess-confessor-savior, we are led to understand, that Miles is lost.

It is possible that there are even faint traces of theological speculation to give additional substance to the theme of salvation and damnation which finally achieves specific form in the sacramentalism of the closing scenes. Less than halfway through the story the governess refers to the children thus: "blameless and foredoomed as they were." By *blameless* she can only mean that she does not have direct, tangible evidence of voluntary evildoing on their part; they still look charming and beautiful; she does not have grounds for a positive placing of blame. Why, then, *foredoomed?* May this not be a suggestion of original sin (which Miss Porter has already seen as an ingredient in the story), an interpretation consistent with the view of Bly as a kind of Eden?

ROBERT BECHTOLD HEILMAN

Three quarters of the way through the story the governess again turns to speculation: ". . . I constantly both attacked and renounced the enigma of what such a little gentleman could have done that deserved a penalty." *Enigma* is perhaps just the word to be applied to a situation, of which one technical explication is the doctrine of original sin, by an inquiring lay mind with a religious sense but without precise theological tools. What is significant is that the governess does not revolt against the penalty as if it betokened a cosmic injustice. And original sin, whether it be natural depravity or a revolt in a heavenly or earthly paradise, fits exactly into the machinery of this story of two beautiful children who in a lovely springtime of existence already suffer, not unwillingly, hidden injuries which will eventually destroy them.

This summary of the imaginative overtones in *The Turn of the Screw* has taken us rather deeply into a view of the book as strongly religious in cast. Yet this very moving impression is produced by agencies that quietly penetrate the story, not by devices that stick out of it, so to speak, and become commanding guideposts. There are no old familiar signs announcing a religious orientation of experience. There is nothing of the Bible overtly; there are no texts, no clergymen; there are no conventional indexes of religious feeling—no invocations or prayers or meditations; all there is is a certain amount of church-going of a very matter-of-fact sort, and otherwise the context is ostensibly secular. Thus the story becomes no bland preachment; it simply "has life"—to use James' criterion of excellence—and it is left to us to define the boundaries and extensions and reverberations of that life. Right where we might expect the most positive assistance, perhaps, in seeking that definition, we find least. Yet even in a few dry and casual ecclesiastical mementos we sense some ever-so-mild symbolic pressures, as of a not-very-articulate wispish presence that quietly makes itself felt.

These intimations of a presence should not be magnified into a solid "character" who demands our attention. But in their small way they collaborate with other intimations. The reading of the story, for instance, takes place during the Christmas season; the framework action begins on Christmas Eve. Quint appears for the second time on a Sunday, a gray, rainy Sunday, just before the governess is about to go to the late church service with Mrs. Grose; after that she is, she says, "not fit for church"; and their only service is then "a little service of tears and vows, of prayers and promises . . ." This is the important occasion on which Mrs. Grose identifies the apparition with Quint. As the governess reflects on the situation, she speaks of the "inconceivable communion" of which she has learned—a Black Mass, as it were. The event next in importance to the identification of Quint also occurs on a Sunday—Miles' "revolution." Miles and the governess are "within sight of the church"; she thinks "with envy" of the "almost spiritual help of the hassock." After they enter the churchyard gate, Miles detains her "by a low, oblong, table-like tomb"—a reminder that Bly was "stricken with death" on the first appearance of Quint. Then Miles threatens to bring his uncle down, and it is he, with fine irony, who "marched off alone into church," while the governess can only walk "round the church" and listen "to the sounds of worship." Here, for once, what we may call the Christian apparatus is out in the open, with a clear enough ironic function.

From this we go on to the most tantalizing body of suggestion in the whole book, less a body than a wraith, indeed, and yet the more urgent for its not falling within the every-day commonplaces of fictional method. Miles' revolution introduces a straight-line action which continues with remarkably increasing tension to the end of the story. James allots forty percent of his total space to this action, which—and here is the notable point—takes only three days. Thus he puts the heaviest emphasis on those three days—Sunday, Monday, and Tuesday. During those three days the governess, the clergyman's daughter, undertakes her quasi-priestly function with a new intensity and aggressiveness. On Sunday night she enters upon a newly determined, if still cautious, effort to bring Miles to confession; she openly asserts her role as savior. On Monday she tries to shock Flora into spiritual pliability—and fails. All her will to redeem, she now

turns upon Miles; in the final scene she fights the adversary directly. She succeeds to an extent: Miles cannot see Quint. But the
end of the climactic triduum of her ordeal as savior is failure:
Quint comes again, as if to "blight" Miles' confession; Miles still
cannot see him—and dies.

The would-be redeemer of the living is called "devil"; in Quint
we see one who has risen again to tempt the living to destruction
—that is, the resurrection and the death. Here, Sunday does not
triumphantly end a symbolic ordeal that had begun in apparent
failure on Friday; rather it hopefully initiates a struggle which is
to end, on the third day, in bitter loss. We have, then, a modern
late-fall defeat patterned on the ancient springtide victory. To
transmit its quality and to embrace all of its associations, may
we not call it a Black Easter?

If this interpretation will hold up, it will crown the remarkable associational edifice which is both a part of and an extension
of the dramatic structure of the story, an edifice which figures
forth man's duality, his living, so to speak, as a potentiality which
may be fulfilled or may paradoxically be transformed into its
radical opposite. This we are told, by implication, through the
beauty which can become ugliness, the brightness which becomes
darkness, the innocence which can become sophistication, the
spring which becomes fall, the youth which becomes age, the
Eden which can be stricken with death, the angelic which becomes diabolic; and through the pictured capacity, whether it be
understood as original sin or otherwise, for revolt, for transvaluation of values, for denial of the agency of salvation. And this
truth comes to us with peculiar shock because we see enacted,
not that imperceptible movement by which man's advance in
age and in corruption becomes endurable, but the transformation
from one extreme to the other in pure state, in essence, in symbolic immediacy. In this poem about evil, youth is age.

James deliberately chose to omit certain matters from his narrative statement. But in his poetic statement he has elaborated
upon his story and given adequate clues to the metaphysical
foundations of his plot. The universality which has stimulated

many critics is the Christian dualism of good and evil; this substance James has projected by poetic method into numerous details of symbolic language and action of which the implications may, in their subtlety, almost be missed. For, like all poetic statements, James' is not direct; even in prose medium it eschews a conventional prose logic; it endows his tale with an atmosphere in which we sense the pressure of so much more imaginative force than meets the casual fiction-reading eye. In attempting to state schematically the origins of that pressure, we fall into much more blunt statements than we ought to make. We say, too forthrightly, that Bly "becomes" a Garden of Eden. As in studying all good poetry, we must resist the impulse to line up, on a secondary level of meaning, exact equivalents for the narrative elements, for such procedure stems from the rude assumption that every part of the story is a precision-tooled cog in an allegorical machine. But we must be sensitive to parallels, analogies, intimations; thus, while preserving the fullness and flexibility of the work, we can investigate its extraordinarily moving tonal richness. And in accounting for tone we necessarily move toward a definition of structure. The verbal and imagistic patterns which have been described do not have the structural finality that they would have in lyric verse. Yet these patterns, which overlap and interfuse in a way badly obscured by the clumsy analytical process, are unquestionably important in the formation of the story and the qualifying of its meaning; they are one of the ways in which the esemplastic imagination, as Coleridge called it, works; and they collaborate closely with the larger structural units—the parts of the narrative as such—in defining this version of the struggle between good and evil.

⊷§ WARREN BECK

For Virginia Woolf

It has sometimes been suggested that Virginia Woolf, in her avowed concern with consciousness as an "incessant shower of innumerable atoms" and in her emphasis on introspection's momentary phenomena, separated her narratives from the main currents of modern life. *Between the Acts* has revived that notion; a few judges find in her last book new support for the anomalous opinion that its author was a great artist, but insignificant. This paradox confesses the difficulty of discerning throughout her shimmering pages any dramatic flow, any progressive overt events involving values of wide concern at present. But though her visions of reality's "luminous halo" have baffled many whom they also fascinate, perhaps *Between the Acts* will draw some readers closer, by demonstrating that introspectiveness in her novels was not willfully esoteric or uncritically glorified, and that she did interrelate subjective individualism and the social order.

In the range of her complete work her last novel seems eminent, dealing in a masterful way with some of the most insistent and difficult contemporary material. The reconsideration of her earlier books which it induces should disclose within their incandescence a similar wiry strength. Virginia Woolf's preoccupation with sensibility has not been an immersion in it. She tried to judge the

NOTE. Reprinted from *American Prefaces,* 1942, by permission of the editors caprices of self-conscious mind as a historical fact, the fruit of renaissance and romanticism, and perhaps also of inexplicable growth in its own due time; she considered these perplexing data now laid on the table by many of those absorbed in social and political problems. In *Orlando*, that dynamic fantasia on the history of England's spirit, Virginia Woolf showed awareness of mutation and specialization in the mind's response to environment; in *Mrs. Dalloway* she made a comprehensive ironic study of modern sensibility, on the two levels of the protected and privileged Mrs. Dalloway's self-indulgence and the shell-shocked veteran's agonizing disintegration. *Between the Acts* amalgamates the themes of both *Orlando* and *Mrs. Dalloway* and explores them further with reference to some typical English people's personal and social status at the outbreak of the second world war.

The issues in this latest novel are new; now no Mrs. Dalloway is exempt from war's shocks, direct and indirect, and if these prove unbearable to cultivated sensibilities, then this England's history may have reached its terminus, Orlando may collapse; or if England endures, then her spirit may pass through modifications even more drastic than the metmorphosis from masculine to feminine which overtook Orlando at the beginning of the eighteenth century. However, *Between the Acts* is far from implying that such adaptations will eliminate the free play of association and sallies of the stream of consciousness. Though Mrs. Dalloway's mental caprices are shown within a milieu that the war has all but destroyed and that the projected peace may not largely restore, they merely take a coloration from her environment, and they show a developed function of intelligence which is not likely to lapse under new political and economic conditions, however painful the transition. This vibrancy of the fancy, this glow of consciousness, is indicated as an emergent human characteristic by its complementary representation in Septimus; his fate is the reverse of Mrs. Dalloway's, by the accident of circumstance, but the two temperaments are of the same metal. If Virginia Woolf doubted the power of either given type to survive as personalities, no matter what happened to individuals among them and no matter what changes overtook their respective classes—if she had fears that the earth was to be inherited by a new race of automatons, impervious to all but authorized and certified stimuli, and incapable of mental vagrancy—she must have put those fears aside, when, with the bombs already falling on England and with Englishmen of all classes uniting to defend personal freedom, she wrote her final testimony.

Between the Acts is a prismatic book, sharply faceted, receiving light from many aspects and refracting the actual into the prophetic. The historical pageant at the Olivers' country house, performed by the villagers and attended by the county aristocrats, extends the narrative in two temporal dimensions: a contemporary cross-section, audience and actors; and an antiquarian fathoming, the theatricals. This alone, as Virginia Woolf executed it, would make a substantial and persuasive novel. In addition, *Between the Acts* persistently moves in a third dimension, the subjective, tracing in several persons the quicksilver flow, the dispersion and association, of introspective consciousness. This material is not only the peculiar product of Virginia Woolf's temperament and her artistic flair; it yields the essence of the book, incorporating a rational view of the reflective individual's present confusion and vulnerability and adumbrating a hope for his survival and further integration. As in *Mrs. Dalloway,* so in this story acute self-consciousness is persistent in widely different characters; but none of these persons in *Between the Acts* is completely overset by his own imaginings, and each has approximated a not too precarious equilibrium, sufficiently responsive to the stresses even of the summer of 1939.

The key characters seem to be three, all women. They are of different ages, stations, temperaments, and purposes, yet their composite projects a symbol. In old Mrs. Swithin, in Mrs. Giles Oliver (Isa), and in Miss LaTrobe there are certainly reflections of the mind of Virginia Woolf herself, but this is not to say that the book is autobiographical in substance or intention. Rather it is fundamentally historical and sociological, representing the English between the acts of appeasement and war, and tracing down the roots of traditional English attitude then being subjected to disturbing strains. Virginia Woolf, besides being highly endowed with the sensitivity she studied in all her novels, was in her culture a complex end-product of English tendencies; and so from different aspects of her consciousness and inclinations she could conceive the several contemporaneous key characters of *Between the Acts,* and through them could epitomize England's ordeal and England's hope. For certainly it is relevant to the modern political tragedy that sensibilities have exceeded resoluteness; and yet the experienced cannot turn from finer psychological ramifications, but must project a social assertion not incompatible with a free, intense personal sensitivity, a fifth freedom implementing the elementary four. This is the problem examined in *Between the Acts,* through the three key characters, each an example of sensibility, and all of them together suggestive of English society's complex mood and motivation.

Old Mrs. Swithin is a Victorian relict, and an aristocrat in whom leisure has allowed reverie to become a kind of profession. Her mind, called vagrant, is like a butterfly, seemingly fragile and even awkward in erratic flight, but forever searching out hidden sweets, and hanging over them poised yet intense, in a mellow illusion of timeless light. In her is crystalline a spirit latent in most of those who, like Virginia Woolf, came of age before 1914, in the autumn of ripeness of a completed period in England's growth. Aware of the past, of history and drastic evolutions not only biological but social, Mrs. Swithin is also religious in a timidly hopeful Tennysonian way, but her chief bent is a nostalgic retrospection. Her politeness to her servants had as counterpart an unexamined faith in the proposition that men's and women's various stations in life are those to which it has pleased God to call them, some at sixteen pounds a year. She was of the generation which doubted Mrs. Manresa's social eligibility because no one knew her family, and when Mrs. Manresa sometimes "referred to an uncle, a Bishop," they were not much reassured, because "he was thought to have been a Colonial Bishop only." Yet Mrs. Swithin's breeding shows positively when she takes the strange unhappy young man William on a tour of the house, and by a lively kindness makes him feel for the moment "healed, made whole."

Her nephew's wife, Isa Oliver, the second of these three women seemingly indicative of elements in the English mind, cannot retreat into her own past, or further still into history. Isa is only as old as the century, thirty-nine, and she feels the future disturbing, shadowing the present. William speaks for her of "the doom of sudden death hanging over us," and says "there's no retreating and advancing." In this impasse Isa, though married and having two children, is dissatisfied and yearning. The murmur of her restless mind talking to itself goes on even as she moves among other people. Thus she is seen during the pageant's intermission:

"What delicious tea!" each exclaimed, disgusting though it was, like rust boiled in water, and the cake fly-blown. But they had a duty to society . . .

The barn filled. Fumes rose. China clattered; voices chattered. Isa pressed her way to the table.

"Dispersed are we," she murmured. And held her cup out to be filled. She took it. "Let me turn away," she murmured, turning "from the array"—she looked desolately round her—"of china faces, glazed and hard. Down the ride, that leads under the nut tree and the may tree, away, till I come to the wishing well, where the washer-woman's little boy—" she dropped sugar, two lumps, into her tea, "dropped a pin. He got his horse, so they say. But what wish should I drop into the well?" She looked round. She could not see the man in grey, the gentleman farmer; nor anyone known to her. "That the waters should cover me," she added, "of the wishing well."

The vague frustrate desire, the dreamy sense of impotence, and the morbid death-wish all are characteristic of the lost generation everywhere, but especially in England, where the stress between cultivated idealisms and imposed evils apparently has been most extreme. So sensitive and responsive an intellect as Virginia Woolf's must have known melancholy like Isa's, and must have formulated it, as Isa constantly does, in an extravagantly elegiac vein. In Virginia Woolf's comprehension, as well as in the generic

English mind this book seems to silhouette, such musings could have coincided with Victorian retrospections like Mrs. Swithin's. The daughter of Sir Leslie Stephen, with a child's familiar access to his eminent serene circle, became one of the advanced Bloomsbury set; and furthermore she led out independently in developing the newest narrative devices for expressing the war generation's troubled self-consciousness. These heirs of all the ages must have found their endowment peculiarly confusing and irksome; the conventionalized optimism and specious equilibrium of late-Victorian life had been left further behind, by more violent reaction, than is usually the experience of a second and third generation. Seldom have children's teeth been more severely set on edge, and seldom has agnosticism been more melancholy. Expression of that emotional experience has been incumbent upon modern fiction. Thus in representing minute and ephemeral apperceptions, even those most characteristic of a socially regressive Victorian minority and a flaccid barren generation of waste-land wanderers, Virginia Woolf often has been more realistic and more cognizant of crucial issues than some judgments of her have acknowledged.

And Virginia Woolf knew far more than Mrs. Swithin's capricious retrospection and Isa Oliver's lyrical involution. She was a gifted literary artist, and perhaps the strongest strand in her complex character was the creative, the visionary, as *Between the Acts* exemplifies it in Miss LaTrobe, the pageant's author and director. Miss LaTrobe is neither a complacent nor a resigned person; her professional anxieties bring out something acid and recalcitrant in her nature, that can resolve itself only in creative assertion. While audience and actors both relax during the intermission for tea, she frets, thinking, "Curse! Blast! Damn 'em! . . . she had agreed to cut the play here; a slave to her audience . . . Just as she had brewed emotion, and spilt it . . ." Her rage turns against herself too. "She hadn't made them see it. It was a failure, another damned failure! As usual. Her vision escaped her." But she is reassured by Mrs. Swithin's tribute, proffered between scenes. Though they failed "in a common effort to bring a common meaning to birth," when Mrs. Swithin, "laying hold desperately of a fraction of her meaning, said: 'What a small part I've had to play! But you've made me feel I could have played Cleopatra!' " Miss LaTrobe thinks to herself, "You've stirred in me my unacted part," and sees herself as "not merely a twitcher of individual strings," but as "one who seethes wandering bodies and floating voices in a cauldron, and makes rise up from its amorphous mass a recreated world."

The encounter between these different women suggests a rapprochement of diverse elements in the English mind, moving toward the further realization of human potentialities, the proper concern today of citizen and artist alike. The grounds of that agreement and a charter for the new England are indicated by the resolute Miss LaTrobe's drastic last scene. The program names it "The Present Time. Ourselves." The audience is purposely kept waiting; finally they are shown a wall partly built, a man and a woman working—civilization in ruins, being reconstructed by human effort. But then to a jangling tune on the phonograph all the players rush out, bearing mirrors which they hold to reflect the audience—themselves, the present. Through a megaphone a voice speaks:

Let's . . . consider ourselves. Ourselves. Some bony. Some fat. Liars most of us. Thieves too. The poor are as bad as the rich are. Perhaps worse . . . Look at ourselves, ladies and gentlemen! Then at the wall; and ask how's this wall, the great wall, which we call, perhaps miscall, civilization, to be built by scraps, orts, and fragments like ourselves?

Yet, the voice goes on,

there's something to be said: for our kindness to the cat; note too in today's paper "Dearly loved by his wife"; and the impulse which leads us—mark you, when no one's looking—to the window at midnight to smell the bean. Or the resolute refusal of some pimpled dirty little scrub in sandals to sell his soul.

Can't we tell what this quality is in human nature, the voice asks? Can we see no reflections of ourselves better than scraps and fragments? Then listen, says the voice; and the phonograph plays—

. . . was it Bach, Handel, Beethoven, Mozart or nobody famous?

. . . Like quicksilver sliding, filing magnetized, the distracted united. The tune began; the first note meant a second; the second a third. Then down beneath a force was born in opposition; then another. On different levels they diverged. On different levels they went forward; flower gathering some on the surface; others descending to wrestle with the meaning; but all comprehending, all enlisted. The whole population of the mind's immeasurable profundity came flocking . . .

Was that voice ourselves? Scraps, orts, and fragments, are we, also, that? The voice died away.

But although at the last she has held and swayed her audience, Miss LaTrobe, in an agony of reaction, has hidden after the pageant's close.

"A failure," she groaned, and stooped to put away the records.

Then suddenly the starlings attacked the tree behind which she had hidden. In one flock they pelted it like so many winged stones. The whole tree hummed with the whizz they made, as if each bird plucked a wire. A whizz, a buzz rose from the bird-buzzing, bird-vibrant, bird-blackened tree. The tree became a rhapsody, a quivering cacophony, a whizz and vibrant rapture, branches, leaves, birds syllabling discordant life, life, life, without measure, without stop devouring the tree. Then up! Then off!

Now as the landscape grew dark, "it was land merely, no land in particular." As Miss LaTrobe looked at it, "something rose to the surface."

"I should group them," she murmured, "here." It would be midnight; there would be two figures, half concealed by a rock. The curtain would rise. What would the first words be? The words escaped her.

But inspiration is not forever evasive; later as she sat alone musing in the bar, no longer seeing the villagers around her, yet "upheld" by them, she remembered how the starlings pelted the tree, and "she heard the first words."

Miss LaTrobe's continued creativity, troubled and tentative on the verge of a mysterious future, parallels a moment from Isa's life at the close of the book, and thus is achieved a further amalgamation of the three women's experiences into a composite symbol. As Isa and her husband sit alone silent after the older

Olivers have retired, Isa feels their enmity bared, but also their love, and knows that they will quarrel and then embrace, perhaps to produce a new life, "in the heart of darkness, in the fields of night." And thus the book ends:

Isa let her sewing drop. The great hooded chairs had become enormous. And Giles too. And Isa too against the window. The window was all sky without color. The house had lost its shelter. It was night before roads were made, or houses. It was the night that dwellers in caves had watched from some high place among rocks.

Then the curtain rose. They spoke.

One reviewer has egregiously complained that the story ended here where it should have begun. But certainly the scene on which that curtain rises has been sufficiently implied, and is moreover of infinite extent, that no book could fully render—their lives went on, and from them and people like them, torn between love and hate, at once selfish and social, moving through shadows across the trackless illimitable unknown of human existence, comes new life, new generation.

Personality in its typical modern constitution may often be isolate and tangential, yet in all creativity there is approach and mutuality. Thus the three variously imaginative women in the foreground of this story merge into a configuration of England's complex spirit, the English mind vagrant and backward-looking, eccentric in ancient pieties and arbitrary habits, like Mrs. Swithin's—the English mind choked with subtle, imperious emotion, like Isa's, involved in duty and privilege, and confused between affection and distaste—the English mind, like Miss LaTrobe's, speculative, sensitive to the inspiration of the hour, often hesitant and fumbling, yet persistently progressive, and unable to live without vision.

However political, economic, theological, and esthetic compulsions may have operated to evolve Orlando through four changing centuries, Orlando as she now stands has a mind of her own, and that mind is in itself a fact, and will be a force, perhaps a decisive one. If in that mind a degree of self-regard and vagrancy of association are the natural complements of creativity, then sensibility is not just a Victorian indulgence in an artifice, it is an element of human psychology and therefore an insistent and even crucial factor in contemporary problems. Certain of sensibility's bents may be discredited, but not sensibility itself. To discount it is not merely to display a puritanical abashment before the facts of life; it is to abet those forces which seek to discredit mind, to dispossess rationality, and by discouraging further freedoms and refinements of consciousness to circumscribe personality and hamper imagination.

To probe the innermost layers of mentation and to describe its persistent characteristics as Virginia Woolf has done in all her novels is certainly as realistic as the method of hard-boiled, dead-pan objectivity; to relate the flow of individual consciousness to large political and social contours of the past and present as Virginia Woolf has done in her last novel is certainly as realistic as narration from the viewpoint of an extreme proletarian sentimentality. Nor is the fictional panoramic anything more than so much scenery unless it includes modes of being and uncovers springs of individual action. Comprehensiveness in the novel demands not only sociological but psychological dimensions, such as those achieved in *Between the Acts,* with its combination of breadth and depth that is almost magical in a work so delicately rendered. The graceful and splendid architectonics of this novel, its scope and incisiveness, its concentration of the essential out of the ephemeral — these qualities are too frequently overlooked in all Virginia Woolf's work on the presupposition that her method is eccentric and its results of no social significance. Meanwhile in many a page of lucid criticism she has written her own defense, not intentionally, much less in controversy, but as a spontaneous expression of her tastes and her philosophy, as in these sentences from "Notes on an Elizabethan Play":

We are not so purblind as to suppose that a man because his name is Smith and he lives at Liverpool is therefore "real." We know indeed that this reality is a chameleon quality, the fantastic becoming as we grow used to it often the closest to the truth, the sober the furthest from it, and nothing proving a writ-

er's greatness more than his capacity to consolidate his scene by
the use of what, until he touched them, seemed wisps of cloud
and threads of gossamer.

The scenes of her last novel are indeed consolidated out of very
tenuous stuff, yet that rendition, seemingly to the careless glance
so evanescent and perhaps even trifling, becomes in its totality
the very substance of human life and the evidence of things not
seen but dearly hoped for. Her book is like an aeolian chime of
painted glass, gleaming in the light, turning and tinkling with
every movement of the air, giving forth no conventionally progressive tune but only a sweet dissonance, responsive to nature,
and yet crying out for a future resolution which human imagination must supply. The curtain indeed rises, and man and woman
speak. The world awaits a denouement. Virginia Woolf has implied that in this drama the proper protagonist is the liberated
and cultivated individual, agent of "the whole population of the
mind's immeasurable profundity." Contradiction would seem to
be not only premature but cynical. Virginia Woolf may yet be
seen as one of the period's most profoundly realistic and discerning artists.

Between the Acts indeed brings England's case up to date.
Moreover, it has disclosed the emergent problem of the modern
individual's fate in terms penetratingly humane and therefore
implicative against totalitarianism's harsh impersonality. Thus
the book should have power, if received, to hearten other artists
who would advocate man's rights and envisage his happiest future, since such concepts are relative to the facts of temperament.
By rendering what she called reality's "luminous halo," Virginia
Woolf has reminded a tragically preoccupied generation of the
dynamic mystery of mind, which becomes the one enduring
source of fortitude and a common hope; and hence remains a
central theme for literary art.

◆§ CHARLES CHILD WALCUTT

The Naturalism of *Vandover and the Brute*

ATTEMPTS to explain and define the naturalistic movement and to account for the "naturalistic" novel have not yet dissipated the fog that hangs over the problem. The vapor, on the contrary, thickens apace and now shows traces of deadly gamma rays from which critics flee. The source of this trouble is the fact that the word *naturalism* now uncovers four or five quite different and often independent trains of ideas, which undergo still further transformations when they appear in what are called naturalistic novels. My purpose here is to indicate some of the scientific, social, and ethical ideas which have been associated with naturalism; to suggest some of the differences between intellectual concepts and the novels in which such concepts are somehow "expressed"; and to illustrate these generalizations in so far as they apply to a particular early naturalistic novel. I want to show that although naturalism can be philosophically defined as materialistic monism, such a definition does not describe or "account" for what is called a naturalistic novel.

The theory says that Being is One, accessible to man as the material universe, which evinces consistent cause-and-effect relationships that he can observe and translate into laws. This belief leads to the rejection of older systems of theology, ethics, and politics—for which new data are now to be found in the order of

Nature. From this beginning, naturalistic thought moves in various directions. For example:

1. Man is good: society is the culprit responsible for man's unhappiness. Or it may be said that tradition is the culprit. Here tradition means the devices by which unenlightened men—men who have not *progressed* to the understanding of their true place in Nature—have preserved the unjust social order in which they are prosperous and powerful.

2. Traditional Christian ethics are "naturally" right (the mythology is incidental) but have not yet been socially realized because of man's ignorance of nature and natural law. Thus man has been confused by his belief in demons, miracles, and dogma; he has not known himself physically (witness the history of medicine) and so has not achieved a proper conception of his "natural" need to live according to the Christian ethic. Furthermore, his struggle with nature for subsistence has produced a social order in which security and individual development are not available to all. Hence the age-old conflict of man against man, in which only a few could succeed; and hence the *physical* impossibility of making the Christian ethic prevail. Science promises an understanding of man and an abundance of the physical necessaries of life, through which the ideals of justice, equality, freedom, and brotherhood will become social realities.

3. Transcendentalism is a great stone in the same arch. Nature is the visible embodiment of Spirit. Man ascends into oneness with Spirit through his understanding of Nature, not through revelation or authority. Thoreau's successful quest for peace through intuition was achieved by a devoted, contemplative examination of Nature: "God himself culminates in the present moment, and will never be more divine in the lapse of all the ages. And we are enabled to apprehend at all what is sublime and noble only by the perpetual instilling and drenching of the reality that surrounds us." Transcendentalism motivates Whitman's early delight in the phenomenal world:

> You have waited, you always wait, you dumb, beautiful ministers, [phenomena]

FORMS OF MODERN FICTION

We receive you with free sense at last, and are insatiate henceforward . . .
> ("Crossing Brooklyn Ferry," 1856)

It underlies the tragic quest of Ahab: "All visible objects, man, are but as pasteboard masks. But in each event—in the living act, the undoubted deed—there, some unknown but still reasoning thing puts forth the mouldings of its features from behind the unreasoning mask" (*Moby Dick*, Chapter XXXVI). It underlies Emerson's definition of Fate as "unpenetrated causes," which, penetrated, will become sources of power and steps toward the realization of the "Beautiful Necessity" by which law and freedom become identical. All these nineteenth-century trends in American thought are on the way toward scientific materialism and are still frequently involved in it, though their presence is not identified by novelists and social theorists who consider themselves to be operating on "scientific" or naturalistic premises.

4. Transcendentalism anticipates the Spencerian philosophy of evolution, which sees man's ceaseless struggle and change as an aspect of the Natural Order by which all forms ascend through higher and higher levels of excellence. Truth and right emerge and "improve" by necessity. Emerson frequently refers to the "aspiration" in Nature: "Striving to be man, the worm / Mounts through all the spires of form." But Spencer was an ardent conservative. He opposed on principle any and all legislative or governmental interference with the natural evolutionary process. The ruthless methods of business he defended as promoting the survival of the fittest. Other Darwinians, like Kropotkin and Lester Ward, dwelt upon the cooperative activities of animals and the fact that many forms of flora and fauna throve best when, as under domestication, they were freed from the struggle for survival. Socialists of course maintained versions of this position. Huxley returned to a sort of dualism by affirming that social and ethical good were to be achieved through man's opposition to the processes of nature. Ethical conduct, Huxley said, was not to be traced to a naturalistic cause.* Thus from transcendental-

* See Richard Hofstadter, *Social Darwinism in American Thought 1860–1915,* Philadelphia, 1945.

ism, through Spencer, Kropotkin, and Huxley, we find such a variety of social applications of naturalistic theory that we have no single program or attitude that can with any confidence be asserted to characterize or control the "naturalistic" novel.

5. Resting on the belief that science shows man to be only an accident and an incident in a cosmic order that is moving toward eventual lifeless rest (entropy) is the "ethic" of ruthless self-expression: man must give vent to his energies and die, for there is no meaningful moral order by which he should be controlled. The superman, who enjoys as many avatars as Vishnu, appears, in some naturalistic novels, as the vehicle of this ethic. The brute superman of fiction is several steps from Nietzsche's conception. Nietzsche denounced *mediocrity,* which he conceived to be fostered by Christianity, determinism, socialism, business enterprise, and Prussian militarism. He wanted greatness of spirit, perfection; but when he had rejected traditional values (the "slave morality" of Christianity) he found himself in an ethical void. It is not, therefore, surprising that others who were already in an ethical void from the effects of naturalistic theory should have invoked his writings to justify ruthless and violent selfishness. When Jack London wrote *The Sea Wolf* (1903) and his earlier tales of Yukon violence, Nietzsche had not been translated into English. London was a devoted Spencerian who could have seen the inevitable and beatific processes of evolution being promoted through these grim struggles for survival. Yet some years later he revealed at once a familiarity with Nietzsche's term and an ignorance of his intent by referring to Wolf Larsen (the Sea Wolf) as a superman. To cap this confusion, London was a socialist. It is quite impossible to *deduce* what he was trying to do in his novels. We can only examine the novels.

6. Attitudes toward the mind reveal the growth of naturalistic theory. In 1865 Émile Zola read Claude Bernard's *Introduction à l'étude de la medicine expérimentale* and straightway concluded that the study of physiology was the first step toward the study of psychology. Medicine, said Bernard, had been an art but now, with the introduction of the "positive" method, would become a science. Fiction, said Zola, consciously paraphrasing, had been

an art but would henceforth be an instrument for the scientific study of man and society. The mind could be studied as a "chemical" function of hereditary and environmental forces, and this positive approach to its working would ultimately make its every aspect and activity *predictable*. A generation later the investigations of Freud and others had led to the discovery that the mind was more complicated than had ever before been imagined. Motives were hidden beneath layer upon layer of "censorship" and compensation. The hope of predicting was abandoned. Psychologists and writers were content to observe and record this fascinating complexity of mental phenomena, happy indeed if they could explain certain human reactions which had previously been attributed to original sin but not presuming to predict anything by the application of mechanistic formulas.

II

Thus the theory of naturalism is not single but several: it is moral, amoral, radical, conservative, optimistic, and pessimistic. When we consider what happens when a theory is embodied in a novel, we find that various considerations of another order complicate the problem and further confuse the deductions which one is tempted to make. A novel is an imitation of an action; its esthetic quality cannot be deduced from the philosophical beliefs of its writer. There is no anomaly in the fact that Zola's best novels are studies in degeneration and failure, whereas his attitude toward science was religious in its fervor—and it was this attitude which controlled the novels. Yet these facts appear impossibly confusing if one approaches them from the conviction that the character of a novel can be deduced from the writer's philosophical beliefs. It is not possible to deduce that a naturalistic novel will be optimistic or pessimistic merely because naturalistic theory as it appears in scientific and philosophical writings is optimistic or pessimistic. The question of whether a novel is optimistic or pessimistic is surely irrelevant. Yet this issue is central in most recent writing about the naturalistic novel.

Another bugaboo is free will. Naturalistic theories of man,

nature, and society have not displaced the element of will from
the novel. They may account for it in theory, perhaps by declaring it a fiction (as behaviorists define mind as "the functional
integration of sensory and motor responses"), but they do not
therefore eliminate it from the novel, which is why statements
of the philosophical or social bearings of naturalistic theory do not
account for what actually takes place in the "naturalistic" novel.
The scientific student of man does not judge and condemn him
for failure to obey moral absolutes. He seeks only to understand.
But the citizen and the artist are used to dealing with their fellow
men as if they were responsible for their actions.

The novelist, furthermore, is working in a genre which has
traditionally employed the concept of free will—or, rather, the
active force of free will. Plots have, in the past, been built around
conflicts between individuals who were assumed to be free to
choose their courses of action. These individuals have been char-
acterized in terms of ethical qualities (honesty, loyalty, selfishness, jealousy, pride) which in themselves embody ethical judgments. To say a man is proud is to use the language of judgment.
The novelist who undertakes to be a naturalist, then, is working
against his own instinctive attitude and against the tradition of
his art. He is hardly to be condemned if he fails to exclude moral
judgment and the idea of ethical responsibility from his novel.
The critic's problem is to describe the outcome of this tension
between theory and practice in the works of the "naturalistic"
novelists. A successful definition will be historical and descriptive, rather than a categorical formulation of certain rules which
have never been perfectly embodied in a novel. The naturalist,
in particular, should be pragmatic in his eagerness to see how his
theory *works* in the solid body of a novel.

Finally, art is always an assertion of human freedom. Even
while it denies man's freedom it asserts it, for it imposes plan and
meaning and order on its materials. The act of writing a naturalistic novel, even one that purports to demonstrate man's utter
helplessness, denies its own intent. All naturalistic novels have
meanings and effects which are not even implied by the philo-

sophical or scientific theories of naturalism. The following section
will attempt to show how these remarks apply to a particular
"naturalistic" novel.

Frank Norris' *Vandover and the Brute* was written for Professor Gates' composition class at Harvard in 1894–95. It was Norris' first long work and an attempt to imitate the method of the
French naturalists with a particularly naturalistic subject — the
destruction of an individual by a degenerative disease. *Vandover*
has not the scope of *The Octopus* or the primordial violence of
McTeague, but it contains some of Norris' most effective writing;
it has, indeed, been considered his most memorable work. It
stands at the opposite end of the scale of naturalistic motifs from
novels dealing with the broad external workings of social and
economic forces. Here the forces are internal and physiological;
the book purports to be a "clinical" study of a disease.

The novelist's reason for dealing with a mental disease would
seem to be his enthusiasm for science. He would, perhaps, be inspired by the experimental zeal which Zola described, the desire
to show in detail how certain psychoneurotic manifestations could
be clinically diagnosed and systematically presented — subjected
to the clear light of knowledge so that man would know for at
least one malady whether he had germs or "lesions" to cope with.
This would, then, be a factual scientific report, rich with informa-
tion vital to human welfare. Its interest would depend upon the
new subject matter and the reader's aroused zeal for human betterment. This hypothetical description, with its implication that
the facts of the case will be scientifically related and established,
leaves no place for an unpredictable element like the free human
will. A disease is strictly physical; it is a problem in material
causes and effects. Spiritual values, morality, or personal struggle
would not *seem* to be relevant to an understanding of it.

Vandover is the son of a prosperous San Francisco businessman.
He is a painter, but he neglects his art. "Vandover was self-
indulgent — he loved these sensuous pleasures, he loved to eat

246

good things, he loved to be warm, he loved to sleep. He hated to be bored and worried — he liked to have a good time." His disintegration begins when a girl he has seduced commits suicide in terror at the prospect of having an illegitimate child. Next his father, weakened by the shock of Vandover's deed, dies. When the reason for the girl's suicide becomes known, Vandover is socially ostracized and loses the love of Turner Mavis, a fine girl who had been a powerful influence for good in his life. After his father's death, his income is greatly curtailed. At this point Vandover resolves to reform, and throws himself into his painting with furious energy. But too late. The disease, lycanthropy, first appears in a terrifying scene when he finds that he can no longer paint, that his hand will not reproduce the image in his mind; and thereafter his descent is rapid and inexorable. The dead girl's father sues him for a large sum. One of his friends, on the pretext of "handling" the case out of court, cheats him of money and property. What is left from the sale of his father's house Vandover squanders in reckless gambling and debauchery, his unnatural life punctuated by attacks of lycanthropy, during which he creeps about naked on all fours, snarling and yapping like a wolf. Finally he is living from hand to mouth, dirty, unkempt, estranged from friends, sometimes near starvation — a hopeless wreck. The story ends with a pitiful scene in which Vandover is cleaning a filthy kitchen for the friend who had defrauded him.

An appearance of factual reality is created by the method Norris employs. The style and tone of *Vandover* suit the commonplace unromantic people and setting of the story admirably. Details of Vandover's life and activity are accumulated with meticulous and dispassionate thoroughness. This was a new note in American letters. The quantity and "meanness" of the detail, with the objective tone, give the effect of authentic "documentation" in the best naturalistic tradition. We are shown, step by step, how "In his idleness he grew to have small and petty ways. . . . It became a fad with him to do without matches, using as a substitute 'lights,' tapers of twisted paper to be ignited at the

FORMS OF MODERN FICTION

famous stove. He found amusement for two days in twisting and rolling these 'lights,' cutting frills in the larger ends with a pair of scissors, and stacking them afterward in a Chinese flower jar he had bought for the purpose and stood on top of the bookcases. The lights were admirably made and looked very pretty. When he had done he counted them. He had made two hundred exactly. What a coincidence!"

Structurally, the novel is not "well-made" or dramatic, in the sense of being organized around a conflict between free moral agents. Instead Norris has conformed his structure to the steady and "inevitable" disintegration of Vandover under a succession of blows from forces over which he has no control. In one passage Norris announces a deterministic philosophy very explicitly. It is when Vandover, after his first attack of the disease, prays for help:

There was no answer, nothing but the deaf silence, the blind darkness . . . there was nothing for him. Even that vast mysterious power to which he had cried *could* not help him now, could not help him, could not stay the inexorable law of nature, could not reverse that vast terrible engine with its myriad spinning wheels that was riding him down relentless, grinding him into the dust.*

There is no climactic choice in the story; it moves evenly on a chain of circumstances.

These elements of style, tone, documentation, structure, and explicit determinism constitute the naturalism of *Vandover and the Brute*. But they do not really account for the novel. In spite of its explicit determinism, the conflict in this novel *is* a thoroughly moral one. It is a conflict between Vandover's free and responsible spirit and a series of circumstantial influences (the disease is merely one of several) which win out over him largely because of his *culpable* moral weakness. Examination reveals (1) that Vandover is morally responsible for his downfall, (2) that the forces which thrust him down are circumstantial rather than inevitable, and (3) that the novel has the form

* 1914 edition, pp. 244–45.

248

and effect of a tragedy. It appears, also, that the tragic effect
would have been stronger if Norris had not allowed so much
moral condemnation to intrude; if, that is, he had held to a more
rigorous determinism!

The tone of moral judgment appears in passages like the following, where Vandover broods on his decline:

And with the eyes of this better self he saw again . . . the eternal struggle between good and evil that had been going on within
him since his very earliest years. He was sure that at the first the
good had been the strongest. Little by little the brute had grown,
and he . . . luxurious, self-indulgent . . . had shut his ears to
the voices that shouted warnings of the danger, and had allowed
the brute to thrive and to grow, its abominable famine gorged
from the store of that in him which he felt to be the purest, the
cleanest . . . [214–15].

Again:

It was gone—his art was gone, the one thing that could save
him. That, too, like all the other good things of his life, he had
destroyed [229].

And:

It was the punishment that he had brought upon himself, some
fearful nervous disease, the result of his long indulgence in vice,
his vile submission to the brute that was to destroy his reason
. . . till he should have reached the last stages of idiocy [243].

Although these passages are presented as Vandover's thought,
they come as auctorial comment also, for it is clear that Norris'
attitude is represented in these and many other passages like
them. One is reminded of Milton's

But, when lust
By unchaste looks, loose gestures, and foul talk,
But most by lewd and lavish acts of sin,
Lets in defilement to the inward parts,
The soul grows clotted by contagion,
Imbodies, and imbrutes, till she quite lose
The divine property of her first being.

Far from illustrating the operation of determinism, Vandover's
degradation is presented as the result of some internal failure

which *allows* the brutish side to grow and thrust out the good. Vandover's moral responsibility depends on his being a person of intelligence and social position; regardless of the author's intention, the naturalistic approach is disrupted because the human being is more important, more intimately known, and therefore more credible than the forces which supposedly dominate him.

There is no established set of forces, either hereditary or environmental, which can bring about his degeneration in such a way that it appears to be inevitable. Vandover is not shown to inherit qualities from his parents that would make him subject to lycanthropy. He does not move in a society that is notable for the pressure it exerts upon its members. He is free from the sort of influences that obtain in industrial areas, or among the poorer classes anywhere. In all these respects he is free from the forces which can be shown, even in the contrived simplicity of the novel, to have shaped a character or bent it toward an unalterable end. Thus the bars which prevent the invasion of his beast must be withdrawn by Chance, that is, by pressures which are not presented as an inescapable part of the milieu; and half of the book is devoted to the impact of various kinds of chance upon him. There is nothing typical, nothing that might contribute to the science of sociology in the course by which he is destroyed. At any time Vandover might take a turn for the better. The events which thrust him down are more coincidental than the acts of fate that destroy some of Hardy's characters. But nevertheless they are presented with such a wealth of convincing detail that the average reader accepts them as probable.

It appears, then, that the Beast—the disease—is an external and adventitious factor like the suicide of the girl or the swindle by the friend. The disease is not studied for its own sake. Vandover does not become a mere organism subjected to clinical examination. The shred of manhood, of free will, that he retains is always at the focal point of attention. The question is not what new form will the disease take, or what does one learn from the data about its growth and operation, but what is the last tiny bit of conscious individuality thinking and feeling and suffering as it approaches the moment of final extinction. The reader's attention is not fixed by the progress of the disease but by wonder and pity at the fact that the human spark continues so long to survive and so to suffer.

The conflict, then, is between a free but fallible individual and a fatal but indefinable enemy. We never see the operation of "That vast terrible engine with its myriad spinning wheels." What we see is a real young man with a well-developed personality and a whole set of convincing mannerisms, who succumbs because of the impact of circumstances upon him—and not the least of these circumstances is the disease lycanthropy, for it is not "scientifically" traced to a source or accounted for. Chance, of course, does not exist in the theory of naturalism. When it appears we know that another frame of reference has been introduced, whether intentionally or not.

There are two extreme points of view which produce inferior art. One extreme is the belief in pure mechanistic determinism. When this attitude is "pure," it is expressed in scientific reports dealing perhaps with pathological or physiological disturbances of the human organism. The "person" being described or examined does not, for the purposes of the report, exist. He is merely a certain amount of tissue, part of which is isolated as a breeding ground for germs or tumors. In pure science, this attitude may be essential for the study of diseases *per se*, although even scientists are not so sure as they were fifty years ago that a disease is anything *per se*, apart, that is, from the nature of the organism in which it lives. The same impersonal attitude is pure in statistical studies of social trends, and it is perhaps approximated in sociological reports. It is doubtful whether it can be anywhere near pure in a work of fiction. Employed by a very cynical writer who despised the human race and delighted to portray the helpless wrigglings of men impaled on the pins of Fate, it would in effect be an assertion of the writer's superiority and spiritual independence. If it were free of such ironic overtones, it would produce a dismal and boring novel with little or no feeling for the dignity of man.

At the other extreme, there is plenty of fiction which fatuously assumes that nature is benign and man is perfectly in tune with it and with himself. From this view come novels which present an easy universe where justice is always done, evil punished (but merely for the delight and beatitude of the Good), and ambitions fulfilled. It is the world of easy pleasure, happy people, and barren complacency. It is a moral world, constructed entirely for the protection of little men. Its perfect "artistic" expression is Hollywood's doctrine of the unique temptation, according to which one has to resist evil only once in order to be forever blessed. Because this sort of thinking cannot or will not acknowledge the power and unpredictability of nature, it can have no true sense of the dignity of man.

Between these extremes moves the tragic view, which underestimates neither man nor the forces against which he contends. The greatest men face the greatest oppositions and suffer most greatly; therein lies the grandeur of the Greek and Shakespearian tragedy — and all great tragic artists show man rising to greatness as he pits himself against forces over which he can never triumph. To acknowledge the might of these forces while not losing faith in the men who challenge them is to possess the tragic view of life.

Vandover and the Brute is in this tragic area. The hero, an ordinary attractive young man, is caught and crushed — not in the "vast terrible engine" that Norris describes, but by social and personal forces which twentieth-century man knows all too well. In so far as he *blames* Vandover for *moral* weakness, Norris moves toward the pole of fatuity, for by doing so he assumes that a moral man would avoid conflict with the moral order. In so far as he talks about the vast terrible engine, Norris moves toward the pole of inhuman mechanism. But in reality the effect of his novel is between these extremes, if only because the reader is pulled in both directions. Vandover is accepted for what he is — not judged — and the reader, I believe, identifies himself with the struggling spirit of the protagonist *as well as* with the social and personal evil which destroys him. The tragic conflict is within the individual and also between him and the society which is composed of the fallible wills of all individuals.

A bold and massive array of external forces demands a corresponding grandeur in the characters who struggle against them. This is Shakespeare's pattern, but it is not so descriptive of the modern dilemma. Instead of man against the cosmos, we now have society against man, which is to say, mankind against mankind. The tragic struggle in *An American Tragedy* and *Studs Lonigan* is similarly conceived. Clyde Griffiths and Studs are modern man, ruined in the milieu which modern man has made, and the reader participates in the tragic *agon,* aware of the dangerous forces within himself; yet in a manner somewhat different from that of the spectator of a Shakespearian tragedy, for the terrible forces against which Shakespeare's heroes contend are viewed with awe and wonder and fear; not only are they unconquerable, they are indeed beyond man's power of comprehension. The catharsis of pity and terror is to be reached *only* through art. The modern tragedy locates the opposing forces in society and the nature of man, where they are not quite so terrible. It is true that the "nature of man" could appear as mysterious and ungovernable as an unknowable Fate, but the fact is that social institutions do appear, in these novels of Dreiser and Farrell, to be subject, however tenuously, to the will and knowledge of man. Hence the conflict they present cannot be as grand as Shakespeare's. The idea of progress, the necessity for social action, creep into these modern tragedies and offer an alternative or added release for the emotions which Shakespeare purges through pity and terror alone. The modern tragedy thus unconsciously presents two orders of symbolic action: One shows man struggling with Fate and his own nature. The other "attacks" the social order as the embodiment of injustice and heedlessness.

Vandover and the Brute is a modern tragedy in a minor and imperfect key. If the book had been more exhaustively "naturalistic," it would have shown more fully the nature of the social (that is, human) forces that destroy the hero—and there would have been correspondingly less need to impose a Sunday school moral censure upon him. Thus the weakness of *Vandover* shows very clearly the potential strength of naturalism as a foundation for tragedy — so long as it is not carried to a point of diminishing returns in lifeless mechanism. In short, so long as it is essentially transcendental naturalism will give full recognition to the power and immensity of the physical world but will also assume a meaning in it that is akin to and ideally accessible to the mind of man; so that man achieves tragic dignity as he strives to penetrate and master his own nature and the physical universe which repeats the tension of actual and potential, real and ideal, fate and will, evil and good, and matter and spirit, that is in the nature of man. Seen in this light, naturalism is no revolutionary departure from the world view of Shakespearian tragedy. It is rather a mode of presenting in realistic "modern" terms the forces, microcosmic and macrocosmic, against which man has always tragically contended. Naturalism is the modern approach to Fate. It is more hopeful in that it suggests rational means of coping with Fate; if it is "pessimistic" it is so only because it has to accord less dignity to man. When it is confused it is so because the polar attractions of mechanism and social action draw it away, in one direction or the other, from the tragic center.

ᴥ§ ERIC BENTLEY

The Meaning of
Robert Penn Warren's Novels

IF AN author makes a deep impression, there comes a time when you are no longer content merely to read his books as they come out. You want to re-read him. You want to know what the body of his writings amounts to. Today for instance, many people must be feeling an interest in the whole body of Robert Penn Warren's writings—not, I hope, because Warren has recently become famous but because one increasingly has the impression that he is the most considerable American writer to emerge since the twenties. As far as recent discussion of Warren is concerned, one's inquisitiveness is sharpened, not by the hullabaloo, but by the strange lack of accord as to the ideas he presents. What has Warren been saying to us? In this sketch of Warren's achievement as a novelist, I shall have that question chiefly in mind. Which is not in the least to imply that it is the most important question that could be asked about him.

I

A convenient point of departure is a meditation on Shakespeare that Warren puts in the mouth of one of his characters. The tragedies, this character says, have all one theme, "the necessity for self-knowledge":

NOTE. Reprinted from the *Kenyon Review,* 1948, by permission of the editors and the author.

FORMS OF MODERN FICTION

The tragic flaw in the Shakespearean hero is a defect in self-knowledge. Macbeth comes to ruin, not because he kills (Shakespeare could scarcely have been so naive as to believe that men have not killed and then ruled in prosperity and dreamless sleep —he had, we know, read Holinshed), but because he does not realize upon what grounds it is possible for him, Macbeth, to kill. Bacon wrote: Knowledge is power. Bacon was thinking of knowledge of the mechanisms of the external world. Shakespeare wrote: Self-knowledge is power. Shakespeare was thinking of the mechanisms of the spirit, to which the mechanisms of the external world, including other persons, are instruments. In other words, Shakespeare was interested in success. By success, he meant: Self-fulfillment. But his tragedy is concerned with failure. Naturally. The successful man . . . offers only the smooth surface, like an egg. Insofar as he is truly successful, he has no story. He is pure. But poetry is concerned with failure, distortion, imbalance . . .

This passage, like many things Warren has said about other writers, fits Warren himself like a glove. That we need self-knowledge is, to date, the alpha and omega of his teaching. Like all moral teachings it sounds simple when reduced to a single statement. Like all profound teachings it turns out to be complex as soon as we try to explain it.

Warren's first novel, *Night Rider* (1939), was also his first large-scale treatment of the theme. It tells the story of a Kentucky lawyer of some forty years ago. Mr. Munn joined the "night riders," a band of men who wrecked the tobacco crop of those of their neighbors who refused to join a would-be monopolistic association of tobacco wholesalers. Beginning with sporadic raids, the riders later organize a kind of army and march on a couple of towns. They are put down by National Guards. Mr. Munn is one of the casualties.

Externally, the book is a splendid adventure story which, in the right hands, would make a first-rate movie. Internally, from beginning to end, it is the story of Mr. Munn's search —unsuccessful as it turns out—for himself. He tries to find himself in other people. It is the impression made on him by the local senator, one Tolliver, that sends him into public life. Tolliver appears to have the confidence, the mastery, the suavity and poise that

Mr. Munn lacks. Only later does it transpire that the appearance
was deceptive. As one of the characters puts it:

Tolliver, talking to people all his life, crowds, never being anything except when his voice was talking to crowds; if he had
anything in him, any life, sucking it out of crowds, talking.
Crowds and women. Never being anything except when he
thought somebody else thought he was something. Just that . . .
like sucking blood, living off something else.

Mr. Munn's awe before the public man—which drags him into
the association and thus into all the catastrophes that ensue—
turns to hate. He resolves to kill Tolliver but, characteristically,
proves unequal to the job. "I thought I could do it," he whispers
brokenly, before going off to let himself be killed by pursuing
troops. In a way the remark is the crowning irony of the book.
For Mr. Munn is not, in general, afraid of killing. He *has* killed
a man. The man he killed (on behalf of the night riders) was
someone he had earlier, as defense lawyer, got acquitted, on
dubious evidence, of a murder charge. Certainly, the fellow had
wished the murder: but was that relevant? Wishing a murder
you have not committed—the crime of Dmitri Karamazoff—is
something Mr. Munn can think about later. The murder he is
being hunted for at the end is one he did not commit.

A more perceptive man might have learned something from
all this about human responsibility. Mr. Munn dies unenlightened
—bewildered, unfulfilled, not knowing himself, and therefore un-
repentant. We cannot, therefore, learn through his consciousness
what Warren has to say. Though the book is Mr. Munn's story,
Warren does not have him tell it. We see him from the outside:
Warren calls him *Mr.* Munn throughout. And the view of life
which the book as a whole enforces is inferred from a whole complex of situations and relationships. We learn a good deal, for
example, from other characters. There are three in particular
who are further along the road to self-knowledge, self-definition.
There is Dr. MacDonald who has in him something of the pio-
neer generations: since the South threatens to stifle him he will
push on west, thus "defining" himself as an intact American.

There is Captain Todd, Southern squire and veteran of the Civil War, whose evident "certainty of self" Mr. Munn envies. And there is Willie Proudfit, an unlettered peasant who, in his pioneering adventures and religious thinking, has lived out a pattern of rebirth which Mr. Munn conspicuously fails to match.

These characters bring home the point about Mr. Munn by contrast. Others — two in particular — reinforce it by parallelism. One is Senator Tolliver: is not Mr. Munn just as hollow as this hollow man? Is not the fact that he cannot kill him symbolic? The other is a spinster cousin of Mr. Munn's, Miss Ianthe Sprague, who is only interested in "the fragmentary, the irrelevant, the meaningless":

And she did not like to talk of the past, and avoided his questions. Indeed, she had little memory of the past. That, too, she had rejected, for out of memory rises the notion of a positive and purposive future, the revision of the past.

Finally, Mr. Munn is "placed" for us by his relation to women. His relation to both wife and mistress reaches a climax and an end in a loveless copulation. Mr. Munn tries to find himself by violently merging with another. (In Warren's poem *Revelation* we find the line: "In separateness only does love learn definition.")

Munn is a failure. We need warmth, but he is cold, and the only half-satisfactory love he can find is with a cold woman. We need wholeness, but he is fragmentary, a helpless prey to conflicting impulses and moods, queer exaltations and prostrating nauseas. The prerequisite of wholeness is continuity with the past and faith in the future, but

because the future was dead and rotten in his breast, the past, too, which once had seemed to him to have its meanings and its patterns, began to fall apart. . . .

He is as discontinuous as Miss Sprague, and, like Tolliver, tries to have others do for him what he must do for himself. The man with no center is a rider in the night of the spirit.

ERIC BENTLEY

II

Warren's second novel, *At Heaven's Gate* (1943), is a more ambitious treatment of the same theme. Here Warren tries to give us a whole group of people of roughly equal importance. He tries to achieve unity, not by the relatively easy device of a protagonist, but by the skillfully patterned interweaving of scenes and by the common theme. There is no romance in this book. These people are not removed from us by time. They are ourselves. *At Heaven's Gate* would be remarkable if it were merely a picture of life in America.

But what we are concerned with here is Warren's *interpretation* of this life. In an admirable study of Warren's first two novels* Miss Irene Hendry has suggested that, while Mr. Munn in *Night Rider* turns outward to other people in his search for meaning, Slim Sarrett in *At Heaven's Gate* turns inward and fails just as miserably. Mr. Munn, Miss Hendry says, tries to define himself by proxy, Sarrett, though always self-regarding, fails to define himself at all. Thus Warren's argument is by no means a simple case for the inner life and against the outer. The intellectual life is as fraught with perils as the life of action. It can be quite as deadly. Sarrett ends as a murderer.

Although the second novel is not so much the twin or complement of the first as all this suggests (Sarrett being no protagonist), Miss Hendry's point is valuable, for *At Heaven's Gate* does take up the discussion where *Night Rider* left off. Mr. Munn is replaced by Sarrett. Senator Tolliver reappears — with differences, with much more blood in his veins — as the businessman Bogan Murdock. Willie Proudfit has a sort of counterpart in the religious down-and-out, Ashby Wyndham: both represent a consciousness that is cruder yet more genuine than that of the more educated, modern, and secular main characters.

Again Warren's main concern is whether the various characters are moving toward self-knowledge or not. Some are not moving; some move but do not arrive. Already in *Night Rider*, the dis-

* *Sewanee Review*, Winter 1945.

259

continuity of past and present had been symbolized by father-rejection—as for example in the "heroine" of the book who shouts at her father: "No, I'm not yours! I don't belong to you! Or to anybody!" The lines just about sum up the "heroine" of *At Heaven's Gate,* Sue Murdock. As Miss Hendry indicates, nearly all the people in this novel have rejected their fathers and, thereby, themselves. Sue Murdock's living through others is worse than Mr. Munn's, for she is hardly even pretending to seek her salvation in them. If she likes a man, it is because, like herself, he is "a mess." Even worse: when Sarrett becomes "a part of her," he is "the part of her she wanted to kill."

Though the novel is called *At Heaven's Gate,* the America it depicts is pretty much of a hell. If night is the pervading image and symbol in *Night Rider,* a characteristic image in the later novel—used at least three times—is that of *pus.* Yet Warren is entitled to say, as Ibsen did, that he goes down into the sewer to cleanse it, not to wallow. "There's something horrible in everybody," says the union leader Sweetie Sweetwater, "till they work it out. It looks like a man's got to boil the pus out." Yet, though none of Warren's characters has passed through heaven's gate, thus leaving his mere humanity behind, some approach it. Sweetwater, for instance, has defined himself, even if the definition is a rather narrow one. If Sue meets with the death which she had, in a sense, asked for, and Sarrett survives in a kind of living damnation, at least two of the people in this novel find something in their long search. In a crisis even the hard-boiled Duckfoot Blake realizes that there are things that matter. The previously bewildered Jerry Calhoun, who had slept with Sue as joylessly as Mr. Munn with his two women, achieves fulfillment. In *Night Rider,* the fulfillment of Willie Proudfit had been symbolized by one of Warren's favorite archetypal patterns, the homeward journey. Here in *At Heaven's Gate* the fulfillment of Jerry Calhoun is symbolized by a similar pattern, and an even greater favorite of Warren's, the return to the father. (*The Ballad of Billie Potts* has it: "And the father waits for the son./ The hour is late,/ The scene familiar even in Shadow,/ The transaction brief,/ And you,

wanderer, back,/ After the striving and the wind's word,/ To
kneel/ . . . At the feet of the old man . . .)

III

Warren's third and most recent novel, *All the King's Men*
(1946), is an expansion of a play he had written about six years
earlier, entitled *Proud Flesh*. The play is possibly the clearest
and most concise statement of Warren's main theme.

The hollow man of action—Senator Tolliver, Bogan Murdock
—is now the protagonist, Governor Willie Stark. He exemplifies
what Sarrett had found in Murdock:

. . . the special disease of our time, the abstract passion for
power, a vanity springing from an awareness of the emptiness
and unreality of the self which can only become real and human
by the oppression of people who manage to retain some shreds
of reality and humanity.

Like Tolliver he seems very much the free and confident man.
He can face and manage everybody and everything—except himself. His son's death brings him to the realization that his own
life has been dedicated to an abstraction, power. (In his poem
Variation: Ode to Fear, Warren speaks of politicians who "would
skin a pig for the pig's squeal.") He hastily tries to patch up his
marriage and purify his politics. But his henchmen will not take
it. Now that he has confronted the *idea* of death, the thing itself
is conferred upon him.

Before dying, Willie gains an insight into the tragic nature of
life. He sees that the "deed in time" is not all, but that "the deed
out of time takes the crystalline form at last"—that is, the mere
flux of events in history is in itself meaningless: meaning comes
from man. But the full significance of the play does not come
from the protagonist alone, but from the interplay of several
points of view. In politics, the Boss stands midway between "the
boys"—the routine politicians headed by Tiny Duffy—and
Adam Stanton, the idealist. The former play a game of pure
power. The latter will tolerate only pure idea. The Boss has persuaded himself that his natural gifts as a wielder of power are at

the service of an idea—in fact, the liberal, humanitarian idea of Adam Stanton's. Thus the Boss is fighting in three directions—with Duffy, with Stanton, and with himself.

In private life, he has also three partner-antagonists: his wife Lucy and his two mistresses, one a carnal affair, the other "idealistic." The carnal affair is simple enough. The "idealistic" mistress, Anne Stanton, is the victim of Willie's illusion that goodness is the root motive of his career. The wife is an almost allegorical—too allegorical—figure, wife and mother, who is practically Warren's mouthpiece, a spokesman for "purgatorical knowledge," self-definition. All these points of view are framed by the point of view of popular scientism, represented by a chorus of surgeons, always on stage.

Warren seems to have realized that the story of Willie Stark, more fully articulated, could be made to convey nearly everything he had tried to say in all his previous verse and prose. Hence (I conjecture) the novel *All the King's Men*.

Thematically, the novel contains everything that is in the play. The few scenes and encounters of the play give place to a carefully articulated and elaborately counterpointed piece of fiction. What previously happened all in a few minutes without much show of realism is now spread over a period of time with full explanations supplied. Beyond this sort of adaptation—which is much what one would expect when *any* play is transformed into a novel—there are two crucial changes. A single narrator, Jack Burden, replaces the chorus. And an apparent digression—the story of Cass Mastern—is added.

Jack Burden may at first seem a pretty exact equivalent of the stage chorus; both make us see the tragic story of Willie through the nontragic eyes of a sophisticated modern cynicism. Jack's floridly figurative prose is a fair translation of the chorus's doggerel. But Warren chose to make much fuller use of his narrator than this. He involved him in the main story, gave him, in fact, his own story, until Willie's career was a play within a play. (In an important article in *Accent* [Summer 1947], Mr. Norton Girault

ERIC BENTLEY

has described the many-sided significance of Warren's narrator.
I must keep to the single thread of my own argument.)

Jack Burden is another of Warren's disoriented young moderns.
We have seen how, in *At Heaven's Gate,* one of them is led back
from his father-substitute (Bogan Murdock) to his actual father
and thus "saved." This happens incidentally, by no means as the
main story of the book. In *All the King's Men,* the saving of Jack
Burden, after a somewhat similar fashion, is the culmination of
the action. Jack had had two pseudo fathers—his supposed
father the Scholarly Attorney and his chosen father-substitute
Willie Stark. His true father turns out to be Judge Irwin, whose
death he has caused. On this last event, *All the King's Men* contains several comments, of which the chief are

Maybe that is the only way you can tell that a certain piece of
knowledge is worth anything: it has cost some blood.

And:

I had dug up the truth and the truth always kills the father
. . . and you are left alone with yourself and the truth, and can
never ask Dad, who didn't know anyway and who is deader than
mackerel.

(*The Ballad of Billie Potts:* "The answer is in the back of the
book but the page is gone./ And grandma told you to tell the
truth but she is dead.")

What of the Cass Mastern story (the interlude that constitutes
Warren's fourth chapter)? It has frivolously been suggested that
Warren put it in because it was too good to be left out; and I
gather that the London publisher will omit it on grounds of irrelevance. Thematically, however, it is central. Even structurally
it seems to me very daring and largely successful—Warren had
perhaps learned from Shakespeare that one could put the whole
theme of a work into one short and strongly symbolic interlude.
Those who cannot read the symbols directly are helped out by
some very explicit phrases like "the common guilt of man," statements like "nothing is ever lost" and "only by the suffering of
the innocent does God affirm that men are brothers." Above all

there is the figure of the spider that is our moral life—wherever you touch its web the vibration shudders through the whole.

This last point is applied to Jack's own story quite overtly. His refraining from the sexual act for fear of breaking his image of Anne is equated with Cass Mastern's evilly performing the act in despite of friendship:

So, I observed, my nobility (or whatever it was) had had in my world almost as dire a consequence as Cass Mastern's sin had had in his.

A less overt link is between Cass Mastern's religious conclusions and Jack's. Cass states a Christian view of the problem of evil: "only by the suffering of the innocent . . ." It is restated in the last chapter of the book by Jack's father, the Scholarly Attorney:

Separateness is identity and the only way for God to create, truly create, man was to make him separate from God Himself, and to be separate from God is to be sinful. The creation of evil is therefore the index of God's glory and His power. That had to be so that the creation of good might be the index of man's glory and power. But by God's help.

Jack does not precisely identify himself with either Cass or the Scholarly Attorney, but he hopes to "understand" the former, and he says of the latter: "I was not certain but that in my own way I did believe what he said."

Jack has achieved fulfillment, identification, definition, self-knowledge. He has been reborn though "the winter had been long."

IV

What does the conclusion of Warren's book amount to philosophically and morally? The philosophy, one might at first be inclined to say, is pure Christian orthodoxy. Undoubtedly Warren finds the Christian scheme of things close to the facts of experience, and it is the directly anti-Christian philosophy of scientism or popular materialism that he is attacking throughout. (The idea "that all life is but the dark heave of blood and the twitch of the nerve" he—Jack, at least—calls "the dream of our age.") Yet the facts of experience seem to be Warren's sole criterion. He is utterly empirical. Or noncommittal. "I was not certain but that *in my own way* I did believe what he said." An orthodox believer might find confirmation in these words. A naturalist might place the italics where I have placed them and feel that Warren helps him to broaden the basis of, and so strengthen, his naturalism.

What of the book's political morality? It was a pity that the reviewers regarded *All the King's Men* as primarily another life of Huey Long to be compared with the other lives of Long and not with the other works of Warren. It must be obvious by now, if my account of the book is halfway accurate, that it is not a political treatise about Long or anything else. Like *Proud Flesh,* it is another study of Warren's constant theme: self-knowledge. Nevertheless, it has political implications—and we may understand them correctly if we see them within the broader frame. Indeed to say that we must see politics within a broader frame— the frame being morality and human life in general—is precisely Warren's thesis. Willie Stark, Adam Stanton, and Tiny Duffy are wrong politically because they are wrong humanly.

This line of thought will be uncongenial to readers influenced by Marxism. Yet to say that it is counter to Marxism—in its insistence that motives *do* matter and that one cannot confine one's attention to the "objective trend"—is to say that it is counter to the political morality of today, Marxist and anti-Marxist, left and right. For the Hollywood war movie, just as much as the Moscow edict, takes politics to be a battle between the Wrong People and the Right People. One judges the man not by his nature but by his affiliation. The same action is good performed by Us and bad performed by Them. All war propaganda depends on this morality, and today we live in a perpetual state of war.

Now if there is anything Warren hates it is this morality. Which is why it was a very sad irony when Mrs. Trilling, in the *Nation,* maintained that the philosophy of *All the King's Men* was a surrender to history and thus an acquiescence in *realpolitik.* To be sure, the war moralist (let the term include Marxists and their opponents) preaches that history is on our side and that the objective trend is more important than the personal motive. But the final conclusion of Jack Burden is: "History is blind, but man is not." The "objective trend" is blind; the "personal motive" is all we have to work with; the person is all we have to see with. This idea is to be found somewhere in the background of all Warren's considerations of history. In *Night Rider,* for instance, where Captain Todd's superior poise is attributed to the fact that he does not look to historical process for moral solace: "he knew things and events were blind." Here again Warren's philosophy is that of the poet with his loyalty to the concrete and the particular and the human, his reluctance to enter the realm of the abstract and the general and the mechanical. Even Mr. Munn saw something of the point when wondering what "the truth" of any historical event is like:

The truth: it devoured and blotted out each particular truth, each individual man's truth, it crushed truths as under a blundering tread, it was blind.

Thus, also, in *At Heaven's Gate,* a distinction is drawn between the sinister, subhuman mob which prepares for a lynching and the human beings which it later breaks up into. The mob, like history, is blind.

But man is not. Whether or not Warren shares orthodox belief in an order of beings superior to man, he certainly insists on the superiority of man to nonhuman nature. For him man is himself a supernatural being. Superior to nature, that is, but not aloof from it, as Adam Stanton tries to be. Tiny Duffy is of course his polar opposite. Unlike Duffy, who really is the surrenderer to history, to what is, to nature, Willie Stark has a marvelous and truly human gift for dominating nature. That is his greatness — which only abject believers in the sufficiency of the "common man" will dispute or regret. Yet, though Willie starts out as a lover of men, he is soon going to work on some of his fellows as if they were brute nature. "My God, you talk like Byram was human!" he shouts about someone he is "fixing," "he's a thing!" This is blasphemy against the divine in man, and Warren appropriately makes it the beginning of Stark's isolation and downfall. One recalls also how Jack Burden reached his lowest point. It was in his first marriage, not when it broke up ("as soon as I began to regard her as a person, trouble began") but earlier:

as long as she was really a part of innocent non-human nature, as long as I hadn't begun to notice that the sounds she made were words, there was no harm in her . . .

"As long as I hadn't begun to notice . . ." Jack was a great one for not noticing. He had heard of Berkeley's philosophy while in college, decided that nothing was real if you didn't notice it, and called this decision his Idealism. It enabled him to stay outside of everything. His rebirth means, as much as anything, a willingness to step inside—to accept responsibility or (since Warren has a predilection for theological language) guilt. The book ends therefore when Jack gives up his narrator's, spectator's, role and resolves to go "into the convulsion of the world, out of history into history and the awful responsibility of Time."

These words are not pious verbiage. If Warren criticizes the mere politician and the master *realpolitiker,* he is equally critical of the idealist who wants to keep a corner of the world clean and is "above politics." Adam Stanton thinks of himself as a genuine champion of the ideal but he is really an idealist pretty much in Jack's sense—minus Jack's awareness of the implications and therefore minus Jack's cynicism. That certain unpleasant things have to be done doesn't matter to Adam as long as he doesn't have to know about them. Thus his sister, in the stage version, can quite rightly denounce him:

Not *his* [Willie Stark's] vanity. But yours, yours now!
Yours, for you'd make the world one thing and the one
Thing you, only the mirror's icy dream, and in darkness;
But the world is warm, and you in your ice-ease. . . .

Adam makes an exception of himself as much as Willie or the unregenerate Jack. He refuses to accept the common guilt, and is therefore doubly guilty. He is thus, in a way, a worse man than Willie Stark, a fact which some idealistic readers cannot be expected to relish.

Action is not something which will be *permitted* to Jack after his regeneration. It is something obligatory. It is dictated by his acceptance of responsibility. Politically, it seems, he will be a moderate liberal, for, speaking at the end of a rather practical reformer who had left Willie when Willie started "fixing" people, Jack declares: "It looks as though Hugh will get back into politics, and when he does I'll be along . . ." Jack is not *returning* to active life. He is taking it up for the first time. He *exists* for the first time. Previously he had lived through others—especially through Willie. But now he is learning to understand Cass Mastern, who said: "It is human defect—to try to know oneself by the self of another." Interpreted politically, Jack's living by proxy puts him precisely in the position of the mobs who gladly let Willie do their living for them.

Not to live by proxy—this surely is a fundamental ideal of democracy; though Warren has been called fascistic. It may indeed be true that Warren is not as sanguine about democracy as some people are. Not that he is against it, but that as a student of human nature he is impressed with the fact that people still *want* to live by proxy. Defending demagogy after his fashion, Willie Stark, in the play, cries: "The *peepul*! The *peepul* is like a girl in her first hot—she may squeal but she loves it!" Warren is not taken in by big talk. But neither is he asking us or "the peepul" to accept the present situation. It is simply that one must not hope for automatic change or for total change. Like Gilbert Mastern, Cass' statesmanlike brother, one should only hope "to do a little justice in terms of the great injustice." One should remember always that no social conflict is ever a crusade—good cause and good men versus bad cause and bad men—because good and bad are always very mixed. "A man's virtue may be but the defect of his desire as his crime may be but a function of his virtue." This is not of course a complete political philosophy, let alone a program. But it is a poet's preface to politics. And today, when many are prepared to reconsider their basic attitudes—"our courage needs, perhaps, new definition"—Warren's books cannot but be pertinent.

ERIC BENTLEY

V

At any rate, since they have to be taken as serious moral docu-
ments, they discredit the current academic view of "tough"
American fiction. In a lecture attacking modern novelists *en
masse*, Professor Douglas Bush of Harvard not long ago declared
that

the conflict within the individual, between his conscience and his
natural self, has been often replaced by a conflict between the
individual and social forces. This may involve a struggle between
good and evil, but it is more likely to show a poor creature destroyed by the environment that created him. Moral responsibility is more or less shifted from the individual to society.

What is there here that Warren does not know? Yet Warren, I
am told, was included in Mr. Bush's spoken indictment. (His
name does not appear in the published version, though Faulkner's
does.) Mr. Bush finds modern novels to be "clinical reports on
the crude or vicious lives lived by crude or vicious people." He
adds: "Indeed we may ask if, in their preoccupation with the
submoral, they [the modern novelists] are not cutting the ground
from under their own feet, since the submoral level of experience
cannot be the tragic level." He finds a formula for the modern
novelist: "toughness plus sentimentality." And he expresses a
strong preference for Shakespeare.

Well, Warren writes "tough" dialogue, and is capable of sentimentality. His five principal works to date—*Night Rider, At
Heaven's Gate, The Ballad of Billie Potts, Proud Flesh*, and *All
the King's Men*—are all murder stories in which neither the
murderer nor the murdered are exactly—to use Mr. Bush's
words—"noble characters, heroic examples." One might ask Mr.
Bush how an artist should be inspired by our sordid world—our
century of the all too common man—to portray nobility and
heroism. How should he avoid that abstraction from the actual
situation which is fatal to literature? After all we have the "noble
characters, heroic examples" of socialist realism to warn us.

Mr. Bush's account of modern fiction is the familiar academic
rejection of the whole naturalistic tendency in modern literature.

FORMS OF MODERN FICTION

(I refer now, not to philosophical naturalism, but to the literary naturalism which we associate with Zola.) Two false assumptions, I believe, are involved. The first is that literature can be moral only through the agency of heroic characters, edifying surroundings, elevated tone, and the like. The second is that naturalism — the naturalistic method, not only of Zola and his disciples, but of most modern fiction — implies amorality, not to say prosaic dullness, excessive and mere factuality. It is true that something like the second assumption — without the pejorative implications — underlies Zola's theoretical writings. It does not, however, underly his fiction or that of any modern novelist of rank. On the contrary, modern fiction, influenced as all of it is by naturalism, has found what Mr. Bush, if he chose, could regard as a moral equivalent of nobility, namely, a rich poetic symbolism. It is not that James or Lawrence or Proust or Faulkner "combine" naturalism with symbolism. It is that a naturalistic picture of things *becomes* symbolic if it is well enough done.

When Robert Penn Warren fails, as he sometimes does, it is not, as Mr. Bush's analysis suggests, because he is too naturalistic, but because he is not naturalistic enough. His symbolism is too often something superimposed. The vehicle which Warren devises to carry his meaning is not always as "natural," as "real," as it should be. The worst thing you can truthfully say about *All the King's Men* is that the almost Hollywoodian thriller which is Warren's vehicle is all too easily separable from his theme That of course is why the book could be a best seller: the public read it *simply* as a thriller.

All the King's Men, the rumor now is, will be a Humphrey Bogart movie. A novel in which so much is derived from Hollywood is given back to Hollywood as to a mother. Consider Warren's characters. *Theatrical*, someone has called them. But Warren's brand of theatricality obviously owes more to the screen than to the stage. Adam Stanton is very much the nice but futile Hollywood professor, Sadie Burke the hard-boiled type, and so on. Stanton embodies an idea, a theme; he has a good deal of the "nobility" that Mr. Bush is after; what he lacks is the natural-ness, the psychological reality, that the modern novelist is after.

If the symbolist in Warren seems not to submerge himself in the naturalist, the thinker in him seems not to submerge him-self in the artist. Trite as it is nowadays to stigmatize an author as a dual personality, I cannot help pointing to a duality in Warren that may well constitute his major problem: it is his com-bination of critical and creative power. I am far from suggesting that the critical and the creative are of their nature antithetic and I am fully ready to grant that what makes Warren remark-able among American writers is his double endowment. The problem lies precisely in his being so two-sidedly gifted; he evi-dently finds it endlessly difficult to combine his two sorts of awareness. There is Warren the critic, the cosmopolitan, the scholar, the philosopher; and there is Warren the raconteur, the Kentuckyan, the humorist, the ballad maker. Sometimes the divi-sion becomes an overt formal separation within a work — *The Ballad of Billie Potts* is the obvious example. *Proud Flesh*, at its worst, wobbles awkwardly from one level to the other. *All the King's Men*, as I have suggested, suffers a good deal from in-complete fusion of theme and vehicle. The choice of such a smart aleck as Jack Burden for narrator may have unlocked Warren's marvelous store of humor, but it sadly limited his chances of rendering (without reporting, without too much explicit com-ment) his theme. And we cannot forgive all the fancy writing, as some critics do, merely on the grounds that the writer is sup-posed to be Burden and not Warren. Burden was chosen and created by Warren. Critics who write the exegesis of a great sym-bolic masterpiece with every detail in place are writing of the book Warren *ought* to have written, not of the one he wrote.

Warren is a faulty writer; but he is worth a dozen petty per-fectionists. Though commonly associated with "formalists" and "classicists" in criticism, he is close to the type of romantic genius: robust, fluent, versatile, at his worst clever and clumsy, at his best brilliant and profound. On the other hand, he is remarkable for self-discipline. The pattern for the American novelist—Sinclair Lewis is the great example—is that he makes the best-seller lists with a youthful tour de force and spends the rest of his life trying to live up to his reputation. Warren did not write a full-length book between 1929 and 1939. He did not meet with the blandishments of the publicity racket till 1946; too late, I trust, for him to suffer from it. He reminds us of the possibility of a better sort of "American" writing than, say, Howard Fast's, a better sort of "Southern" writing than, say, Margaret Mitchell's. At a time when Americanism in writing suggests the ugly cultural nationalism of Van Wyck Brooks and regionalism suggests the ugly cultural provinciality that allows Dante and Shakespeare to be replaced on college curriculums by the poets of eastern South Dakota, it is very refreshing to find a good writer whom one may meaningfully call deeply American and genuinely regionalist. This means, paradoxically enough, that Warren is not *too* American and not *too* regionalist. He has room for the rest of the world, and I think the rest of the world will have room for him. For if you start somewhere you may end everywhere, but if you start nowhere that is also where you will end.

᮪ᱏ MORTON DAUWEN ZABEL

Graham Greene

"THERE was something about a fête which drew Arthur Rowe irresistibly . . . called him like innocence." We meet him in blitzed and gutted London, stumbling on a charity bazaar in a Bloomsbury square, a man alone and a murderer, but fearless because he has made a friend of his guilt: when he gave his wife the poison that released her from the suffering he pitied he did not ask her consent; "he could never tell whether she might not have preferred any sort of life to death." A fortune-teller slips him, mistakenly, the password by which he wins a cake in the bazaar's raffle. But there are others who want it and the thing concealed in its heart. Visited that night in his shabby room by a cripple, Rowe has barely tasted the hyoscine in his tea when out of a droning sky a bomb drops, explodes the house, and blows him and us into a dream of horrors—man hunt, spies, sabotage, amnesia, murders, and suicides: the latest "entertainment" of Graham Greene.

We enter the familiar phantasm of our age, and Greene's expert evocation of it through eleven novels—of which *The Ministry of Fear* is the latest—has justly won him the title of "the Auden of the modern thriller." Here again is the haunted England

NOTE. Reprinted from the *Nation*, 1943, by permission of the editors and the author.

of *l'entre deux guerres,* the European nightmare of corruption and doom, a *Blick ins Chaos* where

> taut with apprehensive dreads
> The sleepless guests of Europe lay
> Wishing the centuries away,
> And the low mutter of their vows
> Went echoing through her haunted house,
> As on the verge of happening
> There crouched the presence of The Thing.

The fustian stage sets of Oppenheim, Chambers, and Wallace are gone with their earlier innocent day. We are in a cosmos whose fabulous realities have terribly condensed out of contemporary legend and prophecy—the portentous journalism of Tabouis, Thompson, Sheean, Gunther, and the apotheosis of foreign correspondence; the films of Lang, Murnau, Renoir, and Hitchcock; the Gothic fables of Ambler, Hammett, and Simenon; the putsches, pogroms, marches, and mobilizations that have mounted to catastrophe in the present moment of our lives. Its synthetic thrills and archaic brutality are ruses of melodrama no longer. Guilt pervades all life; all of us are trying to discover how we entered the nightmare, by what treachery we were betrayed to the howling storm of history. "Mother, please listen to me," cries Rowe to a mother who is dead; "I've killed my wife and the police want me." . . . "My little boy couldn't kill anyone":

His mother smiled at him in a scared way but let him talk: he was the master of the dream now. He said, "I'm wanted for a murder I didn't do. People want to kill me because I know too much. I'm hiding underground, and up above the Germans are methodically smashing London to bits all around me. You remember St. Clements—the bells of St. Clements. They've smashed that—St. James's Piccadilly, the Burlington Arcade, Garland's Hotel where we stayed for the pantomime, Maples, and John Lewis. It sounds like a thriller, doesn't it?—but the thrillers are like life . . . it's what we've all made of the world since you died. I'm your little Arthur who wouldn't hurt a beetle and I'm a murderer too. The world has been remade by William Le Queux."

Every age has its esthetic of crime and horror, its attempt to give form to its special psychic or neurotic climate. No age has imposed greater handicaps on the effort than ours. Crime has gone beyond Addison's "chink in the armor" of civilized society; it has become the symptom of a radical lesion in the stamina of humanity. The hot violence of the Elizabethans is as different from the cold brutality of Hitlerian Europe, the heroic sin in Aeschylus or Webster from the squalid and endemic degeneracy in Céline or Miller, the universal proportions of Greek or Shakespearean wrong from the calculating gratuity of Gide's esthetic murderers, as the worth at which the individual life was held in those times from its worthlessness in ours. A criminal takes his dignity from his defiance of the intelligence or merit that surrounds him, from the test his act imposes on the human community. He becomes trivial when that measure is denied him. So the modern thriller is permitted its prodigies of contrivance and holocausts of death at the cost of becoming a bore. So movie audiences fidget restlessly through "Desert Victory," waiting to be overwhelmed by the edifying bilge of "Random Harvest." The thrill habit, fed by novels, newsreels, and events, has competed successfully with gin, drugs, and aspirin, and doped the moral nerve of a generation.

The hardship this imposes on the artist is obvious. When felony, by becoming political, becomes impersonal; when the *acte gratuit* elicits not only secret but public heroism, its dramatist faces the baffling task of restoring to his readers their lost instinct of values, the sense of human worth. It is not enough that the thriller becomes psychic: Freudian behavior patterns have become as much an open commodity and stock property as spy rings and torture chambers were a generation ago. The thriller must become moral as well.

The Victorian *frisson* of crime was all the choicer for the rigor of propriety and sentiment that hedged it in. Dickens' terrors are enhanced less by his rhetoric than by his coziness. The reversion to criminality in Dostoevski takes place in a ramifying hierarchy of authority—family life, social caste, political and religious bureaucracy, czarist militarism and repression. The horror of *The Turn of the Screw* is framed by the severest decorum,

taste, and inhibition. James—like Conrad, Gide, and Mann—
knew the enchantment of crime, but he also knew its artistic conditions. "Everything you may further do will be grist to my
imaginative mill," he wrote William Roughead in thanks for a
book of the latter's criminal histories: "I'm not sure I enter into
such matters best when they are very archaic or remote from our
familiarities, for then the testimony to manners and morals is
rather blurred for me by the *whole* barbarism . . . The thrilling
in the comparatively modern much appeals to me—for there the
special manners and morals become queerly disclosed. . . . Then
do go back to the dear old human and sociable murders and
adulteries and forgeries in which we are so agreeably at home."
The admonition might have served as the cue for Graham
Greene's talent.

Greene, facing a "whole barbarism" equal to anything in history, has undertaken to redeem that dilapidation from the stupe-
fying mechanism and inconsequence to which modern terrorism
has reduced it. Arthur Calder-Marshall has rightly said in *Horizon* that "few living English novelists derive more material from
the daily newspaper than Graham Greene." His *mise-en-scène*
includes the Nazi underground and fifth column (*The Confiden-
tial Agent, The Ministry of Fear*), organized Marxism torn by
schisms and betrayals (*It's a Battlefield*), Kruger (*England Made
Me*), Zaharoff (*This Gun for Hire*), the English race-track gangs
(*Brighton Rock*), the Mexican church suppression (*The Labyrinthine Ways*), and his *Orient Express* is the same train we've
traveled on from *Shanghai Express* to *Night Train* and *The Lady
Vanishes*. But where once—in James, Conrad, Dostoevski,
Dickens, Defoe, or the Elizabethans—it was society, state, kingdom, world, or the universe itself that supplied the presiding order
of law or justice, it is now the isolated, betrayed, and indestructible integrity of the individual life that furnishes that measure.
Humanity, having contrived a world of mindless and psychotic
brutality, reverts to the atom of the lonely man. Marked, hunted,
Ishmaelite, or condemned, he may work for evil or for good, but
it is his passion for moral identity that provides the nexus of
values in a world that has reverted to anarchy. His lineage is

familiar—Raskolnikov, Stavrogin, Mitya; Conrad's Jim, Heyst, and Razumov; Mann's Krull and Gide's Lafcadio; Hesse's Steppenwolf, and, immediately, Kafka's K. He appears in every Greene novel—as hero in Drover, Dr. Czinner, the nameless D.; as pariah or renegade in Raven, Farrant, Rowe, and the whiskey priest of *The Labyrinthine Ways*; as the incarnation of pure malevolence in Pinkie, the boy gangster and murderer of *Brighton Rock*.

The plot that involves him is fairly constant; *Brighton Rock* presents it in archetype. Its conflict rests on a basic dualism, saved from mere mechanism by Greene's fertility in invention and complex insight, but radical in its antithesis of forces. Pinkie is a believing Catholic, knows hell as a reality, and accepts his damnation; *corruptio optimi pessima* is the last faith left him to live or die by. Ida Arnold, the full-blown, life-loving tart whose casual lover the gang has killed, sets out to track him down: "unregenerate, a specimen of the 'natural man,' coarsely amiable, bestially kind, the most dangerous enemy to religion." She pursues him with ruthless and deadly intention, corners him, sees him killed. The boy is sped to his damnation and Ida triumphs. ("God doesn't mind a bit of human nature . . . I know the difference between Right and Wrong.") The hostility is crucial; it appears in all Greene's mature books—Mather the detective against Raven the assassin (*This Gun for Hire*), the Inspector against Drover (*It's a Battlefield*), the Communist lieutenant of police, accompanied by the *mestizo* who acts as nemesis, against the hunted, shameless, renegade priest in *The Labyrinthine Ways*, trailing his desecrated sanctity through the hovels and jungles of the Mexican state, yet persisting in his office of grace and so embracing the doom that pursues him. A recent critic in the *New Statesman* put the case clearly: "Mr. Greene is a Catholic, and his novel *Brighton Rock* betrays a misanthropic, almost Jansenist, contempt for the virtues that do not spring from grace."

It is this grace that operates as the instrument·which makes palpable its necessary enemy, Evil—and it is by the evil that materializes out of vice, crime, and nightmare in his books that Greene joins a distinguished company: the same evil works be-

hind the psychic riddle in *The Turn of the Screw* and behind the
squalid violence of Conrad's *The Secret Agent,* that parent
classic in this field of fiction, which appeared in 1907 and established the kind of novel that Greene and his generation have
carried to such exorbitant lengths. To fix and objectify it, to
extricate it from the relativity of abstractions—abstract justice,
impersonal humanitarianism, pity, right and wrong, good and
bad—is the ulterior motive of Greene's work. His pursuit of it
carried him among the totems and horrors of coastal Africa, which
he conjures in *Journey Without Maps*—his descent to the heart
of darkness:

It isn't a gain to have turned the witch or the masked secret
dancer, the sense of supernatural evil, into the small human
viciousness of the thin distinguished military gray head in Ken-
sington Gardens with the soft lips and the eye which dwelt with
dull luster on girls and boys of a certain age. . . . They are not,
after all, so far from the central darkness. . . . When one sees
to what unhappiness, to what peril of extinction centuries of
cerebration have brought us, one sometimes has a curiosity to
discover if one can from what we have come, to recall at which
point we went astray.

(An echo sounds here from Eliot on Baudelaire:

So far as we are human, what we do must be either evil or
good; so far as we do evil or good we are human; and it is better,
in a paradoxical way, to do evil than to do nothing: at least, we
exist. It is true to say that the glory of man is his capacity for
salvation; it is also true to say that his glory is his capacity for
damnation. The worst that can be said of most of our malefactors,
from statesmen to thieves, is that they are not men enough to
be damned.)

Greene's progress in his task has not escaped the pitfalls of his
compromise with popularity. His expert contrivance often de-
scends to sleight-of-hand; the surrealism of his action and atmosphere easily results in efflorescences of sheer conjuring; the
machinery of the thriller—chases, coincidences, exploding sur-
prises—can collapse into demented catastrophe. And Greene
drives his philosophical ambition hard. His plots flirt with absolutes—a kind of moral *vis inertiae*—of social and emotional

realities that reappear in the stock humors to which his characters and their psychic pathology often reduce. His great gifts in dialogue, characterization, marginal commentary, and hallucinated scenery run frequently to exorbitance through the uncanny facility which is the danger of his special kind of brilliance.

But there is no question that a major purpose works behind his popular or cinematic effects. He uses horror for what it has signified in every age—Elizabethan, Gothic, romantic, or Victorian—as a medium for exploring the evasions, fears, and regressive panic that may drag us back from the ascendancy of reason or pride to infantilism and brutality, but must always, in any age, be met and faced if salvation is to miss the curse of presumption. "The abyss destroys; the abyss exalts; descend that you may be saved. The enemy we conquer is the enemy we embrace and love." The identity Greene's heroes pursue is the selfhood of a conscience implicated in the full mystery and terror of their natures; if the "destructive element" engulfs them, it is their resisting passion for a spiritual destiny that stains and brightens the flood. And it is because he sustains a dialectic between the oblivion of naturalism and the absolute tests of moral selfhood that Greene has brought about one of the most promising collaborations between realism and spirituality that have recently appeared in fiction, saving his work as much from the squashy hocus-pocus or mechanical contrivance of the common thriller as from the didactic sanctimony of conventional religiosity. In at least three of his books—*It's a Battlefield, Brighton Rock,* and *The Labyrinthine Ways*—he may claim the ancestry of James, Conrad, and Joyce, and the company of men like Kafka, Auden, and Mauriac.

He stands at the threshold of major fiction, a searching, irresistible talent, and a true magician in the words and spells of authentic drama. He has found an instrument for probing the temper and tragedy of his age, the perversions and fears that have betrayed it, and the stricken weathers of its soul. It only remains for him to surmount its distractions and negative appeals more decisively to stand unrivaled as a novelist in the English generation to which history and his high gift of consciousness have committed him.

~§ C. H. RICKWORD

A Note on Fiction

PROBABLY Miss Drew* was wise in not attempting a prolonged
frontal attack on her subject. If sporadic flank incursions, however, are to be at all useful, they should be undertaken with an
eye on the ultimate objective; the possible final synthesis should
be kept in mind. If "the problem of language, the use of the
medium in all its aspects, is the basic problem of any work of
literature," then the merits of the attitudes to sex of D. H.
Lawrence and Michael Arlen are not very relevant. And it is to
topics of the latter kind that Miss Drew devotes most of her
space. Admitting that the pretentions of the majority of novels
to esthetic status collapse as soon as scrutinized, the fact that she
still considers them worthy of appreciative attention shows that
Miss Drew has either not realized this radical worthlessness or
that she has alternative standards.

In pronouncing a bare verdict of good or bad, the critic of
fiction is in no worse case than the critic of verse. And so far as
giving a plausibly objective air to his judgment goes, he has at
his disposal such speciously technical terms as character, situation, incident, narrative, and so forth. But, if he would give his

NOTE. Reprinted from *Towards Standards of Criticism* (London: Wishart, 1933),
by permission of Lawrence and Wishart Ltd. The article appeared originally in
the *Calendar of Modern Letters*.

* *The Modern Novel*, by Elizabeth A. Drew. Cape.

judgment further validity by centering it in the work under consideration, he will find such terms only approximately descriptive of the impressions to be organized. For, whereas rhythm corresponds to an actual excitement in the reader's mind that can be traced to its source in the means employed, character corresponds to nothing so definite. Rhythm is a property of words, character a product that needs analysis before a satisfactory account of its effect can be given in terms of its constituents, and a product, moreover, that invites extra-literary scrutiny. Such scrutiny is fatal to criticism, for, though it may be that the critic's ultimate concern is with the conception of life (the "values") of which the novel is a vehicle, yet he is only so concerned in so far as that conception is made active through art. That that conception is inadequate, to take the negative, which is the more frequent case, is only revealed by a breakdown in the expression, a flaw in the technique, for it cannot be known apart from the form in which it becomes manifest. Obviously, a right apprehension of that "form" depends on a right apprehension of its elements—of which character is generally considered the principal.

However, the impossibility of ignoring this diversity leads to the perception that character has two aspects, a static and a dynamic, "character in repose" and "character in action," each of which can be further subdivided according to whether it is the "inner" or the "outer man" that is presented. But these terms, being descriptive not critical, indicate the angle of presentation but not its success or failure. They assume, too, that at whatever level it is presented, character is to be regarded as a portrait of an imagined human being. If that is the assumption, criticism may either deal with the degree of illusion as such or the significance of the illusion as a symbol of humanity (to praise a novelist for his "knowledge of human nature" is plainly irrelevant; a psycho-analyst or a parish priest might possess as much). Mere degree of illusion, however, provides no adequate test; novelists who can do nothing else are able to perform the trick with ease, since "nothing is easier than to create for oneself the idea of a human being, a figure and a character, from glimpses and anecdotes."

Nor does depth of illusion matter: Raskolnikov is "deeper" than Tom Jones, in the sense that more of his interior is directly exposed, but he is a figure of different not greater significance.

On the other hand, the judgment of "values" arrived at through a consideration of the symbolic aspect of character is unreliable because of the danger, almost the certainty, that attention will be diverted from the symbol to what it may be guessed to symbolize, which, if the artist is incompetent and the critic hospitable and sympathetic, will be much. It is for no other reason than that Conrad's heroes have been discerned by many earnest people to stand for something really tremendous in the matter of soul, that that writer has been so overestimated. Moreover, a novelist who is capable of "staging" a figure of tragic possibilities (by making use of the reader's readiness to objectify that has been noted above) may utterly fail to realize those possibilities. But this conclusion is reached without any direct examination of character as an illusion or as a symbol at all, for "character" is merely the term by which the reader alludes to the pseudo-objective image he composes of his responses to an author's verbal arrangements. Unfortunately, that image once composed, it can be criticized from many irrelevant angles — its moral, political, social, or religious, significance considered, all as though it possessed actual objectivity, were a figure of the inferior realm of real life. And, because the annual cataract of serious fiction is as full of "life-like" little figures of such, and no more, significance as drinking water is of infusoria, it passes critical filters in undiminished volume and unrectified impurity while the meager stream of genuine literature, being burdened with "the forms of things unknown," is anxiously traced to its hypothetical source — a veritable psychologico-biographical bog.

In this connection, the main thing to be noted about the new "subjective" novelists is their increasing tendency to rely for their effect not on set pieces of character-drawing, but directly on the poetic properties of words. The idea of a character's consciousness is created in the reader by the exploitation of the emotive powers of language used to evoke concrete imagery and sensation. The idea so created has unusual reality; the idea of Dedalus, for instance, that is obtained from a compulsory experience of Dublin Beach as he would have experienced it is not unauthenticated by any suspicious connivance of Nature, as when the thunder rumbles conveniently over Egdon Heath.

Miss Drew calls this the "stream-of-consciousness" method—rather pointlessly, for under such a head Henry James must be included—and is inclined to condemn it because "the concern . . . being entirely with the immediate in consciousness, the result must of necessity lack all proportion or perspective as a vision of anything beyond the immediate." Since it cannot be seriously contended that the past is not, in effect, present in the immediate consciousness to be reported if reporting were the whole matter, the fault must be, not in the method but in the writer using it, as, in fact, is shown by the success of those chapters of *Ulysses* in which it is applied. It is unfair to blame the defenseless consciousness for its lack of an "artistic relevance" to which it has not aspired, and one gathers Miss Drew does not really wish to do so. Her label led her astray.

II

Having briefly considered the notions commonly attached in the criticism of fiction to the vague term "character," it may be profitable to examine the almost antithetical set of ideas it is customary to include under the equally wide term "narrative" or its synonyms. The word has one quite technical sense, when it is used of the method of a book. Then it signifies that a course of events is related directly by the author or his mouthpiece, and contrasts with "dramatic" or "scenic," which indicate that events are rendered more immediately by dialogue or other representational devices. In this sense, however, which is descriptive rather than critical, the word is quite unambiguous.

The case is different when it is applied to the whole book to denote the action, as distinguished from the characters. It has an apparently greater critical relevance than the latter term on account of the more genuine objectivity of the quality it designates.

But this advantage is only apparent, for the actual story of a novel eludes the epitomist as completely as character; few great works are not ridiculous in synopsis. And for this reason—that the form of a novel only exists as a balance of response on the part of the reader. Hence schematic plot is a construction of the reader's that corresponds to an aspect of that response and stands in merely diagrammatic relation to the source. Only as precipitates from the memory are plot or character tangible; yet only in solution have either any emotive valency. The composition of this metaphorical fluid is a technical matter. The technique of the novel is just as symphonic as the technique of the drama and as dependent, up to a point, on the dynamic devices of articulation and control of narrative tempo. But, though dependent, it is dependent as legs are on muscles, for the *how* but not the *why* of movement; and, interesting as functional technique may be to the mechanical-minded and to workers in the same medium on the lookout for tips, the organic is the province of criticism. More important, then, than what may be called the tricks of narrative is the status of plot and its relation to the other elements of a novel, particularly its relation to character, in solution.

Modern opinion, commonly assuming that the novelist expresses himself primarily through character, tends to regard story as more or less incidental; either it is scorned as part of the "good old compromise . . . for the entertainment of the reader" or it is looked on as merely the expository structure—the Aintree, as it were, of character or, in less serious connection, a modiste's parlor elegantly set for the mannequin parade.

Hence, though it is stipulated that plot be organic, it is required to be so in the sense that it may be said to arise out of, or be determined by, character. When a book is found satisfactory, this fundamental condition is said to be fulfilled, and "value" is attributed to it or quarried out of character. Only when an imaginative failure is perceived is the plot scrutinized and then only for the, as it were, temporal location of the lapse, whose occasion is still sought elsewhere.

This position is vulnerable from several points. In the first place, in any sense in which the terms used have a meaning at all, it is plain that character, that is, that idea of a human being that is carried away from a play or a novel, is a product of the narrative. Whereas it is impossible to attend to the barest recital of an event, or series of events, without calling up for oneself an idea of the persons concerned, an equally bare description of character invokes no such animated notion. In fact, it is impossible to acquire from words any idea of a person unless that person is defined in time as well as in space. That is to say, action of some sort is indispensable. But, though this be admitted, it may still be maintained that value, nevertheless, resides in the character thus created.

This is, in fact, the usual contention. Professor S. Gaselee, in an essay on the Greek novel in the *Daphnis and Chloe* volume of the Loeb Classics, remarks that "fiction is one of the very few of the inventions of man that have improved in the course of the ages." "Brought up," he declares, "on good novels, we are bored with their rude predecessors of antiquity. . . . Of psychology there is barely a trace . . . any attempt indeed at character-drawing is faint and rough."

I am not concerned to defend Longus and his fellows against their detractor. Certainly, they and their English imitators such as Barnaby Riche and Robert Greene very soon become tiresome. No more speedily, however, than Maurice Hewlett, whose *Forest Lovers* is instanced in the same essay as an example of the good novels that formed the Professor's taste. But the reasons given for the condemnation are interesting. In part, of course, they are the indignant outcry of a sophisticated palate at being fobbed off with thin and pastoral fare. More than that, though, they are also the sincere lament of an unsatisfied appetite. The Professor would like some sauce, but he really needs meat.

If we offered him Homer, even Homer in an English prose version, we should hear, instead of these wails of hunger, the happy noises of prolonged mastication. Now, it cannot be contended that the addition of a little psychology and character-drawing to a chain of events makes all the difference between esthetic starvation and satisfaction, but some quality inherent in those events. And it is this quality that is common to all great works of literature, in no matter what genre. It is a unity among the events, a progressive rhythm that includes and reconciles each separate rhythm. As manifested in the novel, it resolves, when analyzed, chiefly into character and plot in a secondary, schematic sense—qualities that are purely fictitious. Neither is an active element in the whole work in the way that melody and harmony are elements in a piece of music. Perhaps it would be less ambiguous to designate this basic, poetic quality by some such term as rhythm or development; on the other hand, plot or story do indicate its nature—that it is primarily a sequence of events developing in accordance with an inner necessity.

And it is the recognition of this inner necessity that constitutes the recognition of value. To call this organizing principal "character" is to attribute essential importance to what may be no more than a secondary manifestation and is often, even on the face of it, inaccurate. Obviously, the *Odyssey* has this unity; but it does not proceed from Ulysses. So, too, has *War and Peace*; yet Tolstoy makes it, perhaps, even too plain that events develop quite independently of the people they affect, as well as of those who are trying to affect them. And Hardy, in this at least, resembles him. Ultimately, this rhythmic coherence springs from the writer's conception of life and the adequacy thereto of his vehicle.

Actually, then, character is, to borrow biological jargon, an emergent quality of the novel. It emerges from the story, which is itself structurally a product of language, eloquence. An attempt, however, to cut out this intervening stage is marked by the assumption that the novelist's primary creation is of character. And this also indicates what is peculiar in the scope of modern fiction.

By the classic writer, elaborating a given pattern, the individual is seen included within the metaphysical hierarchy, symbolized as Fate, gods, and mortals. To the romantic, however, the individual appears containing within him that hierarchy, so that the writer is compelled to invent his own pattern. And the remoter his experience from the common, and the more personal his values, the more difficult will it be for his creation to make contact with an audience. This task, however, may be left to the character who, however highly specialized, is to be assumed to be a human being with the emotional and other equipment common to such. Whether a skeptical audience that, unmoved by assertion, demands sensible proof will be convinced is another matter.

Historically, character, as we now understand it, is an outcome of the Romantic Revival, a movement that has been discerned by some as one of escape from the mechanistic and indifferent universe of science into the fastness of the individual soul and of an attempt to locate there the limitations that constitute value. In Professor Whitehead's words: "The independence ascribed to bodily substances carried them away from the realm of values altogether. They degenerated into a mechanism entirely valueless except as suggestive of external ingenuity." (There is no reason, however, to suppose, as this phrasing implies, and as it so often suggested, that developments in the esthetic sphere proceed as effects from developments in other departments of thought. The imaginative faculty being supreme, poets themselves, not science nor philosophy, are to blame for any decay of sensibility.)

Such an abstraction of values from the objective universe involves a corresponding restriction of the scope of significant action. In the epic, it is the completed action that animates the bare recital of events and, by unifying them, gives it structural vitality. Since the end is ordained by Fate operating through the wills and passions of gods and mortals, their deeds and speech are adequate to the poet's purpose. There is no need to go behind them to explain their meaning; that meaning is what happened and its inevitability. (The epic poet, like the historian, has also the advantage that, since the events he deals with actually occurred, his narrative cannot be doubted on the score of historic truth, but has only to satisfy as to its imaginative truth, or arrangement, whereas the feigning novelist raises questions of probability. But he, too, pretends to the authority of the past tense, and no one is likely so far to forget the rules of the game as to object unless there is a defect in his arrangement also.)

Problems arise, however, when the overt subject of a narrative is, not the foredoomed destruction of Troy, but the integration of a Richard Myrtle. The scene of action being removed from the external to the psychological world, a technique is required that will manifest the otherwise imperceptible events. Further, a principle is needed that will unify those events when manifested. This principle can be identified with the individual, the "character," and located, by the romantics proper in the emotions, by Henry James in the intelligence, by the followers of Freud — gentle Ruths, gleaning psychology's alienist fields — in the subconscious.

Linked to these questions is that of authority — the angle from which the story shall be presented. Henry James was the first to realize consciously and to state that the interior drama must be shown to the inner eye if it is to be emotively efficient. But it is not vision alone that confers authority; Homer owes his to no sleight-of-hand with the "seeing-eye," but to the internal consistency of that which he offers to it. Nevertheless, visualization is necessary, and it is the problem of objectifying and setting in disciplined motion the subjective narrative that has occupied nearly all English novelists of importance since Fielding, and Richardson before him.

It is curious that, though the romantics destroyed the poetic forms of the previous tradition, yet the novel continued for a considerable period to be written on Fielding's plan. This was, perhaps, largely due to the fact that in England the novel has rarely been the medium of first-rate creative minds and to the not unrelated lack of self-consciousness in the matter of technique on the part of its practitioners. And Fielding's extraordinary effectiveness encouraged such inertia. But the effectiveness of his method proceeded from its entire adequacy to its content, which did not include the individual sensibility. Fielding's attitude was primarily social; he saw people as units in society and estimated their actions by the resultant effects on that organism. Secure of an audience that shared his views, he was able to use objective narrative with authority, though only types emerged from it. Further, being conservative of a tradition that accepted the whole of life as material for art, he was able to base his story very firmly on experience. But for all its permanence and solidity, his art was not heroic, as he himself admitted in calling *Tom Jones* a comic epic. Fielding's single-mindedness, that enabled him to retain so firm a grasp on the more immediate aspects of existence, was dependent on a spiritual crassness that allowed him to remain content with the stuffy metaphysics of his day. The difference between tragic and comic art lies partly in the different attitudes adopted toward the catastrophes ensuing on a collision between individual and collective values. Of course, the great comic artist, such as Congreve, takes his stand above society; his standards are absolute and his own, not those of the herd.

Now, it is the weakness of an art such as Fielding's that it is almost wholly typical. It operates by setting in opposition qualities abstracted from men, so that the response it arouses is only partial. It has the veracity of correct analysis and the further truth of coherent recombination, but the appeal is limited mainly to admiration. If the romantic attention to the individual had meant an extension of the field of perception, the attempt to particularize and subtilize Fielding's structure might have succeeded. Unfortunately, it meant not an extension, but merely a shifting of that field. Consequently, though along with Fielding's method, some of his immediacy was retained, it became increasingly more necessary to expound the meaning of action. Thus the plots of the Victorians became cumbered with a vast amount of not strictly relevant matter, essential to them for their "meaning," but quite unresolvable. For the difficulty in exteriorizing the movements of the individual sensibility is twofold. Outward actions have to be invented that will recreate, and not merely illustrate, inward happenings, and these highly particularized actions have at the same time to be universalized. The necessity for having regard to these two aspects constitutes the real problem. Dostoevski solved it by the violent conjunction of extreme realism in manner to extreme ideality of attitude, but he did so only at the expense of a tremendous amount of will that might advantageously have been liberated for other purposes.

Henry James is often given credit for having been the first to assert that events within the mind might be just as important as those without. The claim is hardly just, but he certainly was the first to realize that the interior drama might be rendered immediately by language without the intervention of circumstantiating physical action at every stage, that the word was as capable of embodying mental as physical movements, and that its latter function was useful only because of its superior vividness.

But James', like Fielding's, was primarily a social art. Truly, the society James contemplated was composed of members far more differentiated and sensitive to other's individuality than any Fielding could conceive, and it was his own creation. It is one, however, in which the maximum development is assured for certain impulses only at the cost of the almost complete omission of others—roughly, the grosser appetites Fielding handled so vigorously.

Thus, though James' narrative is autonomous, it is so only within the boundaries of a limited experience; his action is complete and self-sufficing because it springs from a single source, but it is ultimately invalidated by a latent dualism that is not explicit only because the intractable factor is altogether suppressed. (This suppression is not complete until his last period, but its progress can be observed in his earlier books.) Hence the much extoled purity of his plots is actually of less worth than the impurity of those of the "great" Victorians, in which the presence of large masses of unassimilated matter is evidence of at least an attempt to be comprehensive.

But James' skill in the manipulation of incident, the intricate technique by which events were arranged in varying degrees of relief so that the climax stood out in the round with the maximum intensity and immediacy, was one elaborated to dispose the most attenuated substance in the most substantial manner possible and was dependent on the prose that, apparently aimless, yet with certainty isolated and held up to view the fact on which James wished to dwell. Without it none of James' other devices is sufficient to give more than mechanical form to a novel, as appears from his imitators.

It is notable that Joyce uses no such devices. Nothing in *Ulysses* is, to use Mr. Lubbock's distinction, reported; everything is shown or dramatized. But Joyce contemplates not only the discrepancy between actuality and individual values, between things as they are and as they appear modified by the sensibility; his irony springs from a more profound opposition — that within the subject, the contrast between actual impulse and the appearance that, too, assumes in consciousness. From this profoundly critical standpoint, he is able to exteriorize and objectify vast psychological tracts that as a rule lurk shapelessly outside the action of a novel, perceptible only as unaccountable influences that distort and hinder its progress. And regarding with an equal eye the response both to external and internal stresses, attributing no more value to the one than to the other, he is able to compel both into the same perspective and so set in motion events that, occurring simultaneously on both planes, are in themselves adequate and self-sufficient. Thus the authority and directness of objective presentation is secured for the subjective narrative, Joyce's unit being the consciousness, not its social crystallization, the character. Dedalus and Bloom are but symbols of disintegration; the imminent, never clearly apprehended Ulysses is the hero of this Odyssey, whose significance lies wholly in the completed action and its organic relation to the events of which it is composed.

MIDLAND BOOKS